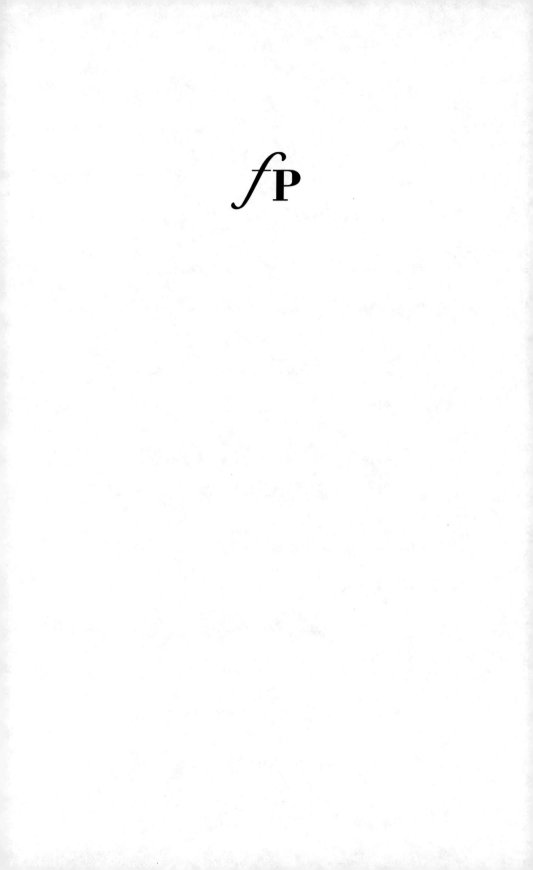

Also by Michael D. Yapko, Ph.D.

Depression
Is
Contagious

How the Most Common Mood Disorder
Is Spreading Around the World
and How to Stop It

Michael D. Yapko, Ph.D.

FREE PRESS

New York   London   Toronto   Sydney

Free Press
A Division of Simon & Schuster, Inc.
1230 Avenue of the Americas
New York, NY 10020

To Diane,
whose effortless ability to light up a room
just by entering it highlights that *love is contagious,* too

Contents

Foreword

Familiar adages appear over and over again because they teach us simple, but important, life lessons. One of these—"the more things change, the more they stay the same"—particularly applies to the pharmaceutical revolution which has misled people to believe that pills can magically replace healthy relationships, make them happy, and cure depression. Forget about it, because that's not going to happen now or *ever*. Notwithstanding our modern technological society, we people are basically what we have always been. Advances made by people are advances made by people; they don't *replace* people.

In fact, people-to-people connectedness can outdo pharmaceuticals in treating depression. To broadcast that news, which is supported by many scientific studies, we need this powerful new book by Dr. Michael Yapko. It will be the tipping point against the present pharmaceutical domination. Dr. Yapko presents a compelling case that the popular pharmaceutical solution is overly simplistic and that we need to look to each other for the antidepressant merits of good relationships.

Dr. Yapko recognizes human relationships as key designers of psychological well-being. In clear terms, citing incontrovertible research described with no-nonsense directness, he brings our attention to the rising rates of depression, a social catastrophe in progress not just in the United States but around the world. Then, most importantly, he identifies human solutions and teaches essential skills for building positive, healthy relationships, framed to reduce the pain and isolation of depression.

The scenarios Dr. Yapko presents rarely reach the therapy office simply because most depressed people don't seek help; paralyzing helplessness and hopelessness define the disorder. But the consequences of depression undoubtedly reach into the hearts of family, friends, fellow workers, employers, customers, and others. The lives he describes are fraught with a variety of dangers, misunderstandings, faulty expectations, guilty self-appraisal, and many other common sources of malaise. But Dr. Yapko provides a professional acumen and sensible guidance with the practical exercises he has developed that give perspective and direction to all people concerned with combating depression.

The study of how relationships affect physical and mental health has a long, rich history. More than a century ago, when psychotherapy first came along, it introduced a stunningly new kind of relationship between doctor and patient. Called a "transference," this special therapy relationship encompassed a lifetime of personal experience, giving it an electrifying intensity of feeling and meaning. The therapeutic effects showed more clearly than ever the impact of a well-designed relationship. *This discovery was at least as captivating then as the pharmaceutical revolution is today.*

Today, however, we require a larger cultural healing process, one that transforms the therapy that works for the few into a social expansion that works for the many. There is a growing awareness that *no one's misery exists alone.* Dr. Yapko provides extensive data that give substance to the all-important point that *depression is both formed and healed in the world of people.* Psychotherapists have always known this but only now have they begun to embrace the paradoxical implication: the culture that *hurt* their patients is also the very culture that could *heal* them. This dual potential effect of the culture—its toxic force and its healing antidote—is accentuated in Dr. Yapko's extensive, detailed exploration of the role of social engagements in the recovery from depression.

He also offers another paradoxical observation: Yes, we humans are biochemical organisms, as pharmaceuticals dramatize, but we are *humanly biochemical.* Dr. Yapko makes the case that a physical and metaphorical "chemistry" is created in person-to-person relationships. To think of the biochemical as *only* limited to a pill, as if it is external to our personhood, obscures the chemistry of human response. If you get angry with me or smile at me, you are creating a chemical synthesis that affects both you and me. Dr. Yapko makes this simple point by highlighting the latest brain research and showing that, in objectively measurable neurological terms, "chemistry" between people is more accurate a description than we could have ever imagined!

Antidepressant medication, though beneficial to many people, is proving to be too narrow a solution to a pervasive problem. With massive profits at stake, the pharmaceutical industry has sidestepped the relational foundation of psychological well-being in order to relentlessly sell its product. As it has flooded the public with oversold claims implying that pills can mimic basic human function, a public too trusting of presumed authority has succumbed to the temptation to believe that "a pill a day will keep the depression away." A countermovement to chemical solutions is now emerging, however, and people are on the threshold of awakening to their need for community and a feeling of belonging.

The work of a new generation of neuropsychiatrists reinforces the scientific finding that relationships not only heal hearts and souls, they heal *brains* as well (Siegel, 1999). People in a relationship experience a neurological resonance, a "harmony" between brains, that fosters feelings of connection and belonging, often beneath the surface of awareness; its effect may be tiny or highly significant, depending on the individual.

Dr. Yapko's many skill-building exercises throughout this book keep the brain's interpersonal circuits "open." They are ways to enhance resonance with relational alternatives to medical prescription. With specific, comprehensive instructions and real-life stories, he helps you understand and address dilemmas of workplace, family, and friends. Dr. Yapko shows how to maximize opportunities for healthful communication and connection and how to rise beyond depressive resignation. Our society now breeds loneliness and despair, but here is how it can offer a guiding light on the road to healthful living—by bringing its members together.

Even in a society that emphasizes individuality, we can attain a communal mutuality because, underneath it all, human beings are communal creatures. Even though we all differ from one another, we are also all in the same boat in important respects. We all need love, security, and guidance in solving problems.

As a teacher of psychotherapy, I have seen communal effects of demonstrations I have given over the years at seminars and conventions. When I conduct these demonstrations, on the surface it seems as though I am engaging with just one person while the audience is "only" observing the session. However, the audience is doing more than merely observing—they drink in the experience, often telling me later how the demonstration with one person resonated with their own experience and helped transform them in some meaningful way. Whether you call that contagion or mutuality or empathy or synchronicity, it points to our commonality as human beings, our indivisible connection to one another, and the ubiquitous energy transformations that keep us alive (Polster, 1987, 2006).

By capitalizing on our desire for a full life without depression, pharmaceutical companies have aroused our hopes for an easy cure for depression. Dr. Yapko documents these exaggerations and shows that medicalizing depression has been damaging when it does not get to the real point of people's misery, when their misery is rooted in painful relationships and dashed hopes. He cites compelling research which reveals that the favorable results of taking pills have been illusory. And he demonstrates that building social connections is pivotal for everyone, particularly those who are isolated and depressed, in order to achieve that full life to which we aspire.

Dr. Yapko's vision for a relational treatment of depression contains two key contributions. First, he sets the stage with his pointedly professional activism. In directly confronting the rising rate of depression as a product of social forces, he challenges us to define the problem as more social than medical. Second, he offers practical hope that a healing connectedness can be restored by first emphasizing people over pills and then developing the skills essential to living well in a world filled with others. In so doing, he joins with a growing number of psychotherapists who are recognizing ever more clearly the social components of every person's healing process. In the face of the pharmacological juggernaut, he illuminates the powerful *human* resources available to undo the depressive isolation too many people experience.

Erving Polster, Ph.D.
Author of *Uncommon Ground*

Introduction

The rate of depression is rising. According to the World Health Organization, the international watchdog of health issues around the world, depression is currently the *fourth* greatest cause of human suffering and disability around the world. That observation alone tells us how serious and pervasive the problem of depression already is. Even worse, however, is the World Health Organization prediction that by the year 2020, depression will have risen to become the *second* greatest cause of human suffering and disability. This unprecedented rapid growth rate is strong evidence that biology is less a factor in its spread and social forces the greater factor.

Is depression really on the rise, or are people just more tuned into depression as a general topic of interest? The best evidence we have suggests strongly that depression is increasing in prevalence not only in the United States but around the world. This is not simply because more people are seeking help for depression or because wary clinicians are diagnosing it more frequently. Rather, the increase appears to be the product of more and more people manifesting the signs and symptoms of depression.

People Can Spread Depression

What we do to each other can too easily become the source of great hurt in our lives and can result in an enduring way of thinking, feeling, and relating to others. But, we are relearning something of vital importance that has been too often overlooked in recent years: Just as people can be a source of pain, they can also be a source of comfort and happiness and a way out of pain. In light of new research, being the strong, self-sufficient "go it alone" type no longer seems the most effective route to personal fulfillment. Instead, science is confirming what we have probably always known in our hearts: *We are built to be in positive, meaningful relationships with others in order to feel good.* Yet, today, our relationships are damaged and suffering in unprecedented ways.

As relationships face more challenges, whether in love, family, business, or friendship, depression is on the rise. Depression spreads in part through troubled relationships and, in this sense, is socially contagious. You can't catch depression in the same way you catch a cold, but the latest research in neuroscience, social psychology, epidemiology, and genetics provides overwhelming support that moods spread through social conditions. Our social lives directly shape our brain chemistry and powerfully affect the way we think and feel. With modern scanning technologies, we now have evidence that our brains change with positive life experiences. In fact, brains can change as much with social circumstances as with medication. Drugs may address some of depression's symptoms, but they cannot change the social factors that cause and perpetuate it.

The Skills for Living Well

What makes for healthy, strong, happy people? Why do some people face stressful and challenging events in life and seem to rise above them, while other people implode in the face of what seem like routine stressors? These questions provide the foundation for much of what I will talk about in this book. The vast majority of research into depression has focused on the pathologies within people that presumably give rise to the disorder, such as character defects, anger-turned-inward, and chemical imbalances in the brain. Only recently has there emerged a different paradigm for thinking about human experience. Known as *positive psychology*, its focus is on what is *right* with people rather than on what is wrong. Instead of studying people who suffer, positive psychologists study people who have overcome adversity and thrived, who are happy, competent, and fulfilled. By striving to identify people's strengths, psychologists hope to help those who are suffering.

One of the first tasks positive psychologists attempted was to develop a new manual that would catalogue and define many of the best aspects of human experience. Unlike the well-known psychiatric manual listing various forms of psychopathology (the *Diagnostic and Statistical Manual*, now in its revised fourth edition, DSM-IV-R) used by mental health professionals to diagnose patients, a new manual called *Character Strengths and Virtues* was developed by psychologists Chris Peterson and Martin Seligman to identify and describe some of the best human attributes. These include the courage to speak the truth, kindness, love, fairness, leadership, teamwork, forgiveness, modesty, gratitude, and many other such positive characteristics. If you reread that list of attributes, you cannot help but notice that they are wonderful human potentials that can *only* be expressed in the context of human relationships. Simply put, *how people develop their best selves is largely, though not entirely, achieved in the context of positive relationships with other people.*

At a time when we are learning how vitally important it is to have positive and healthy relationships, we are seeing such relationships on the general decline. Even a cursory review of recent U.S. Census data shows us the warning signs: More people are living alone than ever before, people wait longer to marry, on average, yet the national divorce rate remains slightly over 50 percent for first marriages, and even higher (about 70 percent) for second marriages. The number of births outside of marriage has risen sharply, and single parents who must work and are thereby too often unavailable to their kids experience and transmit stresses that are widely cited as a reason why children are often struggling emotionally. Millions of children are currently on antidepressant medication, as well as other psychoactive medications for their social and behavioral problems.

As families struggle and marriages wobble, large studies of the prevalence of various disorders in the general population show rates of depression nearly *four* times higher than a generation ago and nearly *ten* times as high as two generations ago. *Social skills have declined and relationships have become less rewarding and effective. As a result, the vulnerability to depression has increased.*

For over half a century, researchers have known that good relationships serve as a buffer against illnesses of all sorts. The evidence is clear, for example, that when you are happy in your primary relationships, you suffer less depression. Furthermore, people who enjoy close friendships and the support of others are happier and more productive. They also suffer fewer illnesses and, on average, live longer. We will explore the health and mood benefits of good relationships with others in the first chapter. What most of this book will be about, then, is how to develop the kinds of relationships that can help you overcome depression, and perhaps even *prevent* it.

Depression Rises as Relationships Fall

Mental health experts have generally treated depression by giving their patients drugs and shock treatments and other newer brain stimulation treatments, or by talking with them about their childhoods. Yet the social conditions that give rise to depression continue unabated, allowing the rate of depression to continue to rise at an alarming rate. New research makes it clear that *depression is not just about the suffering of one individual, as if he or she lived in total isolation.* Rather, depression occurs in a social context; it occurs *within* people, and also arises from the hurts that take place in relationships *between* people.

The pains of rejection, humiliation, the loss of a loved one through a breakup or death, the betrayal of trust, the trauma of violence and abuse, and the many other ways people can wound each other are all reliable pathways into depression. Simply put, depression can be and often is a direct consequence of relationships that are, well, depressing.

Depression doesn't just affect individuals, although it's easy to focus on the person with the symptoms. For every depressed person who gets treatment, at least four more don't. For every depressed person who doesn't get treatment, his or her depression affects the lives of at least three others. For every depressed parent who goes without treatment, his or her child is at least three times more likely to become depressed than the child of a nondepressed parent. *Relationships can spread depression as surely as germs can spread illness.* Depression *is* contagious.

More and better drugs will *not* solve the problem. People who suffer depression, and the people who love them who suffer right alongside them, must also avoid overthinking the symbolic meaning of the depressive experience. Depressed people are usually already quite good at isolating themselves and thinking too deeply about themselves. Instead of examining them even more closely under the microscope, analyzing ever smaller pieces of their psyche, as if depression is just their individual problem, the solution lies in a broader view. We need a *macro*scope. *We need to see depression in its larger social context,* see it for what it is when the world gets more dangerously crowded while people are literally dying of loneliness.

Depression Gets a Lot of Attention . . . but Not Nearly Enough

Few mental health problems have received as much attention as the problem of depression. There are many reasons: (1) Depression has a huge *financial impact* on our society because of the exorbitant economic costs associated with it; these are measured in terms of lowered productivity, more employee sick days, and diminished job performance. Current estimates indicate depression is costing the U.S. economy at least $70 *billion* per year. (2) Depression's cost in terms of *health care expenses* is huge since it is so closely associated with cardiovascular disease, diabetes, smoking, drug addiction, and many other costly health related problems. (3) Depression exacts a heavy toll on *individual lives,* causing high levels of suffering, anguish, unhappiness, and even the ultimate loss of life when people in despair kill themselves. (4) Depression is terribly destructive on the *social level.* Depressed people are often unable to establish and maintain healthy family environments and constructive working relationships with others, or to build loving and positive relationships with others. Some depressed people even destroy and sabotage important social bonds and harm society through antisocial acts.

The power of depression to damage and destroy lives cannot be overstated. We in the mental health professions have worked especially hard to better understand and treat depression and, over the last two decades, our understanding of depression has increased dramatically. In fact, depression has gone from being one of the least understood to one of the best understood disorders that clinicians treat.

A Multidimensional View of Depression: Multiple Paths into Harm's Way

Many things cause depression. Some factors are *bio*logical, some are *psy*chological, and some are *social.* Hence, a *biopsychosocial* model of depression dominates the field.

The *biology* of depression is an extraordinarily complex arena of research. A young field called affective neuroscience is striving to understand the brain mechanisms underlying moods and mood-related disorders like depression. Geneticists are investigating the role of genetics in vulnerability to depression. Psychopharmacologists are striving to understand the role of neurochemistry in mood states in order to better understand how drugs might more effectively be employed in treatment. Some optimistically envision a day when "designer drugs" can be tailored to an individual's unique biochemistry.

The *psychology* of depression is also an extraordinarily complex area of study. Psychologists have always been interested in how people's quality of *thought* affects their mood states and how one's *behavior* increases or decreases vulnerability to depression. The study of factors such as personal history and styles for coping with stress and adversity has generated important insights about who gets depressed and under what conditions. Many previously unrecognized factors that influence depression's onset and course have now been identified. Great strides have been made in developing effective psychotherapies for treating depression which are based on sound scientific research.

Biology and psychology—singly and in combination—play a large role in the development of depression, but considering *only* these domains in treatment has proven less helpful than psychotherapists had hoped. Drugs have become the most common form of treatment, even in the face of the accumulating volume of objective evidence that clearly demonstrates antidepressants—alone or even in combination with other approaches—have numerous problems associated with them. Likewise, the psychotherapy of depression has shown itself to be less effective when it treats depression only as an individual phenomenon. Talking about your depressed feelings or exploring your childhood can too easily miss the fact that *an individual's depression occurs in a social context and is even socially defined.* Your mood and outlook are powerfully influenced by your relationships with others.

No One Is a Biochemical Island

It may seem obvious that our relationships with other people affect our moods, behavior, and quality of life, yet most people focus almost exclusively on the biology of depression when seeking solutions. This is primarily because the drug industry has aggressively marketed the self-serving but unfounded perspective that "depression is caused by a chemical imbalance in the brain." We in the United States are bombarded by television, radio, and print advertising that asserts that depression is a "brain disease" requiring drug treatment. This may be true for a relatively small percentage of depressed individuals, but there is no objective test for depression in existence yet that could prove it. To the contrary, there is growing evidence available to *disprove* it.

As a direct consequence of these relentless, pervasive advertising campaigns, the average person has heard this message that depression is a biochemical problem so many times that he has come to believe it. By continually shining the spotlight on the biochemistry of depression, sales campaigns have left in the shadows other contributing factors. After all, you can't package and sell relationships. Thus, the social domain of depression has largely been ignored. This has been a very costly oversight on the part of the mental health profession. Instead of making sure the value of drugs isn't overstated and seeing that the merits of building healthy relationships are recognized, the drug sales campaigns have rolled right over us, misdirecting our attention from other more important considerations. The damaging message has been all too clear: *You don't need to change your life in any meaningful way. You don't need to spend any time and effort learning new skills to be more effective. You need only change your biochemistry.*

What Medications Can't Do

I am a clinical psychologist who has been immersed in the world of depression my entire professional life. I have treated depressed individuals, couples, and families for more than three decades. My focus has been on developing innovative, safe, and effective nondrug treatments. These are described extensively in professional books and journal articles I have written for mental health professionals. This work has led to my receiving invitations to teach these methods to my colleagues around the world.

Much of what I have learned about depression has led me to emphasize the role of social learning (i.e., what we learn through our interactions with others) in the onset and course of depression. During my career, I have seen depression subjected to intense scrutiny; I have seen professionals dedicate themselves to finding effective treatments; and I have seen the sharp rise in the prescribing of antidepressant medications, now the most commonly prescribed class of drugs in the United States as well as the most common form of treatment for depression.

But medications alone will not and *cannot* address the rising rates of depression. Paradoxically, medications may even *contribute* to depression's increased prevalence. How effective medications truly are is still being argued by mental health professionals, but there is increasing evidence that most of the therapeutic effect of antidepressant medications is attributable to the placebo effect, the response generated by a person's expectations alone rather than a true therapeutic effect of the drug. *Antidepressants may well have succeeded because of good marketing, not good science.*

Even people who maintain an optimistic appraisal of the benefits of antidepressant medications must acknowledge that *no amount of medication can teach social skills.* No amount of medication can teach someone to be a better or more empathetic listener or better source of emotional support for another person. No amount of medication can help someone develop friendships or a support group. No amount of medication can help isolated people who are wary of others become more approachable or skilled in their interactions. Simply put, *drugs cannot solve the problems that lead many people into the pain and despair of loneliness and depression.*

What This Book Is About

Depressed people, and those most at risk for depression, tend to view other people negatively. Do any of the following statements describe you?

- I am frequently hurt by other people.
- I am lonely or more socially isolated than I'd like to be.
- I can't muster the energy it takes to be with others, call a friend or even just answer the phone.
- I generally avoid others whenever possible.
- I have a hard time developing and maintaining healthy relationships.
- I'm often angry at people.
- I am often disappointed by other people.
- I sometimes think people who are happy must be either naïve or stupid.

All the negative thoughts, feelings, and perceptions about other people you may have right now don't just work against them, they work against *you.* By using the practical tools in this book, however, you can change how you relate to others and how you relate to *yourself.* The positive psychology of bringing forth your best self through your relations with others is a clear path to feeling better. *The research makes clear that people who recover from depression have actively learned a variety of new skills that can help them better build the lives they want.*

The Structure of This Book

This book has a simple theme running through it: *positive and healthy relationships are vital to a sense of well-being.* This simple point is extremely complex in its implications. Just telling you how important good relationships are doesn't give you instant access to the skills you need to actually have such relationships. Thus, the emphasis in this book is on helping you understand the links between how you think, the choices you make, the behaviors you engage in and their effect on the quality of your relationships with others, and the depression you experience.

Throughout this book, you will discover two types of exercises meant to help you acquire specific skills. The "Pause and Reflect" exercises encourage you to think about and develop a positive attitude or mind-set that is associated with overcoming depression. The "Learn by Doing" exercises provide structured, active means for developing a specific skill that can help you.

It is important that you become proactive in your recovery from depression. When people get better, it's not by accident. It's because they spent time and energy learning and practicing new skills in thinking, feeling, and relating that make the difference in their lives. The skills described here have made a positive difference to others and I will encourage and support you as you make your way through them. I hope you will be willing to experiment and try out new ideas and behaviors. When you approach people in your social world differently, you are likely to discover how quickly your life can improve as your relationships get stronger or you develop new and better relationships. Other people really can be a source of great pleasure and comfort, if you learn to co-create these characteristics in your relationships with them. Feeling good will be a welcome payoff for your efforts.

Michael D. Yapko, Ph.D.

Depression Is Contagious

CHAPTER 1

Depression Doesn't Arise in a Social Vacuum:

The Social Foundation of Depression

Depression has social causes you must consider in addition to the other causes (such as biological) that typically receive greater attention. I want to show you how to think about depression in more multifaceted, realistic, and *resolvable* ways and how to recognize the role of social factors in depression.

In a single sentence, here is the essence of what's new: *Too many of the leading experts in depression, the ones who shaped so many of our viewpoints, greatly underestimated the role of interpersonal (social) relationships in the onset, course, and treatment of depression.* Biology, both genetics and the "biochemical imbalance in the brain" hypothesis, has been overstated as the cause of depression. Trusted experts can be intentionally deceptive as well as unwittingly biased when billions of dollars in drug company and health maintenance organization profits influence how drugs and other treatments are researched and administered.

Studying relationships just doesn't seem as scientific to people as does studying brain chemistry. People are impressed by brain scans that show changes in brains when people take antidepressants. *But our brains also change in measurable ways in response to other people*, and we can now measure those subtle changes.

We can also learn how to change brains in beneficial ways, but *the brain changes we stimulate socially are simply a by-product of our greater goal: to build the kind of relationships that serve to insulate people against depression.*

Why Focus on the Social Side of Depression?
Because Our *Brains* Tell Us To

The new neuroscience (brain research) shows beyond the shadow of a doubt that we are "hardwired" to be social. Our brains evolved to make us aware of and reactive to others in remarkable ways. Biologically, we're *meant* to be connected to others.

Perhaps the most telling discovery, which first launched inquiry into the effects of relationships on our brains, was made by accident in the early 1990s by a team of Italian researchers led by neuroscientist Giacomo Rizzolatti. Macaque monkeys' brains were "wired" to show which brain cells (neurons) were active while the monkeys engaged in different activities. Specific neurons would "fire" when a monkey grabbed an object, which was expected. But, fascinatingly, the same neurons would fire when the monkey was passively watching another monkey engaged in that same act of grabbing an object. Neurologically, the monkey's brain reacted in the same way whether he was doing it himself or just watching another monkey perform the action. The brain cells would "mirror" each other in different individuals. These brain cells came to be called "mirror neurons."

Humans also have mirror neurons. When we watch other people, a part of our brain actively registers what's going on and portions also actively relate to their experience. Some experts in neuroscience have called our brains "social brains" for this very reason. Interestingly, brain scans of people who show serious social deficits, such as an inability to show empathy for others, show significant differences from the brains of people who can engage meaningfully with others.

Therapists tend to be highly empathetic individuals, and people (like me) who become psychotherapists sincerely desire to help reduce human suffering. Empathy plays a very big role in conducting psychotherapy, a context in which you listen intently to another person and strive to make "a connection" that communicates caring and a desire to help. In one recent study, therapists and their clients were subjected to a variety of measurements during live therapy sessions. Researchers found that during moments of high positive emotion, both clients and therapists had strikingly similar physiological responses, such as synchronous breathing and blood pressure. When these physiological attunements were greatest in sessions, data which clients did not see, of course, these clients later gave higher ratings of perceived therapist empathy. In other words, *the more attuned the therapist and client were to each other in physically measurable ways, the more caring the client thought the therapist was.* The researchers concluded: "This research supports brain imaging data that shows humans are literally 'wired to connect' emotionally. There is now converging evidence that, during moments of empathic connection, humans reflect or mirror each other's emotions, and their physiologies move on the same wavelength."

Brains change in measurable ways through experience, including *social experience.* The relationship between experience and brain chemistry goes two ways, not just one. *What you experience affects your brain at least as much as your brain affects what you experience.* The goal, therefore, is to retrain your brain through seeking out and/or creating new experiences for yourself that will stimulate your brain in new, helpful ways.

Many studies now show the same findings: When people have their brains scanned before treatment, then one group is exposed to drug treatment and another to psychotherapy, and then their brains are scanned again, both groups show specific and measurable changes in their brains. These physical changes have been interpreted by some scientists as evidence that a "biochemical imbalance in the brain" (more specifically a shortage of the neurotransmitter serotonin), exists in depressed peoples' brains that drug treatment may help correct. However, there are indications that the biochemical imbalance hypothesis may well turn out to be entirely incorrect. Cutting-edge research suggests other parts of the brain responsible for the generation of new neurons likely play much more of a role in alleviating depression than do neurotransmitters.

How do antidepressant medications work? No one knows exactly, including those who created them. The newest neuroscience, however, shows clearly that just hours after taking an antidepressant medication meant to increase serotonin levels in the brain (the drugs known as SSRIs, such as Zoloft and Prozac), the concentration of serotonin rises to "normal" levels. Yet, there is no change in mood, no improvement of outlook, no report of feeling better. *Why not?* Why does it take weeks for an improvement to occur *if* one occurs at all in the 50-50 gamble of taking an antidepressant medication? More ominously, why do some people get so much *worse* on these medications?

Drugs seem to work on different parts of the brain than does psychotherapy, but what that means has yet to be fully understood. It suggests there are multiple pathways for achieving specific goals and that what we have previously assumed about antidepressants may be partially or fully incorrect.

Brains also change in response to other people. A remarkable study at UCLA's Neuropsychiatric Institute showed that brains even change in response to the *expectation* that they are going to change by *eventually* taking a drug. This is clearly a placebo effect established *in the relationship* with the researcher. It is reasonable to expect, then, that *the experiences provided here—in the methods of this book—can, in fact, change your brain.* Since no one is hooking you up to brain scanners, or measuring your heart rate or hormonal secretions as you read, the measure of this book's effectiveness will be the *invisible* changes to your brain while you are *visibly* enjoying the improved connections you build to other people.

Why Focus on the Social Side of Depression? Because Our *Minds* Tell Us To

The social implications of mirror neurons suggest we react consciously and unconsciously to the moods and behaviors of others. In fact, social psychology picks up where neuroscience leaves off, studying the direct and indirect effects of being in relationships. Crossing from neuroscience to social psychology, we go from brain to mind.

The essential foundation of social psychology is recognizing that other people influence us in all kinds of ways. For instance, you have seen some people who can walk into a room, spread rainbows and sunshine and make people happier, and others who suck out the life energy of everyone around them. You know that one cranky person can make a situation unbearable for everyone and that others' testimonials lead you to see a movie, buy a book, or go to a restaurant.

In a classic set of experiments by social psychologists Stanley Schachter and Jerome Singer, research subjects unaware of the experiment's purpose were injected with adrenaline and placed in waiting rooms with other people who were ostensibly subjects in the same experiment. In fact, they were actors hired to act out different mood states such as anger or euphoria. Researchers wanted to find out just how much one person's emotional state would affect another's, especially when there was a general physical excitation from adrenaline (increased heart rate, increased perspiration, etc.). The effects were dramatic. When the actor manifested rage, research subjects became angry. When the actor demonstrated a state of blissful contentment, so did the research subjects. *When people didn't quite know what to make of their own internal states affected by the adrenaline, or when their mood state was mild, they essentially adopted the mood states of the other(s) present in the room.*

Emotions are contagious. Social psychologists have proved in a variety of situations that people pick up on each other's feelings and are strongly influenced by what they perceive. This phenomenon is termed the "contagion of emotion."

The *NBC Nightly News* with Brian Williams reported a story recently of a man in line at a drive-thru Starbucks who was impatiently being honked at by the driver behind him. He decided to try to turn the negativity of that driver into something positive, and so he paid for both his own drink and the drink of the irate honker. When the cashier told the "honker" that his coffee had been paid for by the man he'd honked at, he followed suit and paid for the person's coffee behind him! This resulted in a chain effect that lasted throughout the day, each person paying for the drink of the person behind them. When drivers were interviewed, they all talked about the good cheer it spread and the positive feelings associated with rediscovering how "it is better to give than receive."

The Social Spread of Depression

The contagion of emotion is a huge factor in the spread of depression around the world. Cynicism and hopelessness about the future can spread quickly among people who feel marginalized in some way. An entire people can jump on the bandwagon of hate and blame an individual or country for their problems. Much more personally, your own apathy or despair builds when you feel helpless to prevent or get over failures, hurts, and losses.

Yet other people's bad moods don't just "rub off" on you. The process is more complicated and enduring and involves many different kinds of relationships that, singly and in combination, influence how you look at yourself, other people, the world, *life*.

Psychologists use the term "socialization" to describe the process of developing a sense of yourself as an individual while you learn the customs, beliefs, habits, values, rules, and patterns of communication, as well as all the other intricacies of the society into which you are born. No one escapes the overwhelming force of socialization. By the time you realize you have been trained to speak a language that shapes your reality and have absorbed your culture's most basic rules for how to live, these are so deeply engrained in you that you couldn't escape their influence even if you wanted to. I could go live in another country and culture, but I'd still be the *American* living there.

The factors that can affect the onset and course of depression are far too many to list and describe in detail here. I'll mention just a few: *age* (depression is striking at ever younger ages), *sex* (women experience depression at nearly twice the rate of men in the U.S.), *race* (Hispanics and African-Americans have higher rates than others), *culture* (cultures that emphasize strong bonds with others have lower rates than cultures that emphasize individualism), *economic status* (poverty breeds depression), *marital status* (happily married people have lower rates while unhappily married people have higher rates; happily single people have lower rates and unhappily single people have higher rates), and *religion* (generally religion helps lower depression, but can be a double-edged sword and make some people feel *worse*). Each of these factors encompasses many other factors, so the analysis of social factors that influence depression is extensive.

Good Advertising, Unfortunately, Trumps Bad Science: What You Should Consider Before Looking for the Drug Cure

By focusing on only *part* of your depression, you significantly decrease the chances of successfully resolving *all* of it. Realistically, how can you solve *any* problem by only addressing the part of it you happen to find interesting, philosophically agreeable, or easy enough to do something about? For depression researchers and clinicians, this dilemma has practical implications. For you, the dilemma is likely to be quite personal: Should you take antidepressant medications? It is a complex decision and must be made on an informed basis, not just on faith in a drug company's sales pitch to you *or* your doctor.

If you believe that doctors and drug companies are always ethical, responsible, well-informed, and objective, then when you are given a medical interpretation and medical treatment for your depression, you will likely comply solely on the basis of trust. You may believe in your doctor, and you might believe she wouldn't give you drugs that are ineffective or even dangerous. But it isn't so simple. Most antidepressants aren't prescribed by specialists, and nonspecialists don't typically keep up with literature outside their area of expertise. Doctors are influenced by the ads, too! Furthermore, drug company sales representatives visit your doctor regularly and drop off drug samples along with gifts that have been shown to clearly influence doctors' prescribing habits. (The American Medical Association condones gift-taking from pharmaceutical representatives as long as no single gift is worth more than $100. Drug companies find plenty of takers: Spending on marketing to physicians jumped from $12.1 billion in 1999 to $22 billion in 2003, $16 billion of which was in free samples. The numbers have likely increased since then.)

If your doctor wants to be immune to the crass influence of drug company sales reps, and wants to be informed about current research, he may instead rely on prestigious medical journals and presumed objective research data to make treatment recommendations. Some evidence indicates that your doctor's trust may be misplaced. Let me describe just a small fraction of that evidence.

In January 2008, the *New England Journal of Medicine*, widely regarded as one of the top medical journals in the world, published an article that documented the fact that research on antidepressant medications was, for *years*, published selectively. When a study finding was favorable to a drug company, it was highly likely to be published. But, studies that were unfavorable to a drug were very *un*likely to be published. These studies were essentially hidden from view, never analyzed in order to get a more balanced view of the merits of the drug being tested. One doesn't have to go very far in one's thinking to wonder why negative studies would be omitted from consideration and who benefits from such exclusion. This article is staggering in its implications for how science is done and how the results of research studies are published and released to both professionals and the general public. After including these omitted data to their study of antidepressants' effectiveness, the authors stated, "Our main finding was that antidepressant drugs are much less effective than is apparent from journal articles."

How *much* less effective? In February 2008, researchers reported on data they had acquired from the Food and Drug Administration (FDA) regarding the licensing of the six most popularly prescribed antidepressants approved between 1987 and 1999 (Prozac, Paxil, Effexor, Serzone, Zoloft, and Celexa). Their analysis of the data that led to FDA approval of these drugs indicated that these drugs had *a minimal benefit beyond a placebo effect*. The authors concluded, "There seems little evidence to support the prescription of antidepressant medication to any but the most severely depressed patients." Just days earlier, in January 2008, the *Canadian Med-*

ical Association Journal published a study focusing specifically on the merits of the very popular antidepressant, Paxil. This study, done in Italy, compared more than 3700 patients with acute moderate-to-severe major depression with 2687 such patients who received placebo. The researchers concluded that Paxil is no better than placebo in either therapeutic effectiveness or acceptability to the patient in treating acute major depression.

Perhaps the biggest blow to the credibility of the pharmaceutical industry and those who ignore their questionable science and marketing came from the journal widely considered the premier medical journal in existence today, the *Journal of the American Medical Association*, or *JAMA*. In April 2008, two explosive articles were published—one that documented a practice called "ghostwriting" and claimed that drug manufacturers have frequently paid academic scientists to be listed as authors for research articles prepared by company-hired medical writers, and the other about the selective reporting of data. These reports raise serious concerns about how drug companies manipulate the interpretation and publication of medical research purely for profit. Such practices are apparently not uncommon, according to *JAMA*'s editors. In a blistering editorial in the same issue, the editor-in-chief urges strict reforms, including a ghostwriting crackdown and requiring all authors to spell out their specific roles in the research and data analysis. Dr. Catherine DeAngelis, *JAMA*'s editor-in-chief, said, "The manipulation is disgusting. I just didn't realize the extent . . . We're the ones who have allowed this to happen. Now we've got to make it stop."

Recently, a number of important books by highly credible authors have detailed more deception, exaggeration, understatement, and omission of data regarding antidepressants that undermine their status as a first-line approach to treating depression. These include *The Myth of the Chemical Cure* by psychiatrist Joanna Moncrieff of the University College London, *Comfortably Numb: How Psychiatry Is Medicating a Nation* by psychiatrist Charles Barber of Yale University, *Before You Take That Pill: Why the Drug Industry May Be Bad for Your Health*, by J. Douglas Bremner, director of the Emory Clinical Neuroscience Research Unit at Emory University School of Medicine and *Let Them Eat Prozac: The Unhealthy Relationship Between the Pharmaceutical Industry and Depression (Medicine, Culture and History)*, by psychiatrist David Healy of Cardiff University in Wales. These are just a few of the books detailing the shocking lack of ethics in the lucrative promotion of drugs.

Drugs Can Send an Unwelcome Message

There are plenty of excellent reasons to be cautious around antidepressant medications ranging from the way they are tested and approved for use to their limited success in actual use. But here's my message: *The brain changes we look to drugs to achieve have successfully been made in other ways that don't involve the risks that drugs pose.*

These drugs are neither totally safe nor highly effective. Despite how readily our culture has embraced them, they are of limited value, at best. They are serious medications with serious side effects and should be taken only when the need warrants it and with the *general* understanding they are no more effective than good psychotherapy. I agree wholeheartedly with Dr. Moncrieff, author of *The Myth of the Chemical Cure*, who said, "Most doctors and health professionals want to help people to help themselves over depression. . . . What they fail to realize is that every prescription they issue conveys a message of hopelessness and powerlessness. Every time they recommend antidepressants they contradict the message they should be reinforcing about the ability of human beings to overcome adversity."

I'm not against antidepressant medications. I simply want you to know that the issues are complicated and that the ease with which people put these powerful chemicals into their body on the basis of too little good research and *far* too much exaggerated advertising is a legitimate cause for concern. There's a lot we don't know, and that should concern *everyone*. The issue becomes even more controversial when promoting the use of these drugs in children, a practice I will consider in chapter 9.

Learn by Doing: Evaluating the Advertising

Google the word "depression" and visit some of the websites that attempt to offer objective information as well as some that have products to sell (whether drugs or herbal remedies or special fragrances or whatever). Compile a list of the various treatments you come across, including the promises they make, the rationales for their recommended treatment, and any potential harmful side effects they mention. You can also do this with the ads you see for antidepressants on television, and in magazines and newspapers. When you have compiled at least a couple dozen different remedies, what do you notice about the claims? Which of these, if any, seem credible to you? Which seem utterly preposterous? To whom would such ads appeal, and to whom would they be a turn-off? Now the real learning behind this exercise: How do you go about deciding what's sensible and what isn't? The more clearly you understand what influences your decision making, whether a claim is about a product or another human being, the more control you'll have over the process.

A Quick Tour of Depression

What is depression? I've been talking about it all along without yet having defined it. It seems like this should be a simple thing to do, but it isn't. Depression, known to professionals as "major depression," is officially considered a "mood disorder" by the mental health profession and is so categorized in the catalogue of mental disorders and diseases known as the *Diagnostic and Statistical Manual,* now in its revised fourth edition, known as DSM-IV-R. (The *DSM-V,* which will include new disorders and revise others, is tentatively scheduled for release in 2012.) Here I address major depression exclusively. I do not address depression associated with bipolar disorder (what used to be called manic-depressive illness), a much less common and more biologically based disorder. Categorizing depression as a mood disorder is an acknowledgment that its primary feature is an effect on mood. However, the "official checklist" of symptoms the *DSM-IV-R* cites to make the diagnosis of depression includes: (1) sleep disturbance; (2) appetite disturbance; (3) fatigue; (4) feelings of worthlessness; (5) impaired concentration, and (6) loss of pleasure or enjoyment. As two researchers pointed out, this checklist means little, for there are 227 different combinations of symptoms that would all yield a "correct" diagnosis of depression. Depression is a "soft" diagnosis, based largely on subjective perceptions.

Beyond the symptoms DSM-IV-R lists, the more we learn about depression, the more we see its reach into virtually every aspect of a person's life:

1. Depression affects *physical health,* especially cardiovascular disease. In fact, the relationship between depression and cardiovascular disease is

so strong some have suggested that the best early screening device for eventual heart disease may be screening for depression. Likewise, depression has been associated with diabetes, cancer, and Parkinson's disease, among other serious health concerns. Furthermore, depression has been associated with self-defeating habits like smoking, drug abuse, and overeating. Why bother to protect your health if you're too depressed to care?

2. Depression affects *thought (cognitive) processes*. Significant detriments in attention, recall, information processing, and critical thinking have been identified.

3. Depression affects *productivity*. Depressed people perform their jobs less well, take more sick days, cause more accidents, and raise other employees' stress level.

4. The *antisocial effects* of depression include higher rates of drunk driving and workplace and domestic violence, as well as the higher levels of conflict with others, more divorce, and higher levels of social rejection.

Clearly, depression is much more than just a bad mood or unhappy feeling. Depression reaches into and contaminates virtually every aspect of one's life. For psychotherapists, physicians, and those suffering depression, the primary goal is to treat depression quickly and efficiently, *before* a person's life has become painful in so many ways. Another important goal though, is to learn to think *preventively* by reducing people's vulnerability in the first place.

Cynthia was a senior in college when she met Tommy. A serious student then, with some serious ambitions, she planned to go to graduate school to get her master's in public health administration, and she had a pretty good idea what kind of career she'd like to develop. All who knew her had no doubt she'd succeed in fulfilling her plans. She'd gotten excellent grades all along, was grooming her professors for the academic support she'd need to get into grad school, and was the envy of many of her friends and classmates. Cynthia wasn't really looking for a serious relationship, but when Tommy showed up everything seemed to change. For the first time in her life, she fell in love, and she fell hard. None of the casual dating she'd done had prepared her for the whirlwind of Tommy. He was so smart, so cute, so intense, so interesting, so everything, that she could barely catch her breath around him. All her friends liked him, the two of them seemed to blend together seamlessly, and there was no looking back.

Suddenly, school mattered less, career ambitions mattered less, and being with him mattered more. She knew it made no sense, and for once in her sensible life, didn't care. She finished her degree, but her career plans now seemed out of step with the plans they were making for his career . . . and for their marriage. A couple of her friends asked what her plans were for finding a way to pursue her career and still be Tommy's wife, but Cynthia said she didn't know. Maybe they'd start a family first because "Tommy really wants kids," or maybe she'd wait a year and settle into the marriage, let Tommy get his career going, and resume her own career plans then. She just wasn't sure and so the plan was to "wing it."

Five years later . . .

Cynthia and Tommy have two young children, ages one and three. Cynthia stays at home and is a full-time mother. She loves being a mom, or so she tries to convince herself, but she occasionally gets visions of her former life when her old college friends drop by. They play with the children and tell her how good she looks, but she feels the need to tell them how demanding it is to be a mom and what cute thing one or the other of the kids did that day.

One day Cynthia caught herself mid-diaper story and it was as if something exploded inside her. For weeks afterward, she stewed on the question, "How did I get here?" She began to blame Tommy for taking her away from her dreams, and to blame herself for giving in to Tommy's charm and letting herself be diverted from the ambitious life she had planned. She finally admitted to herself with profound sadness that she felt trapped in a life she didn't really want. Now, who can you tell that to? Your husband, the man you gave up everything to be with while thinking you were giving up nothing and getting everything? Your mom or dad, the grandparents of your babies? Your friends who are pushing the same strollers as you? Cynthia went from reassuring herself that this was a temporary emotional block that would soon dissolve to feeling more and more agitated, angry, down, and withdrawn. Tommy couldn't come near her without her growling at him. In his confusion about what was going on with Cynthia, the only thing clear to him was they fought less when he was at work more. He tried to help, of course, but she'd have none of it. The nicer he was, the more enraged she felt. She felt hopeless, despairing, self-loathing, and guilty that she could be so unappreciative of all she had that others might envy. That only made her hate herself even more. She spun the same question around and around in her mind: "How did I end up here?" No answer came, only more despair. Her thoughts turned in directions that scared her.

Now What?

Cynthia was feeling trapped in the wrong life, frustrated and self-blaming, guilty and hopeless, sad and angry, all the while withdrawing from life and having no plan to address much less resolve any of what she's experiencing. She was giving up and sinking deeper into depression.

If *you* wanted to help this young woman, what would you do? How would you attempt to be helpful? Would you want Cynthia to see a physician and get a physical examination to see if there might be something going on medically that might account for her difficulties? Would you want her to see a psychiatrist for an evaluation, perhaps thinking an antidepressant medication might help? Would you want her to see a psychologist and strive to gain some insight into her feelings and reactions? Or maybe a social psychologist who could help her escape the shackles of traditional female role stereotypes. What about other psychologists who might focus instead on expressing her emotions, clarifying her goals, or correcting her distorted thoughts? Would you want her to see a marriage or family therapist to attempt to get communication going again? What about seeing a nutritionist, acupuncturist or herbalist? Or getting a personal trainer or a life coach?

Pause and Reflect:
This Has Been a Test . . .

How you see Cynthia and what you think she should do says something about how you see problems and approach solving them. Each person has a bias, a preexisting belief that shades how he or she responds to different kinds of information and experiences. In this case, you were exposed to an obviously unhappy person, and it likely triggered some reactions in you. Did you judge Cynthia negatively, blame her for her own problems or see her as a whiner? Did you feel sorry for her and want to help? Did it seem clear to you what Cynthia's problem was and what she should do about it? Or, did you perhaps get tuned into the emotions she felt and relate them to times you have felt similarly (trapped, despairing, angry, isolated, etc.)?

Each of us naturally sees things from our own perspective. The challenge we face is how to change perspectives when they end up hurting us in some way.

How you react to everything I will say in this book will be influenced by your beliefs about depression, your own experiences, and your established ways of responding to new ideas, especially if they conflict in some way with your previous ideas. If I simply tell you what you already believe, then you will likely think I'm quite sensible. If I contradict what you believe, well, then what? Will you conclude I must not know what I'm talking about? Will you adapt your perspective according to new data and perspectives? This is a dilemma we *all* face when we encounter new information and new ideas, and how you respond to such dilemmas will define your next move.

Pause and Reflect:
What Do *You* Think Causes Depression?

If we met at a cocktail party and got to talking about the subject of depression, possibly because the latest in a long line of celebrities has publicly disclosed his depression, and I asked you what you thought causes depression, how would you answer? Pause and answer this question before continuing. Now, how would you describe your answer? Is it simple and straightforward? Is it complicated and multidimensional? Does it suggest an effective treatment approach, or does it make recovery next to impossible? How does your viewpoint about depression increase or decrease your own chances for recovery?

If you believe depression is a "biological illness," a "medical disease," caused by genetics and faulty brain chemistry, plain and simple, then a book such as this will seem merely a supplement to the "real" treatments, namely antidepressant medications and/or the various brain stimulation techniques (such as electroconvulsive therapy, transcranial magnetic stimulation, deep brain stimulation, or vagus nerve stimulation). If you believe depression is a personal failure, a sign of weakness, or evidence of some deeper, psychological problem, then you might well strive to find quick insights or strategies in these pages to help you compensate for or perhaps correct them. And, if you believe that depression is more complicated than a chemical imbalance in the brain or a psychological weakness, then you might well strive to develop a broader viewpoint that encompasses more variables contributing to depression. In doing so, you may have to adapt yourself to new ways of thinking about and responding to the phenomenon of depression. New information often requires us to revise our viewpoints.

Untangling Depression from the Biological Knot

As in Cynthia's case, depression features many different symptoms operating on many different levels. In the Introduction, I described the *biopsychosocial* model of depression, widely considered the predominant model of depression, which acknowledges that many different factors contribute to depression. Depression experts typically, and understandably, tend to focus on one aspect of depression more than another. After all, you can't pay equal amounts of attention to *everything*, so you have to prioritize. And, the economic reality is that it's easier to get support money for some research than other research. Some research is also more likely to lead to a product that can mean unfathomable riches to the discoverer.

Today, when sophisticated scanning technologies allow us to see into peoples' brains with unprecedented clarity, and people are so enamored with the seemingly scientific underpinnings of drug research, other seemingly less objective endeavors just aren't as attractive. It's simply part of our culture, and increasingly the world's, to prefer the ease of taking a pill to the effort of having to think critically or learn new skills, even when pills can't do as much as they promise. So, it's been easy for researchers and clinicians to overlook something as "ordinary" as the power of love, the power of human bonding, or the vital importance of other people to our physical and mental well-being. Not anymore, however, for now we know that other people affect our biochemistry as surely as do pills.

Who Is at Risk for Depression?

Everyone is vulnerable to depression. If you are capable of having a mood, you are capable of having a mood disorder. But, studies of epidemiology, the science of studying the prevalence of disorders in different populations, make it abundantly clear that not everyone is at an equal risk for developing depression.

I describe depression risk factors and their implications for treatment and even prevention throughout this book. Each risk factor you learn to identify and address represents an opportunity to help yourself become far less vulnerable to depression. And, each variable you learn to manage more skillfully makes it far more likely that you won't get in your own way, making bad decisions that only make your depression worse.

Truthfully, there are more known risk factors for depression than I can possibly address in this book, but they are not all of equal weight or intensity. *Some risk factors matter more than others in generating depression.* Some are *physical-biological* and include things like poor nutrition and lack of physical exercise. Physical exercise has been shown to have a treatment success rate that matches that of antidepressant medications— *without* the negative side-effects—and with a lower rate of relapse. Some are found in one's *individual psychology* and include things like temperament, personal history (such as early losses of key figures or a history of abuse), and one's quality of thinking (primarily the errors people habitually make in their thought processes, such as jumping to erroneous conclusions without evidence). Some of the risks involve your *social life*, including the social roles you take on (such as husband or wife, mother or father) and the quality of your relationships with other people. If being around other people is terribly stressful, if you can't seem to build or maintain friendships, if you suffer lots of rejection and loneliness, or if you feel like others are always hurting you in some way, you have some of the strongest risk factors for depression there are.

Life in the United States and around the world has grown incredibly complicated, driven by many different forces, of course, but none more significant than technology. Before the Internet, the mass media (television, radio, newspapers and magazines) provided our news, entertainment, inspirations, and our first direct insights into how others lived, even if they were just characters in a TV show. Parents who once worried that their kids watched too much TV now add "too much time in front of the computer" to their list of worries. Today, our view into peoples' lives is much more personal as people place content directly on the Internet through sites such as *YouTube, MySpace*, and *Facebook*. More than half of young people under twenty-one have already put personal content on the Internet, and many thousands more do so each day. Today's average twenty-one-year-old has already sent and received more than a quarter million emails and text messages. Young people meet and interact in ways nearly unrecognizable to their parents.

Adults, too, regularly use computers and do email. We want our computers to be ever faster, slimmer, and easier to carry. We want our cell phones to have service everywhere, take and send email and pictures, and organize our days for us. We want data instantly, and our emails even faster. And we don't just want these things, we *expect* them. The howling you hear when an Internet server "goes down" for even a short while is truly frightening.

We are collectively spending much more time alone with our gadgets, doing things that typically only indirectly involve other people. Too many of us are working longer hours and have less time to be with other people. In fact, in a study done at Stanford University, at least a quarter of the respondents who use the Internet regularly (more than five hours per week) report that it has reduced time spent with friends and family and increased their feelings of social isolation. Time spent with gadgets negatively affects peoples' ability to relate to each other meaningfully. With *YouTube*, anything you do can be on the Internet in front of the world in moments. *MySpace* has become a "rite of passage" for teens, whose Internet bonding through posted messages, pictures, and naïve self-revelation put too many of our young people at risk for cyber-bullying at least and monstrous sexual predators at worst. And, all the while, online dating services tell us that our "soul mate" is just a few clicks away. The Internet is wonderful in many ways, but it can't replace personal contact and good judgment.

Form Over Substance

Our culture, like it or not, has increasingly become one of form over substance: too often image matters more than truth. Many of us are so wrapped up in our solitary pursuits that other people have merely become tools for achieving them. Here's an example: Parents emphasize the importance of getting into the "right" college, which becomes their child's goal. School systems across the country report huge increases in academic cheating. This is form over substance. The child wants an "A" *however* he can get it, convinced that an honest "B" or "C" won't get him entry into the "right" school. When a colleague who teaches at a local university gave a student an "A-" in a class, the student, who felt entitled to an "A," filed complaints with the university about the instructor and made harassing phone calls to her at all hours of the day and night. Many others have told me similar stories of students behaving in threatening, intimidating ways in order to get a better grade than they deserve. A Yale University professor characterized the shift this way: "Students used to come in feeling it was their responsibility to learn. Now, too many come in feeling it is your responsibility to teach."

Psychologist Jean Twenge has captured this sense of entitlement empirically in studies of the attitudes of young people about themselves in relationship to others. She documents a growing narcissism in her book, *Generation Me: Why Today's Young Americans Are More Confident, Assertive, Entitled—and More Miserable than Ever Before.* Young people expect the world to be as programmable as their Ipods, Twenge suggests, and consequently they don't develop tolerance for others' views, empathy for their feelings or needs, or an ability to build and maintain genuine relationships with others that can withstand inevitable conflicts and growing spasms.

Some people's sense of their own importance is so horribly distorted that they feel that someone who insults them deserves to *die*. The tragic massacre perpetrated at Virginia Tech not long ago by a man who felt marginalized by others was horrific to the extreme—and it was one of almost two dozen such shootings just that *month*.

Form over substance; it's how we choose our political leaders, it's how we choose the products whose advertising we know best, it's how we "adorn" ourselves with tattoos and body piercings that we believe look "cool" to others, it's how we lay off loyal long-term employees just before we'd have to start paying their retirement benefits (the "bottom line" matters, not integrity), it's how we raise our expectations of others (and ourselves, too) ever unrealistically higher, it's how we fool ourselves into thinking we can do things we really can't, and it's how we become vulnerable to depression when the substance doesn't match the form.

Depression doesn't arise in a social vacuum. It arises in response to world conditions, family conditions, marriage conditions, *social* conditions. To treat depression as a medical illness that you can cure with drugs misses the point. There will *never* be a drug that can cure depression any more than there can be a drug that cures poverty or racism. Addressing a growing social problem as if it were a disease is destined to fail. *It is already failing.*

Learn by Doing:
Form Over Substance

Keep track of news stories that highlight how far people are willing to go to get what they want, even if it's at the expense of having integrity or compassion for others. How do people justify hurting other people for personal gain? How do they justify revealing bad things about others as in "tell-all" books, or how do they justify lying to or deceiving people to get their vote? Make a list of specific skills or abilities the people in the stories you collect would need to have in order to handle their situations in ways you personally would respect.

Now, in your own life, what examples can you identify of having put the result ahead of your own well-being or the well-being of others? What specific resources or skills will you need to develop in order to handle future situations in ways you'd respect in yourself? Make a list of these and identify the specific behaviors you'd engage in that would indicate you chose substance over form.

Learning Patterns for Making Meaning

I want to focus on one aspect of socialization in particular called "attributional style" that will help provide some focus for the remainder of this book. Attributional style is the repetitive style of thought you unconsciously and reflexively employ to interpret what happens in your life, and it strongly influences your feelings, reactions, and responses.

Let me give you an example: Terri's three-year-old is crying uncontrollably. Now, what does that *mean*? Terri might conclude any of the following: (1) "I must be a terrible mother." (2) "Kids get upset. He'll get over it." (3) "He's always such a difficult child." (4) "He's so sensitive. He'll probably be a poet or a writer or something like that." (5) "I used to cry like that, too. My parents were so unfair." (6) "I hate when he does that. I'm going to give that crybaby something to *really* cry about." (7) "I'll hold him and kiss him and reassure him and this, too, shall pass." Which interpretation Terri attaches to her toddler's crying will shape where this situation—and eventually, through repetition, where the relationship—goes. Her interpretation (called an attribution) dictates her feelings and behavior.

Learn by Doing:
Recognize Your Attributional Style

You have an existing attributional style. You have a characteristic way of interpreting and responding to the events in your life, and your style is going to increase or decrease your vulnerability to depression. It's going to increase or decrease your likelihood of recovering from depression. It's going to lead you to learn the concepts and techniques I'm encouraging in this book, or it will lead you to think everyone else can do it but you can't, and so you won't even try.

Write down five events that occur during the day each day and leave some room to write after each one. Then, for each event, write out a causal statement that begins, "I think this happened this way because . . ." and then fill in the blank. After a couple weeks, go back to your casual statements and evaluate them. Do you typically think when things happen they happen to you or because of you? Or do they "just happen"? Do you typically think these things can change, or that they'll never change? Do you typically think they affect you in just one area, or all across your life? Get a clear sense of how you tend to look at things, since it's your viewpoint that can trap you in depressed feelings for no legitimate reason.

The heart of the problem with depressed people is that *they unwittingly misinterpret or think incorrectly about things that happen in their lives, then mistake their thoughts for the truth.* Research into the thought processes of depression make it very clear that thinking can be dangerous, especially for those who believe that their way of looking at things is the "right" way.

A form of psychotherapy called cognitive-behavioral therapy, or CBT, explores how cognitions (thoughts) influence mood states and behavior. Quite probably the most well researched and scientifically well supported form of treatment, it works well in the treatment of depression (and anxiety as well as other disorders) because of how easily our thinking can mislead us. Most people's thoughts are not extreme, just distorted enough to make us unhappy. So, for example, someone who suffers the breakup of a relationship may conclude, "I'll never let myself fall in love again or let myself be vulnerable to this much pain ever again." What a huge difference between "This loss hurts" (an example of a specific attribution) and "I'll never fall in love again" (a global attribution) in terms of the quality of thinking. To think you can choose a life that will be pain free by never getting attached to someone for fear of being vulnerable and getting hurt misses the bigger picture of what it means to live a life of loneliness, without love, romance, or intimacy. *The idea isn't to avoid being vulnerable. The idea is to be vulnerable with someone you can trust to protect that vulnerability.*

You learned to think and make attributions in the way you reflexively do through the cumulative effect of your socialization history. From the moment you were born, you were exposed to all kinds of experiences, including the kind of parenting you received, the kinds of explanations you received when you asked about things you were trying to understand, the form of religious or spiritual beliefs you were taught, the influence of brothers and sisters and other relatives, the teachings of your schoolteachers, and on and on. These influences all play some role in how and what you think. Understanding those influences doesn't mean blaming others for the way you think; rather, it's meant to help you sort out what you can do to help yourself.

This passing from one generation to the next of vulnerabilities associated with attributional style is what I have come to call the "hand-me-down blues." A primary goal in overcoming depression, therefore, is to recognize how your attributional style makes you, and your children if you have them, so vulnerable.

The Social Lives of Depressed People

Only relatively recently have researchers and clinicians begun to examine the roles that significant people in a depressed person's life play in the onset and course of depression. And we have learned quite a bit about the social lives of depressed people. What follows are just *some* of the findings.

Depressed people tend to have:

- Fewer friends and smaller social networks
- More conflict in their relationships with others
- Less support from others
- Fewer and less well-developed social skills
- Fewer close relationships
- Less rewarding relationships
- Fewer social contacts
- More marital problems and more family arguments
- More pessimism about the future of their relationships

Such findings make a strong case for the negative consequences of depression on relationships with others.

Pause and Reflect:
How's *Your* Social Life?

Take another look at the general findings above. How many apply to you personally? How powerful a force in your own depression are the relationships in your life?

When other people are a primary source of distress in your life, when you find yourself getting hurt by other people in one way or another on a regular basis, or when you "just don't get other people," this book will help you get connected to others in ways that can make a positive difference.

Other people *can* be mysterious and cause you pain. And, other people can be wonderful and bring you joy. What you find in others, no matter what your background might be, will ultimately be a reflection of *you*.

There's a wonderful old story of a man walking a very long road from one village to another. At the outskirts of the new village he encountered a farmer laboring in his field, cutting hay. He said to the farmer, "I have walked a great distance to come to this village of yours. I have left my village looking for a new home, perhaps I will find it here. Tell me, how are the people in this village? What kind of people are they?" The man in the field thought a moment, then asked, "What were the people like in the village you came from?" The traveler replied, "They were uncaring, self-absorbed, cynical and unfriendly. That's why I left." The farmer paused before replying and then said, "I think that's how you'll find the people here, too." The traveler replied, "In that case, I'll just move on and look somewhere else." A couple of days later, the farmer was again out in his field when another man approached him and said, "My village was destroyed and the people scattered. I am looking to find myself a new home, perhaps in this village. Can you tell me, how are the people in this village? What kind of people are they?" The farmer asked, "What were the people like in your village?" The traveler replied, "They were wonderful people. Loving, close, helpful, and I will miss them terribly." The farmer said, "I think that's how you'll find the people here, too."

How do other people perceive depressed people? How do they perceive *you*? How does that exacerbate depression? The answers to these questions lie at the heart of the treatments I will recommend and the skills I will encourage you to develop through this book.

Another well-researched form of psychotherapy called interpersonal therapy (IPT) emphasizes the importance of having positive and healthy relationships and provides skill-building strategies for developing them. There is good evidence that when people improve their relationship skills, their depression improves. When people feel better about themselves, they get better feedback from the world around them. They feel empowered instead of victimized, and they finally feel like they are a part of something more compelling than themselves and their depression.

Rethinking Treatment for Depression

As we observe social conditions around us, including the fragmenting of families and society, we can see that relationships have clearly taken a beating. The divorce rate continues to be high, the length of the average dating relationship is measured in weeks, more people live alone than ever before, and people generally report feeling more cynical about other people. When people feel isolated, devalued, and expendable, it's hard to feel good.

Let's rethink treatment. Our predominant form of treatment, antidepressant medication, is itself a reflection of the larger problem. Let's start to consider how your hurtful circumstances, whether self-generated or not, affect you and your outlook. Instead of taking a pill, take the time to be insightful and proactive in developing skills that will help you to live better. Don't just "wait for the medication to work." If you are withdrawn and unhappy, you can start to connect to others in meaningful ways.

When you have the right tools for a job, you can do it more easily and successfully. This book is about developing the tools to get connected to others in ways that promote a sense of well-being, make a positive contribution to the lives of others, and develop the all-important and wonderfully motivating sense that a bigger world of positive possibilities is out there.

CHAPTER 2

Other People Are NOT Just Like You:

Frames of Reference, Flexibility, and Acceptance

The quality of your relationships affects your potential for happiness and success more than *any* other factor, even your level of intellect or economic status. No matter how smart you are, if you don't get along well with others, you can't enjoy the emotional and physical benefits that come from warm relationships with caring people. No matter how much money you have, you can't buy genuine love.

But depressed people don't typically build or maintain positive relationships with others. To the contrary, depression usually drains people of any desire to connect with others. Depressed people tend to drive others away with their negativity, complaints, cynicism, pessimism, and lack of enthusiasm. Depressed people drain energy from others, and the rejections they suffer, real or imagined, only serve to reinforce their depression.

Barbara, age twenty-eight is miserable. She has no close friends, and she is considered a little "off" by the other people in her office, who generally politely ignore her. Barbara's not obnoxious or unattractive, but she makes no effort to fit in with her co-workers. They are forever swapping stories with each other, but she says little to them beyond pleasant greetings. Barbara genuinely wants to fit in, but feels self-conscious, uninteresting, and fearful that she has nothing to contribute to conversations with others. Occasionally, a co-worker invites her to a social event, but feelings of dread about going lead her to make excuses for why she can't go. To her co-workers, Barbara seems cold, indifferent to them, as if she's above them. Painfully aware she is perceived in this way, Barbara criticizes herself mercilessly. As for the men she works with, Barbara definitely notices them and wants to be liked by them. She'd like to date, but when a guy tries to talk to her she gets so anxious about saying the right thing that she quickly finds a way to escape the interaction. When she does engage in conversation, she talks way too much about the project she's currently working on because it's the only thing she feels she knows anything about. So no one around her really has much of a sense of what she's really like on a personal level. She's not sure even she has a sense of what she's really like and fears that maybe this unhappy, on-the-fringe person is all she is and all she will ever be.

Barbara feels that life is passing her by. Every day she tortures herself with feelings of inadequacy. She wishes she could be like other people, the ones with personality and style who say and do the right things to attract men and have friends. She wishes she could have a personality transplant. Barbara recognizes that her anxiety about other people and her inability to date and build friendships are the reasons for her misery. But it doesn't occur to her that she has the power to change how she interacts with others. Barbara makes the biggest mistake one can make in this regard. She tells herself, "This is just the way I am," and "I'll never fit in because I'm not like other people." She makes the mistake of believing this terribly self-limiting thought, and so makes no effort to change and improve her life and conquer her depression.

Only twenty-eight years old, Barbara has already established a style of dealing with other people that has the potential to depress her even more over time if she doesn't learn to overcome it. She doesn't fit in, *knows* she doesn't fit in, and doesn't do anything about it beyond passively wishing she could be different. Each day she simply collects more evidence of her inadequacy. Well, you might ask, why *should* she try and fit in? Why try to get connected to other people who don't seem to like you, aren't interested in what you have to say, and seem impossible to relate to? Why try to blend in and be like others? Isn't it much more genuine, much more honest, even *noble*, to stand out as an individual, albeit an unhappy one, instead of trying to just be one of the crowd?

If sentiments such as these resonate with your own, then this book is going to be even more important to you than you might have realized. Barbara isn't hostile towards other people, but many people who choose to withdraw from others are. They radiate the anger that comes from the rejection they suffer, real or only imagined, when all they really want, deep down, is to be acknowledged and cared about.

Pause and Reflect: Frustration, Anger, Depression, and Emotional Distance

It is human nature to put down what we can't seem to have. Remember the Aesop's fable about the fox and the grapes? A fox tries to reach a bunch of grapes dangling overhead, but no matter how high he jumps, they remain tantalizingly out of his reach. When he exhausts himself and finally gives up trying to get the grapes, he walks away and proclaims, "They were probably sour anyway." Does this frustration with others shade your view of relationships?

Many people who struggle with depression radiate anger toward others, partly because of their level of emotional pain and partly because they view others as the cause of that pain. Happy people irritate them by being happy; average people annoy them for being average. Yet other people are just who they are, doing what they do. Understanding how to deal with them realistically and even to become closer to some is a worthy endeavor.

Why Bother?

Recently, studies from a variety of fields have concluded that people who are connected to other people in positive relationships have significantly lower rates of depression than people who are not. People in happy marriages, for example, have a much lower risk of developing depression than people who are unhappily single. People who have a network of positive and supportive friends have much less chance of becoming depressed than those who have no such network. Good relationships can provide us with the basic needs we *all* have for love, intimacy and support.

Most people sense intuitively how important it is to have positive and healthy connections to other people. Yet good relationships don't "just happen." People like Barbara, described earlier, who don't fit in well with others for any number of reasons, often become accustomed to being socially isolated from others. They erroneously believe that others will *never* accept them, will *always* reject them, will *never* find them even marginally worthwhile, and will *always* consider them essentially useless. Such damaging beliefs make developing good relationships impossible, and so the social skills necessary to make contact with others and build satisfying relationships never have occasion to develop.

The general health and mood benefits of good relationships now duly noted, let's get a little more personal. Why should *you* bother to try to build relationships with anyone? Why should *you* expend any effort in the direction of getting connected to other people, especially if other people have been a source of hurt and pain in your life? If you're depressed, socially isolated, feeling emotionally scarred by what's happened in your relationships, afraid to trust anyone again, yet also long for friendships or a caring, loving relationship with someone, you are in a dilemma. It's what psychologists call an "approach-avoidance" conflict. It's when you want something ("approach") yet are afraid of it ("avoidance"), and the usual consequence is behavioral paralysis, or "freezing." Here are some easy examples: I want to ask you out on a date, but I'm afraid you'll say no. I want to ask you for a salary increase, but I'm afraid you'll say no or, worse, fire me. I want to paint, but I'm afraid you'll ridicule my painting.

How you resolve this dilemma (or don't), will determine what happens next. If you could filter the fear out of the dilemma, the "avoidance" part of the "approach-avoidance" conflict, what would be different for you? Wouldn't it make a *huge* difference to be focused on what you want, the "approach" part of the equation?

In the realm of relationships, when people put their fear of hurt or rejection ahead of their desire to be connected, withdrawing for self-protection makes sense. But, it's a way to keep things the same, not a formula for change or improvement. It's how time passes, but not depression. It's a mind-set that keeps you afraid, believing something bad will happen to you that you won't be able to handle. Caving in to the imagined hurts instead of learning how to prevent or manage them keeps depression the only constant companion in your life.

This book is about building the skills to manage your relationships with others well. The skills I'll emphasize *will* help you filter the fear out of the equation and focus on ways to get and stay connected to others in meaningful ways. No one wants to take the time to develop skills without good reason. Well, you have good reason: When people get out of themselves, connect to others in a way that directly says there's something about "us" that's more important than just "me," they feel better, get better, and truly *are* better. *When you care and are cared about, you'll feel better.* That, in a nutshell, is the answer to the question, "why bother?"

The Starting Point

Mary, age thirty-four, felt "like I was hit by a truck . . . again." She had been dating Brad for only about three months, but she'd had the "most amazing feeling that he was 'the one,' the one I'd marry and have a family with. . . . I was so sure he felt the same way about me. But, obviously he didn't, because he broke up with me." Mary had been through this before with different men, a pattern of falling in lust or love or *something*, making all kinds of plans for marriage and a family, and then being dumped for one excuse or another. She heard herself tell me essentially the same story with just some minor variations, then posed the earnest question, "Why are men so afraid to commit?"

I asked Mary what indications there were that Brad felt the same way toward her as she did about him. She paused as if contemplating this issue for the very first time before answering, "He laughed a lot when we were together, teased me affectionately a lot, called me almost every day just to say hi, so I knew he liked me." I asked, "Okay, but what made you think he was thinking long term about things like marrying you and having a family with you?" She asked, apparently truly mystified, "Well, why would he call me and keep going out with me if he didn't care about me and want to marry me?"

Do you see the major error in Mary's thinking that leads her to her relationship despair? She misinterprets Brad's apparent interest in her as *evidence of a desire to get married.* Yet Brad obviously could be interested in her without any idea of marriage.

You cannot use your own frame of reference to understand other people. Other people are NOT just like you. Each person reacts from her own unique perspective. If you don't understand another person's frame of reference, then you will have many more difficulties in relating well together. Other people don't necessarily:

- Feel the way you feel
- See things the way you see them
- Care about the things you care about
- Enjoy the things you enjoy
- Hate the things you hate
- Love the things you love
- Value the things you value
- Take an interest in the things you find interesting
- Understand the things you understand
- Want to go the places you want to go
- Want to do the things you want to do

Like Mary in the vignette above, when you think someone else feels the same way you do, and your conclusion is based on your own feelings and perceptions, you are setting yourself up for a rude awakening. You are using your own frame of reference, not the other person's. Mary was using her own feelings and perceptions in assuming that Brad "must" feel the same way as she ("Well, why would he call me and keep going out with me if he didn't care about me and want to marry me?"), not any direct feedback from Brad to suggest he felt the same way.

Mastering this seemingly obvious concept may well be the most challenging task in this entire book. People routinely say, "Yeah, yeah, I get it. Other people aren't like me." Then they promptly ignore that point and get attached to someone who becomes the catalyst for their next depressive episode. So, I want to drive the point home that others aren't just like you in as many ways as I can in order to help you avoid getting tangled up in situations that can hurt you.

Why Do We Use Ourselves as the Reference Point?

It is a reflex, an automatic, thoughtless process, to use yourself as the reference point for your own reactions and behavior. After all, we can only react from within the confines of our own bodies and individual minds. If someone steps on your toe, *you* feel it, not me. If someone steps on my toe, *I* feel it, not you. If I break my arm, no matter how much you might love or care about me, I still have to be the one to wear the cast. Your wearing it for me isn't going to help my arm heal properly.

When you tell someone, "Oh, I know just how you feel," you're intending to be nice, empathetic. But many people get irritated when someone says that, because their first reflexive reaction is to think, "No, you *don't* know how I feel. You know how *you'd* feel, but you don't really know how *I* feel." They have a point: You really *don't* know how someone else feels unless you ask and the person answers honestly.

Using yourself as the reference point is hazardous. It leads you to think you know how others feel when all you're really doing is reacting on the basis of how *you'd* feel in that circumstance. Maybe someone else *does* feel the same way as you—*but maybe not.* You cannot assume anything of the kind.

Your Reference Point Is Social in Origin

Every human being who survives infancy and childhood invariably does so with others' help and influence. After all, every human baby is born utterly helpless. Even an infant senses and comes to learn what conditions are attached to the family: Is nourishment provided on demand, or according to some type of schedule? Is crying responded to on demand or in some inconsistent or unpredictable way? Is the baby held gently or roughly? Is the attitude toward the baby loving, hostile, or indifferent? Is the baby engaged with or mostly ignored?

Through socialization you learn at unconscious, reflexive levels what is expected of you, what is rewarded and punished. You learn what you can and can't say, what you can and can't do. You learn your role in the family, whether you are there to be loved or whether you're there to perform. You learn whether your grades matter more than keeping your room clean, whether it's better to lie or tell the truth, and whether we give of ourselves to others or let others fend for themselves.

I'm not suggesting you need to explore your childhood endlessly, but I am suggesting you will get further in your own personal development if you know that the attitudes and perspectives you hold were absorbed through these all-important relationships. Your frame of reference, the very foundation for your interpretations and responses to life, especially regarding other people, has its origins early in your life.

Learn by Doing:
Values in Your Family

With pen and paper, spend some time exploring some of your most significant memories from childhood as well as examples of "everyday life" in your family. What values were emphasized? What were you taught to think of as important and, in retrospect, what were you taught to believe was unimportant? Here are some examples to guide you: Did you learn to cooperate or compete with others? Did you learn to value structure or spontaneity? Were you encouraged to take sensible risks or play it safe? Did you learn to be a planner or just take things as they come? Was it important to treat others respectfully or were you allowed to say whatever you wanted to? What other perspective-shaping forces were operating in your life that you think have brought you to this point of being who you are right now? Do you tend to assume that other people grew up similarly? What you learned, and what you didn't learn, while growing up, increases or decreases your vulnerability to depression.

The Internal Orientation

The tendency of people in general, and depressed people in particular, to use their own frames of reference in interpreting and reacting to life experiences is called an "internal orientation." The term describes the use of internal experience, such as feelings, beliefs, and judgments, as the sole or primary basis for reactions and behaviors. When your focus, or orientation, is an internal one, it means you are either entirely or mostly engaged with whatever is going on inside of you. Because our attention is limited—there are more things going on at any given moment than we can possibly pay attention to—by having our focus over *here*, it means our focus isn't over *there*. In practical terms, this means that when I focus on how *I'm* feeling, I'm not focusing on how *you're* feeling. When I focus on how *I* see it, it may not occur to me to see how *someone else* sees it. Logically, you would think that these are not "either/or" distinctions, that I can be aware of my feelings *and* your feelings, too. And, while that's true, too often it isn't how many people respond. Instead, they get wrapped up in their own feelings, focused on themselves and their depression, and they miss partially or completely what's going on with others.

In chapter 1, I spoke about the tendency of younger people to be self-absorbed, and I even hypothesized that the rising rates of depression are directly linked to this greater self-absorption. This internal orientation can become so pervasive that it leads directly to an inability to relate well to other people. It is difficult to have empathy or concern for others when what matters most to you is how you feel, for instance. When you become enmeshed in an "It's either him or me" kind of competition, other people become the enemy, the people who can harm you. This mind-set is evident in "hot spots" all over the world. Even in our own presidential elections, we rarely see a respectful exchange of viewpoints about what might be best for the country. Instead, candidates engage in accusation, innuendo, and character assassination. There isn't nearly enough of an external orientation that would lead people outside their own thinking to examine what might be as good as or even *better* about a position professed to be held by "them." If it's the position of "them," it is, by definition, a bad one. It's why people will support mediocre candidates in their own party rather than someone more qualified in another party. Party loyalty prevents thinking clearly or objectively.

I have established an "us vs. them" issue just by writing this book. As a clinical psychologist and an acknowledged expert on depression who is invited to speak all over the world, I clearly and directly suggest in this book that depression is far more a social than medical problem. That's my position ("us"), but other people have a different viewpoint. Some believe depression is a brain disease that requires drugs ("them"). How will you personally reconcile the contradiction when your doctor suggests you take an antidepressant?

Pause and Reflect: Who's Your Expert?

How do you decide to whom to listen, whose opinion to follow? If someone is on Oprah, is that enough for you? If someone is an M.D. or a Ph.D., is that enough for you? When there are so many opinions on everything from the economy to national security to how to lose weight safely, how do you decide whose opinion is valid?

The extraordinary amount of information available today makes it virtually impossible to be an expert across many areas. So, people use intellectual "shortcuts" in their thinking, often adopting the viewpoints of "experts." But, as we are learning the hard way, experts can be bought and experts can be wrong. In areas that directly affect your well-being, from what drugs to put in your body to where to invest your hard-earned money, the more you defer to others, the more vulnerable you are to the consequences of their biases and misjudgments. It helps to know how to gather and weigh information for yourself. Other people are not like you, and they will weigh information differently than you do.

If you want to know what drives people, or you want to know what they are most likely to do, you'll need to understand their frame of reference. In the earlier story of Mary and Brad, Mary's frame of reference is, in essence, that successful dating leads directly to marriage. She distorts available information suggesting that Brad feels differently, then feels devastated when she realizes his ideas are quite distant from her own. Clearly, understanding other people's frame of reference is a vital skill to master in order to avoid the serious and damaging effects of a strictly internal orientation. We'll explore how to do this in the very next chapter. For now, let's keep the focus on your frame of reference and how it influences your mood states and your relationships with others, for better or worse.

Learn by Doing:
Minimize the Risks of Self-Deception

With pen and paper, make a list of times in your life, especially recent episodes, when you found out the hard way that something you assumed to be true, something you really wanted to be true, was not. Perhaps it was believing someone's words and ignoring their contradictory actions, or perhaps it was wanting to believe in someone's honesty and discovering their willingness to deceive. How did you discover you were fooling yourself? How long did it take you to come to terms with having deceived yourself? If you consider many different examples in your own experience and even the experience of others, you'll discover just how human it is to engage in self-deception. Go the next step in your thinking, though. What does this say about your vulnerability to self-deception when you want things to be a certain way? Understanding this process affords you a preventive opportunity. If you know under what conditions you are most likely to try to fool yourself with excuses and justifications, you can much more easily catch yourself in the process and prevent what could be hurtful mistakes.

Internal Orientation and External Reactions

At its best, an internal orientation can lead you to develop greater self-awareness, a clearer sense of who you are, how you feel, what you value, and what defines you as you. At its worst, it can make you self-absorbed, insensitive to others, oblivious to things going on around you, and probably overreactive to every little ripple in your emotional state.

When your focus is on how you feel and even how you feel about how you feel, it becomes considerably more difficult to step out of your feelings long enough to determine whether they have any basis in reality. Cognitive therapists call this distorted style of thinking "emotional reasoning," characterized by the belief that "If I feel it's true, it *must* be true." A primary goal of treatment is for you to learn to distinguish reliably between what you feel is true and what is *actually* true. This is commonly called "reality testing." Sometimes, of course, what you feel to be true will *be* true. Other times you may unintentionally distort things in ways that set you up for finding out the hard way, like Mary, that things aren't the way you think (or hope) they are.

Your frame of reference leads you to react to things the way you do. It's a reflection of your experiences, the values you hold, and the way you interpret things. When you react to someone you've just met, your response is only *partially* based on the actual person. The majority of your reaction is how you subjectively experience that person. If you are focused on appearance and you don't like someone's menacing tattoos, let's say, you can easily dismiss this person on that basis alone. Would you be likely to say, "I didn't like him because of his tattoos," or, "I superficially judge people only on their appearance?" When you say the former, you are saying there is something "wrong" with the person because he has tattoos. When you say the latter, you are admitting to a superficial bias.

An internal orientation leads you to think that your "snap" judgments about other people are accurate. In this case, you'd think there really is something negative about this person simply because of your personal dislike of tattoos. More careful consideration can lead you to realize that tattoos don't define a person's worth.

Pause and Reflect:
Making Judgments

Your frame of reference reflects your many beliefs, values, and attitudes. When you see a movie, for instance, your appraisal of the movie is much more about your subjective reactions than what it actually depicts. When you read a book, your judgment reflects your beliefs more than the author's views. When you listen to the evening news, your reactions to the news stories say more about you than you may realize: Does the story lead you to criticize? Avoid watching future news programs? Spur you to civic action? Make you want to research the issue more? Lead to an apathetic, "Who cares?" Observing what you react to and how you react to it is a powerful way to create greater self-awareness. Through self-awareness, you can make better choices in life that can help reduce and even prevent episodes of depression.

Tolerance is a core skill for building and maintaining good relationships with others. When people feel they are being judged unfairly or negatively, they naturally close down; open, honest communication comes to a stop. Tolerance means being able to contain your negative judgments and communicate acceptance of others' differences and respect for them. You may not like someone's tattoos, for example, but you can accept his or her right to have and enjoy them, appreciating the person is much more than just his tattoos.

Depression and Negative Frames of Reference

You're entitled to your feelings and you're entitled to your frame of reference. But if you are depressed, you need to examine your frame of reference because *depression is a disorder rooted in subjectivity*. It runs on the fuel of a negative frame of reference, a patterned way of interpreting and reacting to life that is painfully self-limiting.

Depressed people tend to see themselves negatively and they tend to see others negatively. They tend to think about the future negatively and they are likely to interpret life experiences negatively. As a direct result, they are likely to *react* negatively to life situations and thereby make their depression even *worse*. This "vicious cycle" of negative interpretations and negative behavior is dangerous to your well-being, so it is critically important that you distinguish between what your internal orientation leads you to believe and what is really true "out there" in the world. Simply put, a negatively focused internal orientation keeps your depression going. *You have to regularly challenge your own beliefs and reactions in order to overcome depression.*

Frames of Reference Are Self-Protective

Challenging your entrenched negative perceptions, whether about yourself or others, requires effort because your world view regulates itself in order to stabilize your beliefs. Psychologists call this stubborn mechanism "cognitive dissonance"—the inability to hold contradictory bits of information at the same time. We filter out information that contradicts what we believe. It's how we justify our actions even when we do bad or foolish things. For example, someone who sees himself as an honest guy overstates his deductions on his income tax. Instead of changing his view of his character, he rationalizes the dishonest behavior: "Everyone cheats on their income taxes, and why should I pay more than the next guy?" Someone else sees herself as a caring and sensitive woman, but gleefully shares the latest trashy gossip about someone she says she considers a friend. She justifies her behavior by saying, "It was no big deal; she's just too sensitive about that kind of stuff." *Mistakes Were Made (But Not by ME)*, a book by social psychologists Carol Tavris and Eliot Aronson, is an informative, funny, and vexing tiptoe through the minefield of self-deception. Reading it will give you a deeper understanding of the broad range of self-justifying behaviors that dissonance can generate.

Let me give you a couple of more detailed examples about cognitive dissonance:

Let's say you consider yourself a "deep" person who "has no patience for superficiality." You see yourself as more sensitive, more thoughtful, more insightful, more *everything* than other people—and you want them to know and acknowledge it. You go to a cocktail party or some such social gathering, and with each interaction you have you get more and more "fed up with how superficial everybody is." Soon you respond to people's polite conversation with sarcasm and rude comments and justify your behavior with the belief that "the idiots deserve it." It would generate cognitive dissonance for you to believe that you, a deep person, would willingly engage in superficial conversation all night. It would mean (gasp!) that you are one of those trite little people you can't stand. So, you maintain your original belief that you are deep, and everyone else is superficial and deserves your scorn. It doesn't occur to you that party conversation is typically superficial. The context dictates the superficiality, *not* the nature of the people.

Let's say you think you are unattractive and "no one's going to be interested in me, so why bother to go to the party?" Because you've predetermined that no one will find you attractive, when someone does show interest in you, you aren't flattered—you actually feel *worse*. Why? Because you "know" that "it's just polite interest" or "someone else put him up to it" or "it's a waste of time because it can't really go anywhere," or you find some other excuse to cut the interaction short. By not engaging, you stand no chance of developing a relationship that would contradict your original belief. It would generate cognitive dissonance to believe no one will find you interesting and then have someone express genuine interest in you. So, you twist the facts and conclude that any display of interest must be phony.

As you can see, cognitive dissonance is a natural mechanism through which all of us strive to maintain our views, whether of ourselves, others, or the world around us. We bend and twist information to fit with what we already believe. If what you believe serves you well, then cognitive dissonance works in your favor. For example, you think you're wonderful, someone tells you you're a jerk, and you conclude, "He must be having a bad day." But if what you believe works against you and leads to depression, then *cognitive dissonance can help keep you trapped in your depression for as long as you don't entertain new and contradictory possibilities.* If you think you're boring and someone tells you she finds you interesting, instead of telling yourself that she must be lying for some reason, you can consider that she really feels that way. You may not understand it, but you can certainly allow it . . . and begin the process of seeing yourself differently.

How you view yourself, how you view others, and how you think about relationships are all part of your frame of reference. It would be exceptional for you to seek out experiences that contradict what you believe rather than filter experiences in a way that confirms what you already believe. In a nutshell, this is what makes trying to make changes in yourself such a challenge. You have years and years of experience to use as evidence to confirm what you believe. When someone or something contradicts this belief in some way, how do you resolve the contradiction? What would be strong enough evidence for you to change what you believe and, as a consequence, change what you *do*?

Challenging Your Internal Orientation: Flexibility as a Goal

Depression drives people deep inside themselves. It leads people to react to their thoughts and feelings as if they were true, and even to justify their depressed thoughts and feelings with the excuse, "but that's just how I am." This statement, "that's just how I am," is a rationale for giving up. It's an excuse you make to resist any new information or experience, and to thereby guarantee that things will stay the same. Psychologists use the term "rigidity" to describe a fixed way of thinking ("cognitive rigidity") or behaving ("behavioral rigidity") that serves to reinforce the problem(s) the person is experiencing.

Many people know that what they're doing isn't working, but they continue to do it anyway. Why? It's easy to say "it's because they're rigid," but I have a different idea. Through my work with depressed, unhappy people, I have learned that they are not necessarily rigid—they simply *do not know what else to do*. There's a big difference between being rigid and simply not knowing.

When I ask someone what she is trying to achieve with a particular behavior, sometimes she knows and can articulate what she's trying to accomplish, but sometimes she needs help trying to figure out just what the aim is, if there is one. Once we have a clear idea what the goal is, however, then it's easy to ask, "So, will doing more of this get you what you want?" When she says, "No, I guess not," then I can ask, "So what else might you do to accomplish this?" And that's when my client looks at me quizzically, and suddenly realizes that she doesn't have the slightest idea what else to do to succeed. People have a strong tendency to keep doing what they know how to do, or what they think "should" work if they just persist long enough, even in the face of repeated failure. What they don't realize is that it takes flexibility, the virtual opposite of rigidity, to be willing to experiment with new ideas and behaviors in order to develop new alternatives for achieving things they hope to achieve. It is wonderfully empowering to learn how to set realistic goals and actively take the steps to accomplish them in whatever arena of life you choose. *Empowerment helps overcome depression.*

The "Pause and Reflect" and "Learn by Doing" sections in this book help you break through cognitive dissonance and allow you to change by creating or observing *direct experiences* without prejudice. In other words, people learn best when they have experiences that nudge them into redefining what they know—or think they know. The exercises throughout this book are structured opportunities for you to experiment with new perceptions and behaviors. They strive to teach new ideas and skills through experiential learning, the most powerful way to learn *anything*.

Your internal orientation can be a basis for self-awareness and serving your best interests when you make decisions with insight and genuine self-understanding in response to an accurate read of the circumstances. But if your internal focus is on distorted and negative perceptions and an inaccurate sense of yourself, your frame of reference can lead you to respond to situations in ways that work against you and make you feel even worse about yourself.

Responding solely on the basis of "that's how I feel" is potentially hazardous. Frames of reference can be self-limiting and even incorrect and cognitive dissonance can lead you to maintain and justify erroneous ideas even in the face of evidence to the contrary. You need to be somewhat flexible in your thinking and willing to experiment with your perceptions in order to develop more effective ways of living your life.

From Flexibility to Self-Acceptance

Psychotherapists are divided in their approaches to treating depression. Some believe that you should strive to change the ways that you pursue happiness, and others believe you should simply accept your circumstances and make peace with your life and feelings. There are sensible arguments for either position. On one side, we therapists recognize the importance of seeking growth, of striving to improve ourselves and our circumstances. That means we acknowledge our weaknesses, examine how we can correct them or strengthen ourselves, and then act to do so.

On the other side, therapists think that much unhappiness is caused by our thinking that we "should" be happy, or that our lives "should" be different and better. As social critic Eric Hoffer said, "The pursuit of happiness is the leading cause of unhappiness." This camp argues that we should strive for greater acceptance of ourselves, our feelings, and our lives. Through greater acceptance, they believe, we can develop a greater contentment with ourselves and our lot in life.

Consider the point on a more personal basis: How much do you criticize yourself for things that you'd be better off accepting as a part of who you are—such as being ambitious or needing more solitude than others or caring about things others don't seem to care about? How much frustration and anger do you feel over the way other people do things when you'd be better off simply accepting their behavior as part of who they are? Proponents of the acceptance model make a strong case for the merits of "not trying to push the river" and learning to "go with the flow."

One of the most valuable techniques associated with this perspective is called "mindfulness," or mindful meditation. Originally a Buddhist practice, it has been adapted by western mental health professionals as a means of teaching a kinder, gentler attitude. Actually a class of techniques, mindful meditation relaxes you and then encourages you to be "present in the moment," simply observing or experiencing whatever occurs moment-to-moment without analyzing it or judging it. You observe your thoughts dispassionately as events: a common instruction is simply to "watch thoughts go by as if they are clouds in the sky" or to "see thoughts as leaves on a stream just flowing by" without either judging or reacting to them.

Mindful meditation teaches you to distance yourself from your thoughts so that you can break the habit of being reactive and judgmental. Learning to accept thoughts and feelings as simply thoughts and feelings removes you from the position of reacting as if you *are* your thoughts and feelings. You're not. It's better to be able to say, "Gee, that's an interesting thought floating by" instead of, "Oh my God! How could I think that stupid, crazy thing?"

Learn by Doing: Learning the Power of Focus

The abilities to relax and focus are extremely valuable and you can develop them in many ways, from practicing yoga, t'ai chi, mindful meditation, imagery, or self-hypnosis. All such methods are comforting, stress relieving, optimistic, and empowering. I encourage you to pursue one or more of them. Get a referral for a competent clinician or practitioner, or acquire CDs or DVDs that teach these techniques. I have created two programs, *Focusing on Feeling Good* and *Calm Down!* that you may find helpful. Information about them is available in Appendix B.

Liking yourself, accepting yourself as you are, doesn't make you a better person. There are plenty of people who are quite self-accepting, even self-loving, who have high self-esteem but are self-absorbed, self-important, insensitive, and even destructive. They can make life pretty miserable for their families and for society. The old adage that "before you can love someone else you have to love yourself first" is *terribly flawed*. Loving yourself doesn't teach empathy, social skill, or good problem solving, the very things you need to form good relationships and overcome depression. The skills it takes to be good for other people are not the same skills it takes to be good for yourself. You want to be able to be good for yourself *and* others. You don't live in a world by yourself, and you, like everyone else, have a responsibility to others, what is aptly called "social responsibility."

A preoccupation with what's wrong with you—your own problems, feelings, wishes, frustrations, hurts, and disappointments—is a hostile internal environment. It makes effective problem solving less likely and healthy relationships less probable. This negative internal orientation fuels your difficulties with people and impedes you from contributing positively to someone else's life. And when your main focus is on your unchangeable past, you're not going to have much of a future.

Such a hurtful mind-set is worth expending effort to change. Strive for a higher level of self-acceptance. Learn to accept the things you can't change, such as your age, sex, or history. Once you accept them, you can begin to learn how to develop them as strengths that you can use in effective and meaningful ways.

Accepting Others

Disturbed relationships with others are often at the heart of depression. The more internally oriented you are, the more you will use your frame of reference as your rulebook for how other people "should" be. The more you focus on how people *should* act, the more likely you are to: (1) miss important cues that could inform you about this person's abilities and values; (2) withdraw from or avoid perplexing people who don't do as you think they should; (3) be disappointed, frustrated, and unhappy when they don't do as you wish; or (4) apply pressure to them to get them to do what you think they should do. As a result, relationships become a source of distress and increase your level of hurt and alienation.

In the next chapter, I address how to assess other people realistically. Being able to "read" other people is usually pretty easy, *if* you know what you're looking for, and it's a vital skill to master because your perception of others determines how you relate to them. If you keep getting hurt by other people, that's not because all other people are "bad," but because you're not reading others nearly as well as you could. Your frame of reference for making accurate judgments about people isn't working.

The Common Denominator in All Your Relationships is *You*

The foundational skill for overcoming depression is the ability to recognize that *each person is unique as an individual.* That sounds obvious, of course, yet it is precisely what is missing in the awareness of many depression sufferers. Without knowing your "blind spots," your particular vulnerabilities that play themselves out in your relationships, you run the risk of trying to latch onto almost *anyone*—or withdrawing from *everyone* out of sheer frustration and fear of getting hurt again.

Depression seems to rob people of an ability to be curious about other people's differences and an appreciation of how those differences will affect their interactions. Psychologists refer to this as an absence of "mindsight." The self-absorbed, internally oriented nature of depression leads people to act as if everyone knows—or should know—what they are feeling, and assumes that others pretty much feel the same way. It leads to shock, disappointment, hurt, and even greater despondency when people find out the hard way that others *don't* feel the same way they do. Other people are NOT just like you. You have to develop a realistic sense of your own needs, strengths, vulnerabilities, values, goals, preferences, and all the other specifics that make you unique and to use your innate gifts to make your life, as well as the lives of others you encounter and come to care about, worth living.

CHAPTER 3

Expectations and Relationship Satisfaction:

Learn to Assess Others Realistically

What single factor most influences how you gauge whether your relationship with someone is good or bad, healthy or unhealthy, worthwhile or a waste of time? The answer: your expectations. *When you have unrealistic expectations of other people, you are at high risk for getting hurt, disappointed, and depressed.* It's easiest, perhaps even reflexive, to blame others for your disappointment and self-righteously say, "That person let me down." Maybe that person *did* let you down, but it's at least as likely that you let yourself down by having unrealistic expectations to begin with. An awareness of your own expectations and the ability to determine whether they are realistic are vitally important skills to develop if you want to avoid suffering the hurts in your relationships that can lead to depression.

Your expectations for how others will see or respond to you can be entirely imaginary, yet still control your actions. Consider these points:

- Depressed people *expect* to be rejected by others, leading them to be shy at least and to have a diagnosable social anxiety disorder at most.
- Depressed people *expect* others to view them badly so when they are given a compliment or are acknowledged in some positive way, they view it as insincere or gratuitous, thereby minimizing or ignoring its merits.
- Depressed people *expect* to be judged negatively by others, leading to harsh and debilitating self-criticism and paralyzing self-doubt.
- Depressed people *expect* others to know how they feel and even expect others to feel the same way, leading to despair and even a sense of

betrayal when others inadvertently hurt them by responding differently than expected.

The evidence is substantial that depressed people too often have unrealistic expectations of others, often without any basis other than mistaking their own fears for truth. They set themselves up for inevitable hurts simply by expecting the worst from others, which further compounds their depression. If you expect yourself to be treated badly, and allow it on the basis of your expectations, you will be. But, not because you deserve it, only because you allow it.

Pause and Reflect:
Are You Aware of What You Expect?

Before you interact with someone, do you consider what you want from him or her? Typically, we want things like gentle support, or a fun, playful response, or an assurance, or an accurate piece of information. If you know what you want before you get into it, how might that influence your response as the interaction unfolds?

Given how much our expectations determine our level of satisfaction with nearly everything from relationships to movies to jobs to restaurants, we all need to become skilled at recognizing what we want—and therefore what we are likely to expect—*before* we interact with someone. What you want and expect is what makes you vulnerable to disappointment when it isn't forthcoming.

Learn by Doing:
Define Your Expectations

On a sheet of paper, make three columns. Label the first one, "What I want from so-and-so" (think of a specific person you will be dealing with); label the second, "What evidence is there that so-and-so can do this?" and label the third column, "Revised expectations."

Think of at least half a dozen interactions with various people you expect to have in the next few days. In the first column, be specific about what you want and expect from the interaction. They may be things such as support, information, sex, fun, money, or a specific course of action you want someone to take. Simply articulating these wants and expectations can be very helpful. The next step is to articulate what you know about this person, what specific evidence you have that this person has the power and will to provide you with what you want or expect. The great danger, of course, is in wanting what someone either can't or won't provide. That's how disappointment and hurt happen. Now, if you realize you need to revise your expectations once you've thought this through, state your revised expectations in the third column. As you'll likely discover, what you want may be understandable, even reasonable . . . just not from *that* person.

Samantha and Her Men:
What's So Special about Feeling Special?

Samantha comes to her very first therapy appointment, a little nervous, unsure what to expect. She fills out a few forms, then picks up a magazine, distracting herself with Hollywood gossip. Soon, the therapist, Susan, comes out to greet her and guides Samantha into her office. Samantha's first impression is that Susan seems a little young for her job, but she came highly recommended by a friend she trusts. Susan also seems nice.

Susan invites Samantha to sit comfortably, and the session formally begins with Susan's asking, "What would you like help with?" Samantha has prepared herself for this and replies, "I came here because men keep leaving me. I want to know what's wrong with me. I want to know why they keep leaving me." Susan asks, "What do you mean exactly when you say men keep leaving you?" Samantha replies, "I get into relationships with men, and as soon as I start to develop a deeper relationship with them, they're gone. Or, they seem ready to commit but then they leave, like my ex-husband did after only three years. And like my last boyfriend did after only a year. There must be something wrong with me. I want to know what it is and fix it, because I really want to be in a long-term relationship. I'd really like to get married again. I'm only thirty-four!" Susan pauses, then asks an important question: "How do you choose the men you get involved with?" Samantha answers immediately, "If he makes me feel special."

Consider Samantha's response, "If he makes me feel special." If Samantha is feeling "special," is that more about her, or more about the guy she's with? When I present Samantha's case to groups of therapists and ask this same question, about half of them will say Samantha's answer is more about her, and the other half will say it is mostly about the guy. This chapter will help you determine how you would answer this question, and whether your expectations for others are more or less likely to be realistic.

An Internal Orientation Works Against Being Observant

If you are anxious, depressed, insecure, or internally focused and self-absorbed for *whatever* reason, then you are less likely to be observant in identifying people's individual differences. Your expectations of others cannot be realistic if you are primarily focused on what you hope to get from them rather than on observing what makes them tick. Consider Bob in the following vignette.

> Bob was assigned to work with a new team of colleagues to design a complex online banking program that upper management expected would take four to six months to complete. If they were successful, the company would make considerable profits, so the pressure on the team was substantial.
> Even after eight years of working for the company, the initial phase of meeting new team members and striving to build cohesiveness with them was always a huge strain on Bob. He wanted to be friendly with his co-workers, but many he'd encountered viewed every job assignment as temporary, and every collegial relationship as transient, a tool for getting the team goal accomplished.
> Bob was interested in other people, though, and asked lots of questions, some of them quite personal, in order to make "genuine contact." He was always unpleasantly surprised at how little others would ask him about himself, making no attempt to reciprocate his interest, but he kept it up, figuring they'd eventually come around.
> The project manager, a fiftyish fellow named Tom, laid out the proj-

ect for the team members in the first of several group meetings. Timelines and individual contributions were defined, and task completion targets built into the team's mission statement and operational procedures.

Bob attended many meetings in the first few weeks, some only with Tom and others with one or two other team members. In each instance, Bob had the uneasy feeling that everybody knew something he didn't, but his attempts to get them to open up and engage with him a little more were met with a casual indifference. Why was Tom so aloof? What about those guys on the team who reported on their own individual progress in only the most superficial, global terms, especially that guy named Jack? Were they screwing up and trying to be evasive? Bob was fearful that his chances for a promotion might be jeopardized by Tom and this team if they didn't succeed.

Bob was becoming more concerned, more anxious, and more vigilant about trying to read the cues about what was happening at work. He did his own job assignment competently, he thought, but each time he approached Tom to ask for feedback about his work and the team's collective progress, Tom told him if he had anything to let him know, he most surely would. Others on the team spoke less and less to Bob, who found himself feeling deliberately isolated and with no clue as to why. He decided to just "ride it out."

Six weeks into the project, Bob got his clearest glimpse into where things might be going. Tom called him in for a meeting, and asked him to report on an aspect of his programming that he hadn't gotten to yet because he was waiting for the piece he needed to get from Jack before he could begin. He expected Tom to understand that "it's in Jack's hands and I'll run with it when he gets it to me," but Tom didn't understand at all. Instead, Tom blew up and told Bob, "You don't get paid to wait, you get paid to write program. What is it with you? You're so busy yakking at people all the time, why don't you yak at them about the damn project? Why don't you lead for a change instead of just being a follower?"

Bob was startled by Tom's outburst, and stung by his criticism. Tom had always seemed reasonably level-headed and even-tempered. Bob wasn't just sitting around waiting for Jack; he was busy with the other things he was supposed to be busy with, getting his piece of the puzzle ready to chip in. After blowing up, Tom crisply dismissed Bob with another admonishment to talk less and lead more. Bob was confused about what had just happened.

In that moment, things changed for Bob. He continued to work on his part of the project, but his heart was no longer in it. He tried to make eye contact and exchange polite greetings with Tom now and then, but Tom had effectively closed him out. Bob was hurt, angry, and unsure what to do. He found himself thinking of little else but his job, his anxiety and despair growing. He had difficulty concentrating at work and sleeping at night and tried to relax by drinking too much.

Bob knew he was at a critical juncture on this project assignment and felt he needed to do something sooner rather than later to try to improve matters.

Bob had been marked as the "team scapegoat" at his job, and both his career and his mental health would increasingly suffer if he didn't handle his situation well. In fact, he was already showing acute signs of anxiety and depression (poor concentration, insomnia, the repetitive spinning around of his thoughts, abuse of alcohol). People in jobs in which they have to justify themselves in the face of inappropriate blame or rejection can be utterly bewildered about how to cope. What is the best way to cope with the negative conditions at work (the external factors) and simultaneously cope with the stresses (the internal factors) of facing such painful circumstances?

Bob might well have had understandable yet inappropriate expectations that set him up to get hurt. It's generally *reasonable* to want co-workers to be friendly, but *this* project leader and *these* team members may have had absolutely no interest in becoming friends and resented anyone pushing them to relate in that way. *What Bob wanted was reasonable in general, but not for those guys in particular.* You have to know whether what you want from someone is *reasonable for the circumstances* and whether it is possible for this person to provide what you want.

Here are some of the key points evident in Bob's story:

- Before you get too emotionally invested in a specific goal that involves others, you first have to determine whether others share your goal and, if so, to what extent.
- You have to assess other people's values, strengths and vulnerabilities evident in their behavior and verbal communications to determine their capacity to support you in your efforts.
- You have to make sure your actions are appropriate for the people

involved, meaning you have established agreed-upon rules for how you will deal with each other.

- You also have to make sure your actions are appropriate for the situation, meaning the specific circumstances support your efforts.
- You need to develop direct, positive ways of coping with stress and disappointment rather than by overanalyzing matters or using self-destructive patterns such as drinking too much alcohol.

Depressed people often feel let down by others who were actually behaving in predictable ways. If the depressed person had simply realistically observed the people who disappointed him, he would not have formed inappropriate expectations.

Starting from the Outside: What Do You Notice in Others?

It's usually easier to see other peoples' character or personality strengths and weaknesses than it is to see our own. It's hard to be objective about ourselves for a variety of reasons, which we'll explore a little later in this chapter. Now, though, we're going to start from the outside and gradually work inward. I want you to consider how you view people in general and then how you "read" and respond to specific individuals. Do other people regularly catch you "off-guard?" Do they surprise you and disappoint you with the things they do? If so, you need to learn how to get your expectations in line and see who people really are rather than who you want or expect them to be. This will be a huge help to your outlook on life and, subsequently, your mood.

Jim Keeps an Eye on the World

My new client Jim, age thirty-one, makes no eye contact when I come out to the waiting room to meet him. He shakes my hand weakly, tentatively, follows me to my office, but says nothing along the way. He sits in the chair I motion him to, and warily looks around the room, his eyes never seeming to focus on any one thing although he is watching me through the corners of his eyes as he scans, obviously preferring indirect rather than direct eye contact. I let him do this without interruption, aware of his apparent discomfort. Eventually he says, with eyes on the floor, "I have a hard time trusting people."

How does someone develop a strong mistrust of people? Presumably Jim suffered some kind of betrayal in his life but he didn't take that as a reflection of that *specific* person's lack of trustworthiness. Instead, he jumped to a much broader conclusion that *all* people are suspect. This is a major point: On the basis of a distorted conclusion, he decided he'd "never trust anyone again." So, now he moves through life alone, suspicious, tensely waiting for the next seemingly inevitable hurt to come his way. Jim thinks he's wisely defending himself against hurt, but what he's really doing is condemning himself to a painfully lonely, stressful life.

Jim's self-imposed mandate to be ever vigilant has kept him looking for signs of danger in everyone he meets. By focusing on potential hazards, he impairs his ability to notice and identify safe, enjoyable, supportive, caring, and good people he encounters. Jim justifies his belief by using his unfortunate history as evidence of its wisdom, but he is needlessly making himself anxious, depressed, and alone.

When I asked Jim how he would know whether someone he met was trustworthy, Jim blankly replied, "I wouldn't." I said, "It's understandable to want to protect yourself from others, but why expend so much effort protecting yourself from people who aren't going to hurt you?" We discussed the importance of assessing other people realistically, sharing information slowly, asking good questions to learn what matters to people he encounters, and being deliberate about giving people a chance to reveal themselves before deciding they are hazardous. Over the span of a few months, very slowly at first, Jim went into more and more social interactions and got better and better at listening to people and learning about them.

I encouraged him to take a class in digital photography, an interest of his. There he met a woman named Cheryl to whom he was attracted but was too afraid to pursue. When she approached him and asked him out, he was thrilled and terrified but managed to set up a time to go out with her the next week. He and I met several times that week just to get him ready for their first date. We discussed what to ask, what to reveal and what to keep to himself, and how to keep things light and pleasant. Long story short, they got along carefully but beautifully. Cheryl was so rock solid, so clear in how she dealt with him, that he eventually came to trust her. I couldn't have picked a better partner for him if I'd tried. With a little bit of coaching from me and Jim's willingness to put both his past and fears aside, he grew into the relationship and for the first time in his life felt connected and worth something. Cheryl loves him, he knows it, and he loves her. It's been almost two years since they began dating, and Jim is a different man. He has developed friendships with Cheryl's friends, and even developed a few of his own. He smiles, he laughs, he looks you in the eye, and he says with sincerity, "I'm happy."

When Jim was looking for the dangers in others, dangers were all he could see. When he looked for stability and sincerity, he found them in Cheryl. It is a basic principle of perception that what we tend to notice, whether in a specific environment or in another person, is what we *expect* to notice. How many times have you overlooked something you were searching for in a drawer, on a shelf, or in a closet but missed it simply because it was somewhere other than where you expected it to be? So often, what we're looking for is right in front of us, physically or metaphorically, and we miss it simply because we're not in the mind-set to notice it.

Having the optimal mindset is helpful, of course, but even more basic is knowing what you're looking for and how to recognize it when you see it. When you're looking for a set of keys, it's easy. When you're looking for something more abstract, like love or compassion, it's much more complicated. *There are wonderful people out there who can be trusted, there are some pretty unpleasant people out there who should never be trusted, and you—and everyone—must learn how to tell them apart.*

Pause and Reflect: Can You Be So Specific You Miss It Right in Front of You?

When people want to get into relationships, they are sometimes told by well-intended others to "make a list of the qualities you want in a person." So, they dutifully make their list ("I want someone athletic with a good sense of humor who loves dogs and watching romantic comedies") and go "shopping" for a partner. Yet it's possible to be so tied to the "shopping list" and the specific items on the list that you overlook good prospects who differ in insignificant ways.

I have seen this happen many times over the years: A potential partner doesn't fit exactly with what a client had in mind and, instead of adjusting expectations to include a fine person who has plenty to offer, the "shopper" sticks to a preconception that leads him or her to miss out. It's not about lowering standards. It's about recognizing a wider array of variations on a theme.

Learn by Doing:
What's Your General View of People?

Pull out a piece of paper and write out a concise statement, perhaps twenty-five words or less, describing your general view of people ("I think people are generally . . ."). Now, how would you describe the qualities evident in your statement? Is your stated view positive or negative in tone? Optimistic or pessimistic? Inviting or hostile? Open or guarded? Logical or emotional?

Maybe you could or maybe you couldn't concisely express a written opinion about people, but you undoubtedly have an opinion. A viewpoint can limit your options. Jim's perspective at our initial meeting prevented him from meeting people and having any relationships, which kept him unhappy.

On the basis of Jim's original viewpoint, he couldn't relax, had to be hypervigilant, couldn't open up to others, and couldn't create new and better relationships. Isn't it great that Jim was able to transcend his past rather than become enslaved by it?

How does your own viewpoint of people enhance or detract from your life?

What Do You Notice in Other People?

When you meet someone for the first time, what do you tend to notice about him or her? Pause and think about your response. Do you tend to notice his appearance—manner of dress, physical attractiveness (or lack thereof), the quality of eyes, hair, teeth, skin, body size and weight? Do you tend to notice her demeanor—smile, eye contact, friendliness, willingness to engage with others, use of touch and personal space? Do you focus on his intelligence, verbal skills, ability to articulate ideas, speed of replies, and grasp of complex ideas? Do you focus on her emotional qualities—easy to laugh, gentle, supportive, seductive? I'm barely scratching the surface of all there is to "tune into" with another person, and listing all the things there are to observe and respond to would take volumes. (In fact, volumes *have* been written about what we notice and respond to, both consciously and unconsciously, in others.)

But some characteristics clearly matter more than others because they have a stronger influence on how other people perceive them and behave toward them. You need to know what you're looking for, and how to understand what people are telling you "between the lines" of what they say, so that you have realistic reactions to them.

The Heavyweight Factors to Assess

Notice my use of the word "assess" in this section's title. It may sound a little cold, a little clinical to you, but I want to encourage you to practice assessing virtually everyone you meet and engage with in some way, whether it's someone you intend to date or marry, someone you're paired with in a team-building exercise at work, or someone you're thinking of hiring or partnering up with in a new business. *Any time you are going to be in a position of potentially being influenced by the actions of someone else, you need to have a better-than-average grasp of how this person does things in order to know how to position yourself with him or her.* By "position yourself," I mean to say that you have to define your relationship with this person in specific circumstances. Is it a relationship of equals, or is it unequal because this person is your boss or your child? You, and only you, can decide things like how much information you will share about yourself, or how much responsibility you will take for what happens. If you're not used to thinking your way through relationships because you assume "everyone is pretty much alike," or "most people have a conscience," or "I'm no bargain so I should be grateful for anyone just noticing me," then you can begin to understand why your relationships may suffer.

Sometimes, people have a negative first reaction to the notion of assessing others. They say, "C'mon, it's just a conversation at a cocktail party," or, "Hey, it's just a temporary project we share at work," or the ever popular, "But, I love him (her)!" They don't *want* to assess people because it seems too detached, too calculating. They want the freedom to follow their heart. But then they complain bitterly when the relationship (predictably) goes badly.

Some people naively think that if they treat the other person well or fairly, they will be treated well or fairly in turn. They are nice people. *Foolish*, but nice. The Golden Rule ("Do unto others as you would have them do unto you") does *not* preclude being insightful and wise about what you do unto others and, in turn, what you allow them to do unto you. If you make the mistake of believing other people are just like you, you will be blindsided when you find out the hard way they're willing to say and do things you're not.

Assessing others doesn't mean being unfriendly or cold or detached. It means being observant, neutral (without prejudging), as you interact with them in friendly, polite, and inviting ways. It means recognizing and considering the implications of what people say and do, and choosing your own responses and behaviors accordingly. Acquiring enough good information about a person helps you be deliberate in deciding just how vulnerable to be with him or her, how much of your heart and soul (and body) to share. It *doesn't* mean being overly suspicious of people (like Jim in the example above). *It means being cautious about making yourself vulnerable until you have a good sense of to whom you're making yourself vulnerable.*

Too many people *don't* do this. They get attracted to someone, perhaps even a genuinely unknown someone they met online in a chat room, their hormones start racing, and their feelings of desire and fantasies of passion and having met someone "amazing" start flowing hot and heavy. The very idea of slowing down and doing some thinking about things can be entirely unappealing. They don't *want* to "cool down." So, they get involved, they get emotionally attached and sexually active on the basis of very little substantive information, and then when they discover this person's "fatal flaw" the relationship comes to a crashing end. Then comes the hurt, the loneliness, and the despair. Or, bypassing that unpleasant aftermath and resisting having to think about its significance, they go out and do it all over again. And again.

This is true not just in romantic and sexual relationships, of course. People can get "hooked" into other people in many different ways. There are countless people who fall for financial schemes ("Become a day trader and learn how to beat the stock market!"), health schemes ("Lose twenty pounds in twenty days!"), and personal fulfillment schemes ("Discover the wisdom of who you were in your past lives!"), all because they trust the promise of someone they naively believe can provide them with what they want. *What you want from other people makes you vulnerable to them.* That's not the problem, though. *The problem arises when you entrust that vulnerability to someone who is willing to abuse it for his or her personal gain.* That is why you have to assess others realistically. When someone "spiritual" tells you to "Send your dollars to God . . . at *my* address," there is good reason to be cautious.

Following are six of the most significant factors to consider in assessing other people. I want to make it clear that these are *my* top six of dozens of possible things to observe about someone else. So it would be wise to pursue this topic further, perhaps with some of the helpful materials listed in the Notes and Appendix sections at the end of the book.

First and Foremost: A Well-Developed Sense of Responsibility

Good relationships are difficult enough between two reasonably intelligent, emotionally healthy people. But, if you don't have a well-developed sense of responsibility, you don't have the foundation for doing all of the other important things that you must do to keep a relationship healthy. By a "well-developed sense of responsibility," I mean that you recognize and accept that your actions directly and indirectly affect others and that you make thoughtful choices with this in mind. The following are examples of what responsibility looks like in relationships:

1. A responsible person commits to performing the tasks that represent an agreed-upon division of labor within the relationship ("I'll cook if you clean" or "I'll research and report on the technology for this new program if you'll write up the proposal we can give to the department head"). One person doesn't get to kick back while someone else does it all.
2. A responsible person does what she says she will do and can be depended upon to follow through on commitments. Her promise is as good as gold. ("I said I'd do it, so count on it.")
3. A responsible person doesn't isolate his spouse, partner, or colleague ("You don't like my drinking? That's *your* problem!"). A responsible person accepts that he is not responsible *for* other people, but *is* responsible *to* them. When one person in a good relationship says, "This is a concern for me," the responsible person helps address it directly and in a timely way.

4. A responsible person doesn't put other people's well-being at risk for her own benefit ("I know I have a family depending on me, but I've always wanted to climb Mt. Everest and now here's my chance").

5. A responsible person doesn't blame other people for the choices he made ("I *had to* hide my mountain of debt from you because I knew you'd be furious with me for spending money we don't have").

6. A responsible person doesn't walk away from an interaction just because it's difficult ("Stop talking, you're giving me a headache!").

7. A responsible person doesn't threaten other people or otherwise try to control them ("Either you cut back on your hours or I'm leaving you").

8. A responsible person doesn't ignore the needs of others who've been led to believe they can depend on her just because her original commitment is no longer convenient ("I know I said I'd be there, but that was before I got tickets to the concert").

The ability to take responsibility for one's actions is often not very easy. Cognitive dissonance leads people to *justify* rather than apologize for some pretty bad behavior. The importance of being able to say "I'm sorry" to someone you've wronged cannot be overstated, and there are few better possible displays of integrity.

Pause and Reflect:
Can You Say "I'm Sorry?"

It never feels good to have to apologize for hurting someone or for having made a mistake that negatively affects others. When you hurt someone, do you acknowledge it and apologize? Do you wait until someone demands an apology and then give it reluctantly or perhaps not at all? How would you describe your typical way of dealing with apologies?

The ability to say "I'm sorry" is a crucial skill to master in a healthy relationship. No one is perfect and you will, of course, make mistakes from time to time. How quickly you acknowledge and take responsibility for them is what, in part, defines your sense of moral responsibility.

Now, translate this into something you can actually assess in others. When a potential love interest reports on something she did, or was a part of doing, where does she place responsibility? For example, did her prior marriages fall apart because "those husbands turned out to be defective people," or because "*I* chose badly because I was so desperate?" If she tells you the former, I'd advise you to run away *now*! She is blaming her former spouses for the demise of the marriages as if she had no role whatsoever in what happened. In fact, though, she was *half* the marriage. On the other hand, if she admits to some responsibility, she *may* be okay, but you need much more information before you can safely conclude that.

Second: A Relatively Realistic Self-Awareness

How well do you know yourself? Some of the most depressed people I've treated became depressed by trapping themselves in circumstances where they really just didn't belong. With eyes wide open, yet not really seeing, they ignored their own basic nature and got absorbed in situations that violated that personal nature.

Here's an example: One of my clients, Joyce, is depressed, divorced, and in her mid-thirties. A self-described "nester," she claims she wants nothing more than to find the right man and settle down into a long and healthy marriage. But she has not been dating, socializing, or putting herself in situations where she can meet eligible men. Why not? Because she has gotten herself into what I consider a bad situation with two different men who are her "friends." Joyce calls these men "friends with privileges." Even though they are "just friends," with no illusion on anyone's part that the relationship is going to turn romantic and possibly culminate in marriage, they are having sex together. Joyce says, "It's casual, there are no strings, it's nice to be held, so what's the harm?" This extremely high level of self-deception keeps Joyce depressed, feeling very bad about herself.

What is a "nester" doing in this kind of exploitive relationship? She wants marriage but is in a kind of relationship that saps her motivation to go out and meet new people. Although she claims to value depth and commitment, she engages in intimate behavior that is in direct violation of those values. As a direct result of this "solution" to her lack of a love life, she pretty much hates herself, feels cheapened by it, yet feels stuck in it because of all the conflicting emotions involved. She is depressed because she is violating her self-awareness and sabotaging her own goals.

Knowing yourself is difficult. It requires that you think clearly about your desires and values and then acting in accordance with them. Making moral compromises, getting lost in the need for contact or approval, selling out for a raise or a promotion are pathways to unhappiness. You want to know yourself well enough to be able to stay out of situations that are attractive on one level, but violate your sense of yourself on another.

How can you assess how well someone else really knows himself? When he says, "I'm ready for a commitment," that sounds good, but is it true? When someone says, "I can complete this for you by Friday," should you believe her? The key point is this: Most often, but not always, people are telling you *what they believe to be true* about themselves. Some people intentionally lie and know they're lying, but for most people it's not about lying. *It's about self-deception.* It's about wanting, even needing, to believe we're better than we really are. No one is going to say to you, "I'm a superficial person who callously uses other people for whatever I can take from them, so will you sleep with me?"

It takes some time to determine how well someone you're assessing knows himself because you have to talk a lot and listen to what this person says about his or her character, temperament, or nature. *You don't need to believe, nor do you need to disbelieve, what you hear.* You simply note it. Over time, you watch for how well the things people *do* fit with what they *said* they'd do. The more consistent they are, the better it speaks for their level of self-awareness. Even when they're inconsistent, if they're responsible about it, they'll acknowledge and try to mend the inconsistency. If they're not responsible, they'll make lame excuses for it.

This is why you don't want to rush into things with people. *Until you ask a lot of questions, until you observe the relationship between what someone says and what he does, you just don't know how much of what he tells you will be true.* Until you see someone in a variety of situations and moods, you won't really know whether he can be respectful when angry or sensitive when stressed.

Third: It's Vital to Know What Someone Values

The deepest core dimension of a person is his value system. A value system is the framework by which you decide what's right and wrong, what's desirable and undesirable, what is and isn't worth doing, what is and isn't important, and how things should and shouldn't be. Our values are the single greatest predictor of what our behavior will likely be. That doesn't mean they're not a perfect predictor, of course, but most people are quite consistent in behaving in ways that reflect their values.

Values can be stated directly, or they can be inferred. When you meet a woman with three kids who gushes about how wonderful it is to be a mom, you don't really have to ask her if she values the family. When you meet someone who works way too many hours, who is the first one in and last one out, you don't really have to ask if his priority is his job. Instead of recognizing that his commitment is to work, not relationships, however, too many people will take it as a challenge to change him. They self-deceptively think, "Well, once we're together he won't work as much so we can spend more time together." Then they're miserable when he sets the relationship aside because of work. How could they *not* see it coming?

If you know what matters to someone, *really* matters, you will be able to adjust your expectations accordingly. If you know someone is a sexual opportunist (a "playboy"), you won't expect a commitment (and, if you're truly wise, you won't sleep with him, either!). If you know someone is deeply religious, or political, or humanistic, or if you know she is extremely competitive, you'll know much more about what kinds of behavior to expect.

It takes time to learn what someone values. It takes time to find out how well she knows her own values. It takes time to find out how stable or enduring someone's values are.

Fourth: The Ability to Accept Inevitable Differences

We generally are attracted to people who are like us. We meet people and go through the typical questions of who we know in common, the places we've both visited, and other shared experiences. *While our initial attractions may be based on similarities, however, it is how we deal with our differences that determines whether this relationship will be healthy and lasting.*

No matter how similar in values, background, or goals two people might be, there will, of course, be individual differences between them. These differences can range from the superficial to the profound: One person prefers tea over coffee, one has more social interests than the other, one has a lesser sex drive than the other, and so on. The fact that there are differences between people is to be expected, but when a couple is in distress, one partner tends to try to impose his or her preferences on the other. He says, "I wouldn't spend my money on that crap. Why do you?" Or she says, "Why do you hang around that loser? He's such a jerk!" The essence of the message is, "If I don't like it, neither should you. *You should be more like me.*" It's a very destructive message, one that devalues your ability to make your own choices and live your life according to your own standards. It makes you feel as though you are being controlled by someone else and not being true to yourself. Such a relationship crushes your spirit, makes you doubt yourself, and will lead you to feel trapped and depressed.

When you assess someone, you want to assess his level of acceptance so that you can know if he is able to acknowledge and respect what's different or unique about you. You're assessing his ability to respect the boundaries—the limits you set, the lines you draw that cannot and should not be violated—that define you both as individuals, even if you are a couple or a team at work. As long as you are effective in what you do, it is not for someone else to tell you what your interests should be, how you should spend your time or money, or anything else that is a matter of personal preference. In relationships, that "we" that evolves makes anything that affects you both something to be discussed and negotiated, not imposed by one on the other.

Respecting boundaries means not invading someone's space (such as looking through their drawers or email), not imposing your will on someone else through manipulative tactics because it makes you feel better ("You may be twenty-seven, but I'm your mother and I forbid you to get a tattoo"), and accepting the choices someone else makes even if you don't agree ("I'm not coming to your wedding because I don't like who you're marrying").

As you share ideas and perspectives, is someone openly critical or judgmental about the things you say? Does she say some variation of, "If you had any sense you'd see things my way?" Does he start to punish you (pouting or turning a cold shoulder) if you have a different opinion about something? It's fine to disagree, but if you want to have a relationship that has mutual respect built into it from the very beginning, evaluating someone's capacity for tolerance is vital.

Fifth: The Skill of Impulse Control

Controlling your impulses allows you to "think before you act"—to pause and evaluate the merits of a response before reacting. Someone who lacks impulse control says whatever flies into his head with no consideration of how it might affect others. Impulsive people instantly react to people or situations, far too often making things worse. They say something terrible in the heat of anger that causes permanent damage.

Impulse control means having the ability in a split second to anticipate the consequences of a statement or action and to decide *whether* to say or do it and, if so, how best to say or do it. It is one of the most valuable skills in life to be able to *pause and reflect for a moment before saying or doing something that can't be undone.* It may be exciting (temporarily) to let yourself be seduced by your attractive neighbor, but the cost when your relationship implodes will annihilate any fond memory for the episode. It may be exciting to meet someone in a bar to go home with for the night, but the cost when you discover the sexually transmitted disease you've been left with squashes the probability of any involuntary smiles coming to your face when you think about it for the rest of your life. It may seem harmless and fun to "do the wild thing," and sometimes it is, but until you think through what the likely consequences are going to be, good impulse control means *temporarily* doing *nothing.* I wish I had a dollar for every time one of my clients said to me, "But it seemed like such a good idea at the time."

Assessing someone's degree of impulse control isn't difficult. Does the person often say rude and thoughtless things and only later (if it all) recognize their hurtfulness? Does she spend money she doesn't have on momentary, even silly pleasures? Does he react instantly and storm out the door, or hit a wall violently, or throw or break things when he is angry? Even if someone takes responsibility for the act and apologizes later, how many times do you want to go through the cycle of hurt followed by an apology? The power of impulse control is in its ability to prevent people from saying and doing hurtful things they'll have to apologize for later.

Many people not only don't exercise impulse control, *they don't feel they should have to.* They think they should be able to say and do whatever they want, regardless of whom it might hurt. Their attitude is, "if someone gets hurt by me just being me, then that's *their* problem." It's what allows people to engage in antisocial or socially reckless behavior—driving drunk, sleeping with someone else's spouse, or shoplifting an item they want. *Combine poor impulse control with a sense of entitlement, and you have a relationship that simply cannot do anything but produce misery.*

Self-absorbed celebrities are obvious examples of people with poor impulse control: they party whenever they want, buy whatever they want, and sleep with whomever they care to, believing that they're important and should be denied *nothing* that provides personal gratification. They display no sense of awareness about their action's negative effects on others. Fortunately you can take note of behavior in "regular" people *before* you get attached to them and prevent disappointment, hurt, illness, and depression.

Sixth: Adaptability and Problem-Solving Skills

Relationships are naturally going to change over time. Organizations evolve, staffs turn over, company priorities shift as new ideas come in and current ideas become obsolete. Marriages and other long-term committed relationships also change over time. People age, bodies change, babies arrive, children become adolescents, young adults leave home, grandkids arrive. Adaptability indicates how well someone accepts and responds to the inevitability of change. "Rigidity" describes the difficulty some people have in adjusting to change. The more rigid someone is, the more energy he expends trying to keep things comfortably the same. The rigidities can range from relatively simple ones ("Don't ever sit in my chair again!") to much more complicated ones ("How can I live without you?").

Rigidity surfaces in relationships when a change of some sort is needed. For example, Max consistently shows up late for meetings with his team at work. His supervisor lets him know politely that he's done that one too many times and his tardiness will no longer be tolerated. Max says, "C'mon, gimme a break. I'm busy with things! Besides, the first ten minutes of these meetings are just silly small talk, anyways." Max is given the feedback that his behavior is unacceptable. Instead of changing it, he defends it and thereby indirectly states his intent to go on as before. Someone else may use foul language that you explain you find offensive, but he defends his right to use it. Someone else is impolite and refuses to use good manners because she thinks they are unnecessary in a good relationship. Examples of how people refuse to change unacceptable behavior and defend it are endless. You can defend it, but you're not helping the relationship any when you do that. Someone has already told you it's offensive behavior. Your defending it isn't likely to make that person change his or her mind. It only creates an uncomfortable impasse.

In assessing people for relationships or business, you would be wise to observe how well they adapt to feedback and to changes in circumstances. When someone is so rigid that he demands that a plan stay the same, for example, even when it's a poor one with predictable negative consequences, it doesn't bode well for future interactions. When people are so rigid that they'd rather brush off your concerns or wishes than hear them and adapt to them, the relationship is guaranteed to suffer.

A "stay-the-course" philosophy can be a sign of stability, but it can also be a sign of rigidity, particularly when it polarizes people and makes them dig in their heels even harder. In healthy, long-term relationships of any sort (business or personal), it is a constant challenge to keep the lines of communication open enough for one to say to the other, "This isn't working for me anymore." And, someone tuned in and responsible may sigh and wish to avoid the rest of the conversation, but will instead do what's sensible and figure out how to make things workable for *both*. When the relationship isn't working for one of you, then it isn't really working for either of you.

If you know someone who would rather avoid problems than solve them, this is going to make your relationship *far* more complicated. *Problems don't get solved and people don't become better problem solvers by avoiding them.* It isn't fun to have to pay attention to problems, but it is necessary to acknowledge them and move through them as quickly and efficiently as possible. Drifting off into getting drunk when things are tough is not a good problem-solving behavior. Slamming the door on your way out and disappearing for a couple of days out of spite is not a good problem-solving behavior. Refusing to speak or giving someone the "cold shoulder" escalates the anger rather than helping to solve problems.

The rigid pattern of avoidance, or disappearing, instead of facing and solving a problem makes moving forward next to impossible. It becomes extremely burdensome—and depressing—to be the person in the relationship who's always saying to the other, "C'mon, we need to deal with this!"

From Outside to Inside: Assess Yourself

The six key things to assess have a huge impact on the quality of the relationship you form with someone. Listen very carefully to what people say. Watch their behavior. Learn all you can about what makes a person tick so you can adapt your expectations for the relationship in more realistic directions. You can save yourself a lot of despair when you make good assessments before you get invested in someone. But the other half of the relationship is you. What makes *you* tick?

It is often easier to be more objective about others than yourself, because:

1. We live with ourselves; we're constantly absorbed in our own thoughts and feelings; we know our history, our disappointments and failures, our fears and doubts, and we know our successes. We know when we seem to fool others with displays of competence or bravado that we don't really feel. Simply put, it's sometimes hard to know what the "real" us is, or if there even *is* a "real" us.

2. We each have limited awareness, a field of consciousness that is relatively narrow in terms of what we can be aware of at any given moment; thus, we *all* have "blind spots." We also have substantial gaps in our awareness that we're occasionally startled to discover about ourselves ("Whoa! I never realized I was so clueless about that sort of thing!").

3. We're actually *motivated* to ignore our own contradictions or inconsistencies. It's hard work to continually revise our self-image and so we tend to form an idea about ourselves pretty early on in life and then filter information through that self-image. Cognitive dissonance leads us to ignore, manipulate, distort, and misrepresent information that is at odds with an established belief or perspective. It's how we maintain a stable sense of ourselves and our world. Once we decide, "I'm this way" or "The world is this way," we resist reconsidering that entrenched belief.

Awareness of these six key characteristics can change how you approach relationships (if you're willing to be adaptable) and increase your success in them. *These same six patterns also determine how well **you'll** function in a relationship*: how you deal with issues of responsibility, whether you have a realistic self-awareness, a coherent value system, flexibility, impulse control, and a tolerance for others' differences. Just reading the previous sentence is going to pose a challenge to you: How realistic are you in your appraisal of yourself?

I'm not talking about self-esteem, which refers to your view of yourself, whether you like and respect yourself. I'm talking about how well you really understand your own way of thinking, feeling, and behaving. Many people have a view of themselves that was formed years, even decades, ago and they think of themselves as still being that same person. They hear an angry dad from a childhood episode say, "You'll never amount to anything!" and believe it, but as an adult never revise it. They remember a childhood episode when their overwhelmed mom, who had three kids and worked two jobs said, "I wish I'd never had you!" and absorb it. They never consider it from an adult perspective in order to revise it.

What do you believe about yourself? When you consider the organizing principles of relationships, how well can you identify where you are on each continuum?

One of the most reliable pathways into depression is to trap yourself with rigid ideas of how you "should" be rather than developing a healthy awareness of how you really are. You can always strive to improve yourself, of course, but you can like, rather than dislike, yourself enough to want to do that.

To minimize unrealistic expectations and depression:

- *Strive to be responsible for yourself.* What you say and what you do is up to you. What others do is outside of your control, but when *you* make the choices, they are *yours*. If they hurt someone, it helps to apologize. Blaming others for your choices is destructive to relationships.
- *Live in a way that's consistent with your values.* Every time you choose a course of action that violates some value you hold, you will like and respect yourself less. It's just not worth it.
- *Be tolerant.* If you don't like what someone stands for, if you don't like or respect the choices someone makes, then this isn't the person for you to partner up with beyond the most superficial level. Instead of trying to change someone in big ways by pressuring or trying to control them, let him or her be and keep a respectful distance. Respect your own boundaries and those of others.
- *Pause and reflect.* Before you say or do something, especially in emotionally charged situations, exercise impulse control by stopping to deliberately, silently list multiple options for responding. Choose the one that will lead to a better outcome, not the one that will make you feel better but make the situation worse.
- *Expect and allow for change in your relationships.* Big or little, changes are going to happen. That's normal and even *desirable* since that's how relationships deepen and grow stronger and more intimate. When

doing things the same old way doesn't work anymore, don't waste a lot of time wondering why. Use the information to craft a new response and get on with implementing it. It's an extraordinary way to let people you care about know that you're "tuned in" and you care.

- *Be self-aware.* Take the time to explore yourself. Read books, go to lectures, take classes that encourage greater self-understanding. The greatest benefit is you get to make better choices about what you will and won't do. The value of prevention cannot be overstated.

CHAPTER 4

Thinking Too Much and Too Deeply:

Learn to Take Action

An old Irish proverb says, "You'll never plow a field by turning it over in your mind." This chapter explores one of the most disabling aspects of depression, a pattern called rumination—the tendency to think passively and repetitively about your concerns and negative feelings, essentially spinning around and around and around in your mind your worries, doubts, and despair. The merry-go-round of unproductive stewing is directly related to the onset and course of depressive symptoms. It also directly relates to depression's most common companion, anxiety.

It may seem counterintuitive to you at first, but there is a measurable danger in thinking too much. This is especially true when the thinking involves a self-absorbed preoccupation with inwardly focusing on your negative or unhappy feelings and outwardly expressing them to others.

Beth Wonders:
Is There a Deeper Message in Marti's Comment?

Yesterday at a business luncheon, Beth sat next to Marti. It had been a reasonably pleasant luncheon, a notch above the usual rubber chicken meal, and the guest speaker was informative yet entertaining. She talked about how things would soon be changing in their field, how new technologies would be integrated into the work environment, and what to expect in the coming months as obsolete protocols were rapidly phased out. Marti made a comment to no one in particular about the frustration of always having to make adjustments to the latest technology, making whatever she currently knows outdated. Everyone at the table nodded in good-natured agreement.

The comment struck Beth as insincere coming from Marti, who was a department head. Extremely bright and well-respected, Marti was always the one ushering in the changes she was now taking a potshot at. Beth wondered if there was some message in there that she was supposed to pick up on. Was Marti indirectly saying she should be striving to stay more current? Was she suggesting Beth wasn't catching up to new changes as quickly as she should? Was Marti surreptitiously watching who reacted to her comment to identify who was struggling with adjusting to the company's frequent changes and therefore might warrant closer monitoring?

Beth couldn't sleep that night, fearing she'd missed something deeper she was supposed to catch in Marti's comment. Then she wondered if she should ask Marti directly what she thought of her and mentally played out different scenarios of how to best approach her and ask for direct feedback. Then she feared she'd be drawing negative attention to herself and thereby set Marti up to watch her more carefully. Then she thought Marti might appreciate her interest in getting feedback and make her seem more dedicated to the job. But then she thought she might be viewed as too needy for approval. By the end of the week, Beth was miserable, anxious, and unable to sleep, yet no clearer about whether Marti's comment meant something (or not) and whether she should say something (or not).

Research on rumination shows that depressed people typically hold the mistaken belief that by thinking, analyzing, and contemplating, they are engaging in problem solving. Ruminators may *think* they're being insightful, but they are really only delaying taking effective action. *It is a basic truth that in order to overcome depression, you must be proactive (not passive) and **do** something—take an effective and timely course of action that makes a positive difference.* You must make good decisions and implement them as soon as it is helpful to do so.

Passivity fuels depression. Beth could end the spinning by making the sensible decision that if Marti has something important to say to her, then it is up to Marti to make the time and find the appropriate means to say it. It's Marti's responsibility, and Beth isn't in charge of Marti. Decision made, let it go, end of rumination. Getting out of rumination involves the skill of knowing when to let go and move on.

The Ruminative Process

Rumination is a style of coping with life stressors and negative mood states that features a very strong internal orientation, a process of engaging in self-focused attention on one's negative feelings and perceptions at the expense of taking effective action. It's the basis for what many understandably call an "analysis paralysis."

Learn by Doing:
Focus on It and It Gets Bigger

One of the most basic principles of perception is this: What you focus on you amplify. As a quick exercise you can do right now, stop reading and notice a sound in the room you've been "tuning out" as you've been reading, just some routine background sound that's been there all along, and focus your attention on it. You'll notice it becomes more prominent in your awareness. You have amplified your awareness of the sound by focusing on it.

It's especially important for you to *consider how you decide what to focus on.* Do you even have a sense that you decide, or do you feel it "just happens?" Do you tend to notice what's wrong or what's right in your daily life experience? Good things happen in your life every day, perhaps not hugely dramatic ones, but good ones nonetheless. You meet nice people, see beautiful trees or clouds and countless other little things that you could notice and amplify that would lead you to conclude, "Life is *sometimes* hard, but there are lots of good things that happen in my life, too."

Now, knowing that the quality and direction of your focus amplifies your experience of whatever it is you're focusing on, consider that *a self-focused attention on one's negative feelings and perceptions* is one of the most powerful contributors to depression. It plays a vital role in the onset of depression, as well as in how bad it gets, how long it lasts, and how likely it is to return after an episode comes to an end. Thus, I want to emphasize in the strongest possible terms that it is important for you to master ways to break out of rumination and take action in order to reduce the frequency and severity of depression in your life and even to prevent episodes of depression from taking hold. *The most important skill is to know when to stop thinking and when to follow a well thought out plan for taking effective action.*

Rumination as a Coping Style

A coping style is pretty much what it sounds like—an enduring, patterned way of coping with the challenges and difficulties that life hands you each day. The way to evaluate a particular style of coping is by assessing the benefits and drawbacks associated with it.

Learn by Doing:
Develop a Positive Coping Style

Stress is inevitable in life: job deadlines, difficult and even unfair people, health setbacks, losses, unwanted burdens of one sort or another, and even our own reactions that sometimes make matters worse. Developing a variety of positive ways for managing stress and coping with your problems is one of the critically important skills for keeping hard times from turning into depression that hurts you and affects the other people in your life. I especially encourage going out of your way to find and be with supportive others.

How do you typically cope with stress or the difficulties you face in your life? Do you engage in negative coping behaviors, such as drinking too much alcohol, eating too much junk food, or withdrawing from people? Or do you engage in positive coping behaviors, such as regular physical exercise, practicing some form of relaxation, and spending social time with supportive friends? List as many positive coping mechanisms as you can think of that would help get you through tough times. Then strive to use them!

Just Because You Ask It, the Answer May Not Come

The ruminative person thinks that if he asks the same question enough times, eventually a satisfactory answer will emerge. But there are some questions that simply cannot be answered in a definitive or satisfying way no matter how many times you ask them. Why isn't life fair? Why do innocent children get fatal illnesses? What happens after we die? Such questions can launch lifelong searches for some people, but they are no closer to answers at the end of their lives than when their search began. It helps to ask good questions—questions that can actually be *answered*. A good first question to ask about your questions is: *Is this question answerable?* Is there some path to follow to get a definitive answer, or will *no* amount of research or information gathering provide an answer?

Rumination is related to, but not exactly the same as brooding, pouting, wallowing, or just feeling sorry for yourself. It is less about specific life situations, which tend to come and go over time, and is more about being a stable, predictable way of handling stressors across different kinds of situations. When one situation resolves, on to ruminating about the next one . . .

Rumination, like other coping styles, develops early in life and becomes a deeply engrained, reflexive pattern for responding to negative situations. The fact that it is reflexive means it is a contemplative process launched unconsciously. And, as the principle of cognitive dissonance you learned earlier would predict, people who engage in rumination naturally defend it and rationalize it, typically by saying they're *not* ruminating, merely "analyzing all the possibilities."

Thus, there's a rationale for rumination that actually serves to keep it going: *The people who ruminate tend to believe they're gaining insight through the process of rolling an issue around and around in their minds.* Realistically, thinking something through *is* desirable generally, particularly when it is an exercise in impulse control. But there comes a point when thinking becomes *over*thinking, and where your ability to solve a problem with decisive action becomes impaired rather than enhanced. The goal, then, is to know where that point is in a given circumstance so that you can decide on and take effective action.

The Detriments of Rumination:
How It Feeds Depression and Anxiety

Reflexively, as soon as people who engage in ruminative thinking start feeling bad, they start asking themselves broad questions such as:

- Why is this happening to me now?
- What does this mean?
- What does it say about my life?
- What does it predict for my future?
- Why does this *always* happen to me?
- Why can't I *ever* be happy like everyone else?

On one hand, these questions may seem reasonable or even insightful, but they invite you to selectively review past hurts and extend them into the future as negative expectations, leading you to believe your problems are both insurmountable and inevitable. Instead of focusing on a problem, you may get wrapped up in your depressed feelings, analyzing them, linking them to more and more problems and thereby making them ever larger and more complicated. This isn't how you recover from depression. *It's how you get more depressed by getting depressed about your depression.*

You do not want to focus on depression in ways that make it bigger, more complicated and unsolvable. You want to "divide and conquer," to break "depression" into its components and address each component in effective ways that neutralize it. In fact, it's what you're doing by following the exercises in this book: breaking the social aspects of depression into components that you identify and then developing effective skills to manage them.

The research shows quite clearly that people who ruminate:

1. Have higher levels of vulnerability to depression. Someone who ruminates compared to someone who does not ruminate is considerably more likely to become depressed over time.
2. Have more severe depressions because they become paralyzed with indecision and stop taking effective actions to help themselves. It's one of the primary reasons why only about a quarter of depression sufferers even bother to seek help. They decide *in advance* it's hopeless, and give up without even trying.

3. Have more chronic depression and more relapses. Instead of taking effective action, they sit around doing nothing to help themselves.
4. Are more likely to suffer anxiety in combination with their depression, what is called a "comorbid" or co-existing condition. The anxiety caused by wondering, "Will I ever be normal?" or "What if I never get better?" complicates matters because there is no immediate way to answer such fear-inducing questions.

Rumination increases self-doubt, which also increases anxiety. If you feel you can't make a decision because you don't know what to do, and even if you did know what to do you fear the decision would be wrong, then you can appreciate how freezing into inaction can come about. The pattern of "second-guessing" yourself raises self-doubt, feeds rumination, and increases anxiety. Learning to be a good decision maker, trusting yourself to make sensible, well-thought-out, and timely decisions, is how good self-esteem gets built.

Rumination and Sleep Disturbance

The most common complaint people have when suffering through episodes of depression, and perhaps even between episodes, is some form of insomnia. They may report difficulty falling asleep, staying asleep, or they may complain that they wake up too early and find it impossible to fall back asleep. It is no surprise, then, that fatigue is the second most common symptom depressed people report.

Sleep can be affected in depressed people for many different reasons. But depressed people with sleep disturbances routinely report that though they're exhausted, they still can't shut off their streaming thoughts.

When you lie in bed, what do you think about? People who sleep well almost invariably answer, "Nothing." People who don't sleep well almost invariably say, "*Everything*." Rumination features greatly in sleep disturbances, causing physical, cognitive, and emotional arousal. As you contemplate whatever is bothering you as you lie in bed, it triggers the release of stress hormones, causing your thoughts to race faster and faster, and gets you emotionally upset. Any one of these alone would be enough to affect your sleep, but together they make sure good sleep isn't going to happen.

The goal is to learn effective mind-clearing strategies. People who say they sleep well and think of "nothing" don't really mean "nothing" in a literal sense. They mean that what they think about is so trivial it may as well be nothing. They're not thinking about their problems. Instead, they're focusing on how good it feels to be in bed, or how much they're going to enjoy sleeping. Their thoughts are about nothing of significance, and that is a model of what you're striving for if you're ruminating instead of sleeping. The goal is to learn methods of clearing your mind and focusing on things that will soothe you. Something as silly as counting sheep actually works because it's monotonous; it doesn't generate physical, cognitive, or emotional arousal.

Learn by Doing: Improve Your Sleep

How is your sleep? Good sleep is vital to mental and physical health, but the research on sleep shows that too many of us are working more and sleeping less, and that the quality of our sleep is diminishing along with the quantity. Keep a sleep log for a few weeks. Write down when you go to bed and when you wake up, how many times you awakened during the night and how many hours of sleep you actually got. If you're not getting at least seven hours of sleep, you're not getting enough. Some people need more, some need much more, but very, very few people can get by on less and still function well.

William Dement's book, *The Promise of Sleep*, provides great insights into the mechanisms and importance of sleep. Read it and you will discover how important it is to go to bed about the same time each night and how important it is to increase not only the amount of sleep to around eight hours, but also the efficiency of sleep, meaning that for eight hours you set aside for sleep, you actually get those eight hours. It takes time and practice to develop good sleep patterns, and learning to relax and focus away from problems and on soothing thoughts and images paves the way for healthy, restorative sleep. Learn the skills of natural sleep and you won't need to take sleeping pills.

Learning to manage rumination to improve your sleep is healthy, empowering, and helps generate the energy that lets you do other helpful things.

Rumination Damages Relationships

Have you noticed your effect on others when you rehash the same old issues and keep vowing to do something but then never follow it up with effective action?

It's wonderful to have friends and loved ones who care about you and in whom you can confide. It isn't clear, however, whether confiding worries and complaints is good for you or the other person. It's also not clear how much support you can ask for before it becomes too burdensome to others. "Reaching out" and "seeking support" from others is generally desirable, but it can easily slip into "wallowing" and "misery-seeking" behavior.

A common complaint of the co-workers of depressed employees, or the friends or relatives of depressed people is that "I get burned out listening to them complain all the time." Depressed people are often shocked to hear this, erroneously believing that the more they talk about what's wrong, the more support and feedback they'll get and this will move them closer to actually doing something about their depression. The evidence contradicts this, though, because in fact rumination *delays* action while simultaneously increasing self-doubt.

Some mental health professionals find the idea that you can think too much philosophically unacceptable and believe idealistically that the more you analyze things the more insightful you'll become. "Deep, insight-oriented" psychotherapy may encourage you to examine the details of your childhood and adulthood in a process that can go on for *years*. Analyzing your life and developing a relationship with a therapist who promotes insight can be worthwhile, of course, but is best done *after* depression lifts, not as a means to try to get your symptoms to remit.

Yet these "deep" clinicians ignore the massive evidence that treating depression by emphasizing skill building has a higher success rate than approaches that encourage analysis. This determined oversight is a deeply disturbing display of cognitive dissonance within the profession.

I tell you this to help you put rumination in a larger social context, since some psychologists actually *encourage* rumination by telling you that analysis is "deeper" than decision making and insight is preferable to taking sensible action. This approach can prevent you from getting past your depression. The actual clinical evidence is quite clear. *The therapies that have the highest treatment success rates in treating depression all focus on teaching people specific skills that encourage them to take timely and effective action.*

Women, Men, and Rumination

Research in epidemiology, the study of the prevalence of a disorder, has consistently shown that women tend to experience depression at a higher rate than men. In the United States, the rate of depression is almost double for women, and in some cultures it is almost *triple*. Naturally the question arises as to what general biological and social vulnerabilities women have that men don't share.

Women have some biological vulnerabilities; at least half of women report significant changes in their mood on a monthly basis because of their menstrual cycle. A significant number of women also experience some degree of postpartum depression, the "baby blues," partly due to the dramatic hormonal shifts that take place during pregnancy and childbirth.

The greater vulnerabilities to depression for women, however, tend to be social rather than biological. Women are treated differently than men. Distressed girls are more likely to engender "rescuing" behavior in their parents, unwittingly encouraging a greater sense of helplessness in them. Psychologist Mary Pipher's exceptional book, *Reviving Ophelia*, provides many sensitive insights about the challenges of growing up female. Studies suggest that parents are more likely to encourage and even inadvertently reward sadness in girls more than in boys by giving them extra attention and support. Women are more likely to suffer sexual abuse as children (a pattern evident in the histories of ruminators), lifelong sexual harassment, and inequitable divorce settlements. They generally live closer to the poverty level, and are limited by the so-called "glass ceiling" in business. Men face their fair share of difficulties, too, such as higher levels of drug abuse and completed suicide when depressed, as Terence Real's book about men's depression, *I Don't Want to Talk About It*, sadly reveals. But women's more passive, ruminative style when facing adversity adds an extra layer of challenge to the process of overcoming depression.

Perhaps the greatest factor, though, is the socialization process that encourages women to be more *thoughtful* and men to be more *action-oriented*. Women are generally taught to be sensitive, attuned to others, more emotionally aware and expressive, less impulsive and self-concerned, and more "other-oriented." The implicit message is, "Be a good daughter, be a good wife, be a good mother." A reliable path to personal happiness is making others happy, but this concern for others can't be at the expense of being decisive and active in living your own life.

One of the top researchers in the field, psychologist Susan Nolen-Hoeksema of Yale University, began studying the sex differences in depression many years ago and wondered why women suffered more depression than men. Her research into the sexes' differences led her to explore their different coping styles. Her high-quality research highlights the detriments of rumination and further identifies rumination as a key factor in elevating women's vulnerability to developing depression. Her superb book, *Women Who Think Too Much: How to Break Free of Overthinking and Reclaim Your Life*, focuses on women's greater tendencies toward rumination, but her findings about its detrimental effects apply equally to both men and women.

Pause and Reflect:
Your Strengths Can Give Rise to Effective Action

Earlier I mentioned the focus of an emerging positive psychology that strives to expand people's strengths. Positive psychology researchers often study people with valuable skills in an effort to identify exactly what they do that seems so effective in order to make it learnable for others. If a researcher were to study something you do well, a skill that could be taught to someone else who could benefit from having it, what skill(s) might that be?

No matter how much people seem to be struggling with some part of their life, they are more than their problems. Taking the time to identify your own personal strengths is crucial for living and relating well. I encourage you to find more ways of recognizing and using strengths you already have. It takes some vision, though, to see beyond only your limitations.

Managing Rumination

The strategies I describe in this section can help you get some relief when you start to ruminate. You can keep yourself from getting overly wrapped up in your negative focus and thereby prevent yourself from sliding into bad feelings. I will also help you overcome rumination as a coping style.

Distraction Strategies: Benefits and Liabilities

Numerous research studies consistently show that when ruminators are given tasks to perform that distract them from their negative focus, *they feel better* by the time the task is complete. Simply put, interrupting the downward spiral of negative thoughts and feelings helps people feel better.

In times past, when someone felt bad, others might say to him or her, "You think *you* have problems? You want to see some people with *real* problems? Go volunteer at the hospital!" Okay, it wasn't the most sensitive and supportive advice, but it often *worked*. People would go to the hospital, volunteer their time, and they'd feel better as a result, perhaps because they put their own problems into perspective or were actively, positively contributing to others' lives, or they were no longer negatively self-absorbed, or because of *all* these possibilities.

Researchers in positive psychology have discovered scientific support for what the great spiritual teachings across the world's religions have been telling us all along: If you want to be happy, you need to make other people happy. If you want to be admired, you have to recognize and point out to others what is admirable about them. If you want to be appreciated, you have to notice and share what can be appreciated in other people and in the world around you. *The things that have the greatest potential to lift your spirit, and your mood along with it, can only be done in the context of social relationships.* The goal is to get absorbed in things that are worthy of your time and energy, things that are *good for you, good for others,* and *good for the world* around you.

Learn by Doing:
Doing for Yourself by Doing for Others

Positive psychology confirms the wisdom of the ages, that "It is better to give than receive," at least as far as mood and life satisfaction go. For the next month or more, make a point of doing at least three things a day to make someone else feel good, even if only momentarily. Pay someone a compliment about her pleasant demeanor or even just his appearance, or thank someone for a job well done, or acknowledge a skill the person has and ask with appreciation how he learned that skill, or write a thank-you note for some kindness someone extended to you, or make someone's day by telling him how he made your day. When you look for opportunities to say and do nice things for others, you'll find them. Going even further by volunteering an hour or two (or more, if you can) each week to some worthy cause would be great. And remember, the nice things you say and do shouldn't just be reserved for strangers. Your family and friends can certainly use some of your kindness and generosity of spirit, too.

Initially, it might seem a little bit phony to you to do things for others just to try to feel better about yourself. I'm willing to bet that what's right about it will quickly overtake what's wrong, and you and others will come to appreciate it.

Realistically, you can't always distract yourself in order to avoid ruminating about bad and hurtful things. You wouldn't want to even if you could. Distraction isn't meant to make you avoid a negative situation that you need to address. Rather, distraction means pulling yourself away from useless ruminations and doing something else that interrupts the downward spiral of negative thoughts and feelings. If you avoid problems that you need to solve, eventually they will escalate until they force you to attend to them—at which point they're likely out of control. Thus, you want to handle things *before* they become urgent, *before* they're "on fire." Avoidance prevents your timely response and adds a great deal of unnecessary drama to your life.

Distracting yourself in order to "get out of yourself" can be a very good strategy, but bad strategies include drinking alcohol to excess, eating too much, or getting lost in meaningless pastimes, such as web surfing or video games. These self-destructive behaviors then give ruminators more to ruminate about, and so they engage in even more self-destructive behavior in order to further divert themselves. Consider the rise in obesity and associated overeating that leads to a preoccupation with weight loss . . . which leads to excessive focus on diet and body size . . . which leads to self-criticism and feelings of unhappiness . . . which overeating comfort foods tries to soothe. It becomes a vicious cycle.

Exercise

Physical exercise has been shown repeatedly to be one of the most effective means for overcoming depression. There is no doubt that physical activity can distract you from ruminating. Yet there is something therapeutic about exercise that goes beyond distraction and that is not yet understood by mental health professionals. In studies comparing depressed people who exercise and those who simply receive antidepressant medications, the findings are remarkably similar: People who exercise regularly, defined as at least three times a week for at least thirty minutes per time, show *a level of improvement that matches that of antidepressants but with less than half the rate of relapse!*

Perhaps exercise stimulates certain biochemicals that improve mood, but no matter how old you are or what shape you're currently in, the benefits of regular exercise accumulate quickly. Last week walking just a quarter of a mile took the wind out of you, and this week you can walk half a mile comfortably. Such rapid gains help people who don't tolerate frustration well and who otherwise give up pretty quickly if things don't change right away with just a little effort. Regular exercise can provide significant improvement in depression very quickly, which is rewarding; when you're depressed, rewards for your efforts sure feel good.

Learn by Doing:
Take a Walk and See the World

People say, "I know I should exercise, I know I'd feel better if I did . . . but I don't feel like it." Making exercise a social process rather than a solitary one can help whenever you don't have the drive to do it yourself. In the next week, ask friends and neighbors whether any of them are interested in taking an occasional walk with you either around the neighborhood or somewhere else of mutual interest. I'd suggest asking several people and setting up walking times with them so no one person becomes the only person you can walk with. It's wise not to have all your "walking eggs" in one basket. Maybe you even want to go beyond walking and check out a workout facility, like a gym. You can make that a social process as well. Finding or creating a "workout buddy" can keep both of you showing up and doing the exercise together, whatever it might be. Setting up friendly competition, establishing a commitment to each other to keep showing up, doing things to keep it fun and interesting are all ways to make exercise both social and productive. Move your body and change your life!

Mindful Meditation and Hypnosis

Besides distracting yourself from rumination that triggers or traps you in depression, you also want to identify and correct negative and distorted thoughts. However, it's not always the distressing thoughts that are the problem. The problem is that you actually *believe* them. Thus, it may make more sense to simply learn how to step back from your thoughts and let them float by without taking them in and believing them.

Mindful meditation, described earlier, helps you learn to focus your awareness in meaningful ways. It helps you to redirect ruminative thinking into calming, relaxing images while also detaching from your thoughts as triggers for emotion. For example, a common imagery used in mindful meditation is to picture your thoughts as fallen autumn leaves floating down a gentle stream. From a safe and comfortable distance, such imagery allows you to see your thoughts ("I'm so screwed up!") go by in a detached way, thereby losing their power to make you feel bad. The thoughts become objects of curiosity rather than triggers for bad feelings. In essence, mindful meditation teaches you to be aware of and then accept and use your thoughts in new ways rather than fighting against them. Through calm, focused experience, you discover that *you are more than your thoughts*.

Hypnosis similarly involves a focusing process. People in hypnosis are highly attentive to a specific focal point, whether the soothing words of someone guiding them through the experience, or a specific idea, image, or symbol. It could be almost anything the person focuses on as a means of relaxing and getting absorbed in the experience. Too many people seem to have misunderstandings about and a mistrust of hypnosis, which is unfortunate. One misconception about hypnosis is that people will have less control over themselves. In fact, skillful applications of hypnosis *increase* the degree of control people can attain over their experience.

Of all the things I have studied in depth in my lifetime, I have been most impressed with hypnosis for its ability to help people develop greater self-mastery. Modern clinical hypnosis has become a core component of behavioral medicine and psychotherapy programs all around the world because it can help you control your thoughts, feelings, behavior, and even the level of pain you experience in your body.

Hypnosis is about building frames of mind. A qualified clinician (state licensed health care professional) who uses hypnosis has the professional background and training to teach key skills that can reduce anxiety and depression. The experience of hypnosis is relaxing, and people in hypnosis hear and can respond to anything and everything going on. They are active participants in the process, and can more easily absorb new ideas and learn helpful skills when in that relaxed, focused state.

With self-hypnosis you can learn to focus and relax yourself independently. As in mindful meditation, you learn to control the direction of your thoughts, but self-hypnosis actually goes a little further than mindful meditation by emphasizing specific skills and more personalized ways of overcoming depression. (I emphasize these skills in the hypnotically based CD programs for depression and anxiety I've created called *Focusing on Feeling Good* and *Calm Down!* which are described in Appendix B.) Working with a knowledgeable professional with these methods is a great option, and when that's not feasible for one reason or another, having professional CD programs as a self-help guide can be an excellent alternative.

Doing exercises in mindfulness and hypnosis, and developing new strategies for coping and making decisions actually changes your brain. Plenty of good neuroscientific evidence shows that brains change in measurable ways from experience. Seeking out and creating deliberate experiences that retrain your brain are sensible treatments, and provide yet another reason for being positively action oriented.

Pause and Reflect:
Get Off the Merry-Go-Round

Having structured and deliberate ways to calm and focus yourself on things that soothe you is invaluable. Are you aware of particular images that you find especially relaxing? Perhaps a pleasant memory or an imaginary place you create, or a special place you like to revisit in your mind. The human spirit can be remarkably resilient in the face of great challenges, and can become even stronger with conscious nurturing. Take the time often to relax and detach from the ongoing flow of life and thoughts, and remind yourself of your true nature and how to be faithful to it. Make such a meditative practice a regular part of your life. It will strengthen you and help you deal with everyday stresses as well as potentially greater challenges the future may hold.

Overcoming Rumination

Learning to overcome rumination as an ongoing coping style is an even more worthwhile goal than managing it with distractions, exercise, and focusing strategies like mindful meditation and hypnosis. To do so, you learn to develop "discrimination," which in this context means choosing between two or more alternatives that have the potential to fulfill some wish or need. If you need a new car, for example, you will have to discriminate between many different available options in order to choose the one car that you believe will best meet your needs.

Throughout this chapter, I have presented you with a key discrimination even though I have not explicitly labeled it until now: *How do you distinguish between useful analysis and useless rumination?* By now, you may have arrived at the best answer: *If it doesn't lead to meaningful, effective action, then it's useless rumination.*

Decision-Making Skills

Anything that reinforces passivity works against your recovery from depression. Anything that reinforces a sense of helplessness, victimization, or powerlessness reinforces depression. *You must take effective action in your life if you want to reduce and prevent depression.* Now, consider these skills that go into taking effective action: Defining the problem, developing a timeline for resolving the problem, gathering relevant information, developing potential solutions, weighing the merits and liabilities of various alternatives, implementing a solution, and adjusting an approach as need dictates. These are the skills of effective decision making.

There are many different ways of going about making decisions, and each style has a value *depending on the circumstances*. The problem with depressed people's decision making is that it tends to be one-dimensional: They typically make decisions on the basis of how they *feel* and communicate (with words or behavior): "I feel attracted to you, so I'll go ahead and be vulnerable and sleep with you even though I don't really know you." "I'm afraid to fall in love again, so I won't." "I want to go back to school and develop a new career, but I'm afraid I won't be able to learn at my age." "I know I'd feel better if I exercised, but I don't feel like it." "I know I should tell my kid I love him more often, but I can't because it makes me uncomfortable to say it."

Pop psychology tells people to "get in touch with your feelings and trust your guts," but some of the most important personal gains come from using good information *instead of your feelings* to decide things. *Your guts can deceive you.* Your feelings can misguide you. Your intuition can be flat wrong. It leads to another discrimination you will eventually have to master: How do you know when your feelings can be trusted, and when they are misleading you? The only way to know is to use information, gather facts as much as you possibly can, whenever you possibly can, in order to *make an informed decision rather than an emotional one.* As I said at the outset of this chapter, it may seem counterintuitive to say that there's a danger in thinking too much, but now you know why it is so. Intuition can be wrong, and so can unchallenged assumptions.

I used the example of buying a car a little earlier. If you were going to buy a car, how would you decide which car to buy? Would you choose according to the price? The looks of the car? Its resale value? Its safety record? Its gas mileage? Its ecological impact? The comfort of its feel? Its country of origin? The one your dad recommends? Obviously, there are many different ways to decide which car to buy, and how you go about deciding will determine which one to buy. This is the artistry of decision making: *Which framework is the best framework for the decision at hand?*

Depressed people have to guard against using a decision-making process that unintentionally works against them. When someone decides, "I don't want to ask for help even though I'm suffering terribly," he doesn't want to continue to feel bad, but he's made a decision out of fear of the unknown, or a paralyzing belief that no one can help, or an expectation that he'll be given medications he would never take, or that asking for help is an admission of being crazy or weak. Any decision made according to an emotion-based internal orientation almost guarantees that you'll get worse. *Using your feelings to make decisions is very risky to do when your feelings are depressed.* They can too easily lead you to overanalyze things, miss options, respond halfheartedly, overestimate risks, underestimate yourself, and otherwise misstep.

You Can Learn a New Style of Decision Making

In order for you to make good decisions, you want to become aware of your feelings and take them into account, but not be governed by them. They're a part of you, but they are not all of you. *You're more than your feelings.* When your feelings encourage you to give up without trying, lead you to believe there's nothing you can do to change either yourself or your circumstances, or allow you to isolate from or damage your relationships with other people, then it's obvious you're giving your feelings too much power to run your life in ways that hurt you. You can be emotionally aware, but still develop a different means for making decisions: *Make your decisions according to the result you want, not just the way you feel.*

You're more than your feelings. There's more to your life than whatever is going on in it right now. There's an entire future that has yet to unfold, and how it will unfold will depend on the sensible actions you decide to take now.

CHAPTER 5

Don't Bring Others Down with You:

Learn to "Lighten Up"

If you walk into a crowded room, get everyone's attention, and take an impromptu survey ("All those of you who like hanging around depressed folks, please raise your hands . . ."), you'll discover one indisputable fact: Very few, if any, people like being around people who bring them down and make them feel bad. Be honest: Do *you*?

Jenny came home from work a little later than usual. The morning meeting with the project team leaders had lasted much longer than planned, and it caused her to run behind all day while rushing to get caught up. Jenny hated days like this, but fortunately, they were pretty rare. Today was simply a stressful exception and there was no need to make too big a deal out of it.

When Jenny got home, she poured herself a glass of wine and flipped on the TV while she contemplated what to have for dinner. After a couple of slices of spinach quiche she decided to take a bath to unwind. She soaked in very hot water with a new bath oil, and by the time she came out of the tub, she felt like a new woman.

Once dried off, Jenny realized that she hadn't checked her voice mail. She picked up yet another message from her friend Connie, this one even more miserable than the last couple dozen such messages. Jenny supported her friend in every reasonable way she could: They talked for hours on the phone, in coffee shops, at the park, wherever. It was always the same old issues coming up, and Connie was no closer to actually doing something to resolve them, which made Jenny feel as though she was talking to a brick wall. Tonight, especially, Jenny just couldn't

muster what it would take to listen to Connie say all the same depressing things over and over again. Jenny felt a little guilty at first, but then
felt relieved as she said to herself, "I'm not calling her back. Nope,
tonight is all about self-preservation."

Connie is reaching out to Jenny when feeling depressed. She is right to
do that. Jenny is protecting herself from negative influences on a day that
has been stressful. She is right to do that. This vignette raises complicated
issues addressed in this chapter: When is it a burden to others to talk
about one's feelings, and how available should someone be to someone in
need?

When you're depressed, would you rather be left alone, or would you
rather be around others? Some people know that when they're depressed,
being alone is a bad idea. They know they're vulnerable to wallowing in
emotional pain and drinking or plowing through a quart of ice cream and
making things even worse for themselves. They think of other people as
"lifelines to sanity," and deliberately seek out caring, supportive others to
be with when they're feeling bad. Generally, this is a very good idea, especially if it helps you focus on something more helpful than how bad you're
feeling.

Ricki had never faced depression before. In fact, she wouldn't be facing
it now if her husband of more than twenty years hadn't abruptly left her
for a woman almost half her age. One day he was there with her as he
had always been, and the next day he was gone. Ricki was devastated.
Living alone now for the first time in her adult life, she was suffering not
only the depths of depression, but also the heights of anxiety. She barely
slept and ate, couldn't concentrate, couldn't sit still, and couldn't stop the
endless flood of tears.

This went on for about a week, and then something snapped. It was
as if she floated outside herself and saw herself from a distance. She did-
n't like what she saw, either. She saw a weepy woman terrified of being
alone, a woman who acted as if she had nothing—no family, friends, no
career, nothing. Yet, that wasn't even close to true. She had a loving family, dedicated friends, and a successful career. In that moment, she
decided to stop hiding herself away and get back out among the living.

Ricki called friends and filled her calendar with social dates. She
was touched by their concern for her and whatever fear she had that she

couldn't face them after what happened evaporated instantly. At first she just needed them to be there, and their company provided some desperately needed contact comfort. It helped her at the deepest levels. She made a point of not burdening any one person too much so that she wouldn't "wear out her welcome" with them. She joined a local walking group and developed new friends while enjoying getting to know the nearby state parks. There were times she felt too anxious to go, but she went anyway. She discovered that it calmed her to be out in nature. Ricki's anxiety and depression diminished over the next few months. She was still deeply hurt by what happened, of course, but she realized that her life would go on in new ways that would perhaps be even better than before. To Ricki's credit, she reached out to others, got lots of emotional support, and she used it to rebuild her life.

By reaching out, Ricki experienced directly the healing power of good relationships. Instead of giving up, she challenged herself to grow. It can seem impossible to push yourself out the door and do something, *anything*, when in the grips of depression. *But this is what people who overcome depression do and no one else can do it for you.* Ricki handled one of the most painful life experiences with a plan, a *sensible* plan that kept her connected to others in beneficial ways.

Unlike Ricki, unfortunately, most people tend to isolate themselves when they're depressed. They typically find it takes too much effort to have to talk, think, answer questions, engage in small talk, pretend to be interested in someone else's life when their own life is crashing. It may not sound nice, but it's honest: Depressed people tend to get wrapped up in their depression and focus on how bad they feel. They view other people, especially *happy* people, negatively. So, depressed people stop going places where they'll be around other people, and typically end up sitting at home, watching television or gazing out the window and making lists of things that bother them, which only makes them feel worse. They stop doing things that require any energy or enthusiasm, believing they don't have any and, in thinking that, drain the little energy they do have.

People generally want to be around people who make them feel good. We want to be around people who inspire us, appreciate us, enjoy us, and can have fun with us. We tend to like people who are upbeat, friendly, and who openly express their positive feelings. We typically like people who are fun to be around, easy with their smiles, and who show an enthusiasm for whatever they're doing or whomever they're talking with.

Depressed people are often so "heavy" to be around that others end up avoiding them like the plague. The depressed person's perception that others don't like them or want to be around them may not be entirely imaginary. Negativity does, in fact, drive others away. Thus, it becomes vital for you to master setting aside your depressed feelings in order to positively engage with others, especially in certain sensitive social contexts. Knowing when to open up and when to keep your mouth shut is a great skill. It's important to do both, but at the "right" times.

This chapter is about how to maintain your relationships and keep them going along reasonably well despite your depression. I'll be drawing your attention to the importance of making sure that when your depression lifts, which it is likely to do, those relationships you most value are still there and undamaged. If you withdraw from others, or you spew on them with your unbridled negativity, there's a good chance they won't be there for you when you're ready for them to be. It's not as simple as dismissing them as "fair weather friends." It's deeper than that, because everyone needs relationships that provide comfort, and when you're depressed, you naturally have a much tougher time providing it to others. To preserve their own well-being, a responsibility each person has to him or herself, people who are not depressed sensibly pull away from those they fear may pull them down. *Rather than blame them for that, the more worthy goal here is to avoid putting them in that awful position.*

Pause and Reflect:
What's Your Effect on Others?

Consider this question carefully: What are the effects of your depression on others in your sphere of influence? Answer this as truthfully as you can; be careful not to overstate or understate your impact. If you're not sure, would you consider actually asking them? Be careful—it may be hard to hear what they have to say. By considering how your depression affects people around you, you may find that you're managing things pretty well or that you need to revise at least some of what you do in order to improve your relationships.

As Dr. Erving Polster insightfully wrote in his Foreword to this

book, no one suffers depression alone. I emphasize in my clinical trainings for other professionals the importance of bringing spouses, children, even friends and neighbors into a depressed individual's therapy in
order to give each person a voice. It helps the depressed person get more
realistic perspectives and support from others, and it helps others learn
what to say and do to help themselves and the suffering person they care
about.

Why Isolate?

When you're depressed, pulling away from others may feel natural. When
you're feeling lousy, being around others may seem like much too much
work. Even if you *want* to be around other people you may declare
yourself "unfit company" and isolate yourself as a sensitive means to
protect other people from you. As we will discuss later in this chapter, that
may well be a smart thing to do on an occasional basis—but it may also
be a means of perpetuating a sense of self-sacrificing martyrdom that can
make things worse.

Many depressed people got that way through failed and hurtful
relationships, so being around other people *isn't* what they want to do.
They feel anger, a sense of betrayal, and helplessness in the face of other
people's cruelty. They may hate themselves and everyone else. When
you're preoccupied with hating yourself and everyone else, other people
can seem stupid, superficial, and selfish, apparently too clueless to appreciate the depth of your suffering and all the good reasons you have to
justify being depressed.

When my new client, Ted, came in for help with his longstanding
depression, he told me he wished he was "like other people." Specifically,
he wanted to be "oblivious the way everyone else seems to be oblivious,
too blind to see the hypocrisy in the world, too stupid to know they are
sheep being sold the newest silly gadget they're convinced they just
gotta have, too blind to see that their silly little lives don't mean a
thing." Geez, you spend a few minutes with Ted, and any pleasure you
may find in living flies out the window! Does he really feel this way, or
is it his depression doing the talking?

There's a peculiar form of self-righteousness that allows many depressed people to feel there is something intelligent, even *noble*, about being depressed. They may think they are smarter or more insightful than other people, which is why they see the deep, depressing problems others don't. They may think their depression makes them more creative or artistic in trying to express their pain. Or, they may think they have suffered more profoundly than anyone else. They feel justified in their depression, as if no one else has a clue as to what's really going on that, to them, defines their depression as *sensible*.

This unfortunate frame of mind virtually guarantees things will stay painfully the same. Whatever basis there is for depression, it isn't where you want to stay. *Depression isn't what you want your life to be about no matter what's happened to you.*

When someone's outlook is so negative and condescending towards others, when his depression seems so rational to him or even evidence of a "higher consciousness," no wonder isolation seems a reasonable path to take. Other people isolate themselves because they feel others can't understand or relate to their special form of (depressed) wisdom. This reinforces their belief in their distorted viewpoints and deepens their depression. Others simply find it too draining, too much work, to have to be with other people when they feel bad. All of these issues will be addressed here.

Isolation May Not Be Possible for You

Isolating yourself by avoiding other people is a lot easier if you live by yourself, work by yourself, and shop online. You can create extra layers of distance that insure nobody will try to talk to you by simply avoiding eye contact with others, being expressionless, speaking in monosyllables, scowling, rolling your eyes in obvious contempt, and doing lots of other little things that tell people in no uncertain terms to stay away from you. You probably see other people as uncaring without seeing how *you inadvertently trained them to be that way.* If you are alone and lonely, depressed and isolated, this chapter can help you learn how to keep depression out of your interactions with others.

If you are married and have a family you'd like to hold onto, or a good job you'd like to keep that involves a boss and co-workers, or friends you value who call or stop by and actually care about you, even if you're unsure why at the moment, this chapter can help you conduct your relationships with people who are a part of your life, and were there before you became depressed. The essential message I want you to remember is this: *Your depression has come and it will very likely go, but your most highly valued relationships with family and friends can and will endure if you take deliberate steps to make that possible.*

I said that your depression is very likely to go. Research on recovery rates indicates that the chances are excellent that you will recover from your depression if you continue to read and learn about depression, if you take advantage of the help qualified experts can offer, and if you strive to develop the skills you as an individual need to better manage the life challenges you face. *Depression is a manageable condition provided you don't ignore it, justify it, passively accept it, blame others for it, or otherwise respond to it in ways that are likely to aggravate or perpetuate it.* It's why having a realistic understanding of depression precludes an unrealistic hope that "a pill a day will keep the depression away." There's more to it than that.

Pause and Reflect:
How Should Others Treat You?

When you're depressed and other people are already a part of your life, such as your spouse, friends, or your kids, what do you think is the most effective way for them to respond to you? Should they tiptoe around you and show you lots of extra consideration so as to not upset or stress you further? Should they just go on with their own lives and leave you behind? Or should they go out of their way to try to make you happier? What are your expectations, and how do you get these expectations across? Is there any reason for you to reevaluate your expectations?

It is a challenge to find the right balance for any one individual as to how much simple acceptance versus how much "push" he or she should get from others in order to get better. There's no "one size fits all" answer to this, and so any answer you eventually discover for yourself will come from careful consideration and honest communication with the people in your life. The key consideration, though, is how you train people to treat you: You need to change anything that either disempowers you or hurts others.

Caution: Temporary Depression
Can Cause Permanent Damage to Relationships

How you answer the questions in the "Pause and Reflect" above shapes how you experience and act toward other people in your life when you're depressed. How do you think *you* act around others when you're depressed? Are you quiet and withdrawn? Irritable and even hostile? Approachable or radiating "stay away from me" messages? How you treat others when you're feeling bad is a vitally important issue for many reasons, but one is especially compelling: *To respond to others from your emotional pain is to treat others in ways that drive them away from you.* It isn't usually a straightforward approach to pulling away from people ("I hereby end this relationship"). It's an indirect way of detaching from others through behavior that pushes them away. Thus, there's a great probability that even if you manage to convince yourself you don't care if others leave you when you're depressed, when they actually do leave it will very probably make you feel worse. You probably won't be happy about how you handled things, and you certainly won't be happy with those who left you when you were down and out. It's a "lose-lose" scenario.

Perhaps you've decided you'd be better off without someone you think is hurtful to you, but is that your depressed thoughts leading you to those conclusions? Will you feel the same way when your depression has lifted and that person is actually gone? You have to be clear-minded in deciding to end a relationship, and not do it out of either depressed hostility or apathy. It's more important to make such a decision when you are clear that the decision is valid and implemented for the right reasons.

"Just Keepin' It Real, Dude"

The largest group of depression sufferers in the United States is currently between ages twenty-five and forty-four. (That may change if depression continues to strike at younger and younger ages.) One of the many characteristics of this age group that feeds their higher rates of depression is their belief that they should be able to say what they think and say what they feel "just because." Just because they feel a particular way, they think it's important to "put it out there." The common attitude is, "Ya gotta keep it real." Roughly translated, that means you have to speak the truth as you see it, telling people how you feel or what your reactions to them are in a given moment. Never mind if your viewpoint is hurtful to others, never mind if being "real" sends out the wrong message, especially to more vulnerable children, that "this is the way it is." There's a significant sense of entitlement wrapped up in this behavior.

Learn by Doing:
Trash Talk

Watch a few trashy talk shows on television (if you can bear it). You'll see people openly confess to outrageous and destructive behavior, you'll see the mocking of the victims and the booing of the perpetrators, while the audience yells for more. It is terrible stuff to watch, but there's a point: These people illustrate some of the worst of human behavior, and they strut proudly while doing so. They offer their pathetic justifications and their thoughtless rationales and, frenzied studio audience aside, they seem to have no idea that the rest of the civilized world sees them as the worst possible examples of human beings. It can reinforce for you the need to have boundaries about what you will and won't say, what you will and won't do. Define high standards of integrity in dealing with others and live by those standards.

There are some who grow up believing that people really do talk to each other in the style of trashy talk shows, asking very private, rude questions, and they don't see anything wrong with it. They think you should be able to say *whatever* you want to *whomever* you want, regardless of how crass, tasteless, insulting, or mean-spirited it might be. With no boundaries in place, their relationships limp along at the lowest level of quality.

I raise this point for a reason: You have to decide what you're willing to say to people, what you're willing to disclose to them, and what you're willing to let them say in your presence. You're going to have to decide where to establish the boundaries that define just how much "letting it all hang out" you're willing to tolerate in yourself and others. If you believe you should be able to say anything you want to others, especially the people closest to you, then you'll end up saying things to people when you're hurt, angry, or depressed that have the potential to destroy the relation-

ship. Your bad feelings will come and go, but that person will hear the echoes of those poisonous things you said for years to come.

Pause and Reflect: The Merits of Authenticity

Some people justify their negativity—their constant complaints, cynical comments, or criticisms—by saying, "Well, it's how I feel. It would be phony to act like everything's okay when it isn't." Do you think it's generally more important to be honest or to be easy to get along with? Under what specific conditions do you think it's more important to be pleasant than authentic? And under what conditions would you say the opposite is true?

There is an important distinction between honesty and discretion. You don't have to say everything you think or share everything you feel. There are situations in which it is more important to get along (avoid unnecessary conflict) than it is to be honest. That's true in families and it's true in the business world. When there is nothing to be gained, when the situation is a one-time event unlikely ever to be repeated, or when the person you're complaining to can't do anything about it ("I can't stand your family!"), you're likely to be better off just keeping your feelings to yourself. When the situation is an ongoing one, when this is someone you're going to have to deal with repeatedly, and when there's something this person can actually do about the problem and has shown an inclination to be helpful, then it may well be worth saying something respectfully.

Impulse Control: Know When to "Put a Lid on It"

There's a skillful in-between that separates keeping your negative feelings "locked up inside" and simply blasting people with your frustration and despair. The in-between lies in developing enough impulse control to hold your tongue just long enough to decide *whether* to say something and, if you determine it's important to, *how* to say it for the best possible effect.

Impulse control means taking a pause, a deliberate and measured pause, before you say or respond to something in order to consider the implications and possible consequences of what you want to say. What may be only a three-second pause according to the clock can be a very long time subjectively, long enough for you to consider your options and deliberately choose the one that you think will be most helpful in the circumstances. Learning to pause before you reply prevents "snap" reactions that can make things worse when you impulsively say something hurtful to the person or fan the flames of anger and escalating conflict to an even higher level. "Getting it off your chest" may feel good initially but you may feel even worse about yourself when later, after you cool off, you realize you were out of line. Once you've said something thoughtless, it's been said. Once the bell has been rung, you can't unring it. You might apologize, and your apology may even be graciously accepted, but the interaction will still be remembered as a negative that could have been prevented with some impulse control and forethought.

Depression adds an extra layer of complexity to this issue. When people are depressed, they typically feel tired, defeated, and barely able to cope. Having to expend energy to watch what you say can seem like a huge effort and the apathy of depression can lead someone to think, or even say out loud, "who cares?" When the depression lifts though, and he's ready to resume the relationship on a more positive basis, he may discover the relationship has been damaged, perhaps fatally. So, just when he's starting to feel better and wants to reengage, he takes a hit that might well lead to feeling like a bad person, a loser, someone who "always ends up alone."

It *does* take effort to watch what you say. It *is* extra work to have to consider other peoples' feelings and analyze whether a given situation is best handled with no comment or by saying something purposeful. It takes extra thought to consider different ways of saying something, and then decide which way to say it, but the outcome will probably be better. This is how impulse control leads to the development of judgment, and how judgment evolves into a trust in and higher regard for yourself. As you get better and better at controlling what you say, and as you get more skilled in saying things that "hit the mark" in your interactions, your self-esteem will grow. Good self-esteem evolves as you review important interactions with others and you get to say to yourself, "I like what I said and did there. I like the way I handled that." When you're able to say that to yourself most (not all) of the time, you're doing well.

The Self-Esteem Cart *Doesn't* Go Before the Horse

Often people ask, "Well, don't I have to feel good about myself *before* I'm able to say and do things better?" The question seems to have a certain logic, but the answer is unequivocally no. This is what I call a "sequencing" issue: Which comes first and what comes next? Does someone's good self-esteem allow him or her to have impulse control and be more effective in choosing what he or she says? Or, does developing impulse control and being more effective in choosing what to say gradually build self-esteem? If you wait until you feel good about yourself before you start developing and applying the skills I'm encouraging in this book, you've put the self-esteem cart ahead of the horse. That isn't how it works.

The self-esteem issue is a complicated one only because people have made such a huge issue out of it. The mental health profession got this one wrong, and now knows it and is trying to correct for the damage done. For a long time whenever someone engaged in bad behavior, it was made out to be a self-esteem problem. So, people who joined gangs and acted violently toward others were told they did so because of their poor self-esteem. People who cheated on their spouses were told they did so because of their poor self-esteem. Students who got lousy grades were told they underperformed in school because of their poor self-esteem. The one-dimensional answer to nearly every problem was to raise self-esteem.

On the surface, it may sound like a reasonable perspective: If people felt better about themselves, they'd be nicer, less violent, more compassionate, more loyal, more generous, more *whatever*. But, here's the problem: Self-esteem is a personal appraisal of how you feel about yourself, *but not necessarily an indicator of how good you really are.* Lots of people in the world have a very high self-esteem—and they *shouldn't*: gang members who think they're great for having killed two cops, thieves who think they are unusually clever for the way they scam people, political leaders who think they're above the law, and religious leaders who think they have a divine right to do things they really shouldn't. Lots of other people, too, like themselves a lot but are not good people.

When Self-Esteem Works Against Relationships

We've raised a younger generation to believe it's important to have good self-esteem. Many of them are rude, insensitive, and worse, but they still get lots of reward stickers at school just for showing up and looking reasonably alert. The heart of the problem lies in what I've been describing: The self-esteem cart *did* go before the horse for these young people. They were rewarded for doing nothing, and told they should feel good about themselves even though they didn't do anything to warrant it. Schools took competition out of their gym classes so there wouldn't be any "losers," and tests could be taken over again until the student passed. This does nothing to prepare people for the real world where there *are* winners and losers. Not coincidentally, young people are now the fastest growing group of depression sufferers.

A popular bumper sticker says, "Think education is expensive? Try ignorance!" At a time when technology is more sophisticated than ever and life is more complicated than ever, the educational system has to fight for every dollar. But instead of giving teachers and schools what they need to provide the best, most well-rounded possible education, programs such as "No Child Left Behind" emphasize only mainstream courses and the goal of elevating test scores. Consequently, kids don't learn to value information simply for the sake of having information. They whine, "Why do I have to know this? Is it going to be on the test?" Unless it is immediately relevant for them, they don't value simply knowing something.

Lots of people of all ages, not just kids, apparently don't want to expend the effort it takes to think and learn. But the fact that so many people can manage to have good self-esteem despite being uninterested in anyone or anything that doesn't fit within their narrow field of interest doesn't bode well for their future. Thus, we can (and do) make celebrities out of people who get rewarded for doing *nothing*.

Good self-esteem doesn't make you a good person, nor does it make you an effective person. Personal and social skills do. Telling people, "You deserve the best" may be a good advertising hook, but it works against people doing anything to actually *become* deserving. It's a pathway to self-centeredness and a sense of entitlement, neither of which counts as a positive social skill.

Perhaps the worst part of this culture's tolerance for and even celebration of undeserving people is that people learn they don't have to produce anything of any value. They learn that they can engage in bad behavior and may even be rewarded for it. Consequently, they don't have the perspective or the social skill to build the kinds of relationships that can insulate them against depression. Predictably, they will want to get connected to others, as most people do, but they will have few of the actual skills needed to make it possible.

If you want to have relationships that are satisfying, healthy, and which enhance your life, you have to continue to develop the skills that make it possible. It's not about waiting until you feel better to start developing the skills. It's about developing the skills I've been describing all along (impulse control, selectivity, not using your frame of reference to predict others, clarifying the goals for your interactions, assessing others realistically, and so on) so you'll feel and *do* better. These skills will also help to make sure you don't bring others down with you. It's all about raising the standards of behavior.

Getting Past Being Entitled to Your Feelings

Feeling entitled to special considerations because you think you deserve it gets in the way of good relationships and leads to anger, rejection, and the depression that comes with feeling abandoned and alone.

Clients will often say to me, "But I'm entitled to my feelings!" or "My feelings are my feelings and no one has a right to judge them." Your feelings may well be valid. Let's assume for the moment that your feelings are perfectly understandable and appropriate for whatever's going on in your life. But what defines how well you do and how good you feel is what you *do* with your feelings. Think of all the possibilities: You can ignore them, wallow in them, use them as a catalyst for effective action, blame them on other people, contemplate deeply why you feel them, self-medicate them with alcohol, drugs, or food, pray about them, and whatever else occurs to you to do with them. Whatever you do with your feelings, remember *you're more than your feelings*.

Learn by Doing:
Feelings as a Choice

Just above, I've listed a few possible responses to your feelings. None of these alternatives suggests being unaware of your feelings or negating them in some way. All of them suggest making a deliberate choice of what to do about them, if anything. See how many alternatives you can add to my list of things to do with your feelings. The goal in saying that you're more than your feelings is to encourage you to think beyond them sometimes so that you can make good choices in other ways. That implies that there are times when focusing on your feelings may not be the best option. Next, make as long a list as you possibly can of contexts in which acting on your feelings is likely to be counterproductive, even harmful. For example, getting into your frustration with the government is not a good thing to do on April 15th. You're better off sending in your income tax check without exploring your feelings about where it's going.

Depressed people tend to focus on their feelings and then use them as the guide for what to do. That's potentially a huge mistake. When you make the big decisions in your life, how do your feelings influence your decision making? A relatively young field called "affective neuroscience" studies the relationship between emotions and brain functions, in particular how people's mood states affect the quality of their decisions. For example, when people are afraid, their decisions will likely be conservative, even overly cautious. When people are angry, they're more likely to be aggressive and take bigger risks. Depressed people are more likely to make short-sighted decisions that reinforce their depression: "I know I'd feel better if I exercised, but *I don't feel like* going to the gym" or, "I know I should be more attentive to the kids, but *I don't feel like it.*"

When someone makes a bad decision according to her mood state, is she "entitled" to her feelings? Should people be told to "trust their feelings?" When someone behaves irresponsibly because he is depressed, neglecting his spouse and kids, or saying cruel things to them in anger, is he "entitled" to this behavior? People justify bad behavior and bad decisions by saying their feelings led them to act badly. *Your feelings are not more important than your responsibility or integrity.*

Give Others a Voice

When I'm working with couples or families in therapy and everyone is struggling to deal with one family member's depression, giving each of them a voice is one of the most important things I can do. By this I mean creating space for them to say what they think and feel. When the spouse of a depressed person is able to talk about how this person's depression affects him or her, and when kids get to talk about how mom or dad's depression affects them, it is often a turning point in the treatment process. Often, depressed people don't have a clue how frequently their mood leads them to say mean things they don't even remember saying. Too often, the depressed person doesn't know that others are both deeply concerned about them and afraid they won't get better and worried about how difficult they're making life for everyone. *Giving family members a voice is a vitally important way to make sure no one is isolated, forced to be silent, and thereby become a victim of someone else's depression.*

When I'm working with couples, the spouse of a depressed person usually says how hurtful the words and actions of the depressed spouse are. When the depressed person responds, "But, I'm depressed," I will jump in and say something such as, "I'm sorry you're depressed. I *really am* sorry you're depressed. But that doesn't excuse saying such terrible things to your spouse or anyone else." As you can imagine, it isn't what the depressed person wants to hear. Actually, he or she was hoping I'd offer support, understanding, and even approval for saying or doing whatever. But the first step to getting the marriage and family back on a healthy track is to define what you can and can't say to someone, depressed or not. *Even when you're depressed, you have a responsibility to others to treat them respectfully.*

People seem to forget that depression isn't just an individual problem. For each and every depressed person out there, there are *at least three* other people directly and negatively affected by his or her depression. *All of us* are affected indirectly by depression in so many ways, from the people who cope with depression by drinking and then driving drunk to all those who jack up the price of health care because they need, or simply want, on average, four times as much medical care as nondepressed people.

I hope I'm enlarging your perspective of depression. I hope I'm encouraging you to give the people in your life a voice. And, I hope I'm encouraging you to think twice before you hurt people you love by saying thoughtless and hurtful things when you're depressed. Even when someone else says or does something thoughtless and hurtful, you build your own self-esteem by responding in ways that *you* respect. It's another opportunity for you to say to yourself, "I like the way I handled that."

Learn by Doing:
Set a Limit on Down Time

Spend a week keeping track of how often you and your closest confidant spend talking about you, your feelings, your depression, your worries, your problems. Keep track of the total time you spend together and how much of that time is spent addressing your feelings and issues. Does it seem like too little, too much, or a reasonable amount of time to spend in this way? What about to your partner, friend, co-worker, or family member? (Have you ever asked?) If it seems like a lot to you, it probably seems even more so to the other person. Set up a specified time and amount of time to focus on your concerns, and strive to stay within those limits for a few weeks. Experiment with setting a limit on how much negative sharing you do while simultaneously striving to increase the amount of positive focus in your time together. To do this, I'd suggest creating a context for positive interaction: Go for a walk, or go out for dinner and a movie, or invite your co-workers to lunch, or invite some friends you've neglected lately over for a visit, or do something else of your own choosing that can help you keep the conversation light and easy and avoid the negative. How might this improve your relationship?

How Much Should You Reveal about Your Depression?

Just as you should exercise discretion in what you say to people while you're depressed, you should also consider *whether* you should even tell people you're dealing with depression and whom, if anyone, you should tell.

Historically, depression has been something that people were ashamed of suffering. They'd rather report a bad back than depression because depression was and *still is* viewed as a personal weakness or mental illness by too many people. Both are incorrect, of course, but there is a stigma associated with depression that still prevents far too many people from getting help. Only about 20 to 25 percent of the people who need help for depression are likely to seek the services of a mental health professional, an unfortunate statistic that highlights how many people don't want to openly acknowledge and get treated for their depression. Many people simply don't recognize their depression. They think they're stressed, over-worked, bothered, harassed, irritated, in a really long bad mood, but *not* depressed.

In an effort to get more people to seek help, some professionals thought that calling depression a disease seemed a good way to reduce the stigma. Telling people in TV ads that "depression is a disease just like diabetes" was meant to take away any self-blame and encourage them to seek medical help. In essence, the message was, "depression happens, you don't have any-thing to do with it, so just take these pills and it'll probably go away."

The campaign to get people to see themselves as "diseased" has been less than successful. They may think they're stressed, but most people just don't think of themselves as diseased. Personally, I'd like to end the disease campaign and just talk to people who are coping with faster, more com-plicated lives while living in a culture that unwittingly teaches people the very patterns of thought and behavior that make them more vulnerable to depression. I want people to know they can develop skills and relation-ships that can be more helpful in the long run than the pills can.

I'd like to offer some guidelines for helping you decide how much you should tell people about *your* depression. It's a delicate issue with some serious implications, not the least of which is how receiving a formal diag-nosis of "major depression" may affect your future job prospects, your ability to obtain health insurance, and even the quality of care you get from your doctor. If these issues concern you, you should discuss them directly with your doctor and a qualified therapist to determine the best way to handle them.

As a general principle, *it's best not to give other people information they really don't need.* You're allowed to have heart without wearing it on your sleeve. If you have only a casual relationship with someone, such as a co-worker, there isn't any good reason to mention something so personal.

The first person to whom you should open up about depression is your physician. Ask him or her for a thorough physical examination, since there are diseases and conditions for which depression is a likely conse-quence. Some medications cause depression as a predictable side-effect. Level with your doctor and share your observations and concerns. Make him or her aware of what's going on with you since it might well lead to a different diagnosis and treatment. Seeing a mental health professional is also a great idea, someone with an advanced understanding of depression, including its onset and its consequences. Revealing as much as you possibly can about the factors affecting your depression is a vital step in designing an individualized program of treatment for you. When you're in therapy, don't hold back anything that may affect your recovery.

You can tell your family what's going on in a very general way, by saying, for example, "I'm going through a difficult period and, just so you know, I'm taking steps to get the help I need and that's as much as I want to say about it right now." Or, you can be more specific and say something such as, "I am dealing with depression, as you probably already know from my mood and behavior. I am taking steps to get help. Is there anything in particular you want to know or say about this?" Listen to the concerns, answer questions if you can, but most importantly, provide the reassurance everyone needs that you can and will function and that you are actively getting sensible help.

You can decide whether to be general or specific in what you disclose by following the lead of the person to whom you're talking. If someone asks for more specifics, you may want to provide some. It may help reduce other people's anxiety if they can ask questions and have a sense of knowing what's going on and what to expect. If someone accepts the general disclosure and asks for no further information, you can invite questions. If he or she doesn't pick up on the invitation, you can simply leave the door open for further discussions by saying, "If any questions come up about this for you later, feel free to ask."

Be sensitive to the age of your listener. Young kids aren't going to ask many specific questions because they don't really know what to ask. Be aware, though, kids can and do pick up on parents' mood states, so don't fool yourself into thinking that your child doesn't have any questions. Most likely, he or she just doesn't know what or how to ask.

Your spouse or your partner deserves special consideration. This is the person who most likely knows you best and whom you most directly affect with your words and actions. To deny something is wrong when it's obvious to him or her that something is off, to refuse to get help when your partner is telling you how concerned he or she is, or to get angry when he or she is trying to get you to open up are all unfortunate ways of making sure the relationship will suffer. *If you know something is wrong and you just don't want to face it yet, get some courage from someplace and face it anyway.* When others are telling you that you are affecting them negatively, you owe it to them and yourself to get this problem resolved as quickly as possible. Waiting for something to come along and "fix" you isn't much of a plan. You can do much better than that.

If your relationship with your spouse or partner isn't good and even contributes to your depression, then opening up about what's going on may not be a very good idea. Not everyone is supportive and says or does things with sensitivity. Some people take the things you reveal in a moment of honesty and throw them back at you later, using whatever you revealed as a weapon against you. If you are in a relationship that isn't healthy, then it may be best to keep your answers general and save your detailed conversations for a mental health professional (psychologist, psychiatrist, counselor, etc.).

Some people will intentionally and maliciously try to kick you when you're down, but most people aren't that mean-spirited. Most will see your depression empathetically simply as a vulnerability you have. In an effort to be helpful, and to protect you from life stressors, some may exclude you from family discussions about kid or money problems until little by little you get treated as the "sick" one. That may eventually become how you see yourself, which will keep you depressed and make you weaker, not stronger. Help your family understand you don't want to be treated like an incompetent or invalid just because you're going through a period of depression.

Friends, neighbors, and regularly encountered acquaintances are probably going to know something is going on so use your judgment about how much to reveal. If you don't want everyone in the neighborhood to know your business, then don't tell it to the gossip next door. If you have a good friend you trust to keep whatever you discuss between you, then talking to a friend can be a great way to get perspective from someone who knows you. Make sure you don't "burn out" your friends, though, by asking them to listen to your problems more than is comfortable for them.

Learn by Doing:
Who to Tell What

Make a list of all the people in your life you expect to encounter in the next few weeks. Include your family members, friends, colleagues, neighbors, customers, everyone. Now, spend a little time thinking about how much, if anything at all, you want to tell each person on your list about what's going on with you. As you'll discover, most people don't need to know anything, many don't need to know much, and only a very few need some level of detail. Think about how you will answer direct questions ("Is something wrong? What's going on with you, anyway?") and prepare a number of specific responses that cover the range from minimally revealing to open self-disclosure. You need not be caught off guard without good answers ready to go. Here's another chance to prevent saying something impulsively you'll regret later.

You're More Than Your Mood

By now you must have noticed the common theme running through my advice: Be thoughtful and deliberate. When people make decisions solely on the basis of their feelings, they are much more likely to make mistakes that cost them dearly. Peoples' feelings lead them into fistfights, one night stands with total strangers, bad investments, expensive purchases that give them "buyer's remorse," and silly and destructive arguments with people they love. The worst things that human beings do to each other *don't* have their origins in logic. Be aware of your feelings and use them as information and as a factor to consider, but don't allow them to determine your actions. You are not your feelings.

Your heart, your guts, your brain, every part of you, can deceive you. There will be times your gut feeling is right on the money, and times when it's way off base. If you don't know when to listen to your feelings and when to override them, it may help to follow these guidelines.

1. When you don't have facts or adequate information about someone or something, you'll make an emotional guess that may well be wrong. Override your feelings and get relevant facts and information if you can possibly do so. Sometimes it may not be possible, but often it is.
2. When your reflex is to take something personally that may not be personal, override your feelings and consider multiple viewpoints. There is a difference between something that affects you personally (such as a job layoff of many people, including you) and something not personal (the layoff wasn't about you)

3. If strong feelings will lead you to make an irreversible decision you may regret later, override them and think logically first.
4. When you stand a chance of losing money, getting hurt emotionally, hurting your reputation, or getting hurt physically, override your feelings and choose the more sensible alternative.
5. If following your feelings will affect others negatively and cause them potential harm, override your feelings in order to evaluate the best course of action. This is especially true when the other person is someone who is dependent on you, such as a child.

As you see, it's fine to follow your feelings when the results of your decisions don't hurt you or anyone else and the feelings fit the circumstances. But if you give yourself the room to follow feelings that hurt you or others, you will make poor decisions that feed into your bad feelings about yourself—which can keep depression going. When you handle your feelings well and see yourself making good choices about how you respond to people, you get to walk away from those interactions thinking, "I like what I did there." Remember, *you're more than your mood.*

Develop an Attitude of Protectiveness Toward Others

When you're in a relationship with a family member or business customer, you have a responsibility to that person. If it's a child, you not only have a responsibility *to* them, but a responsibility *for* them. In any enduring relationship, there's a "me" and a "you," but more importantly, there evolves a "we." Two people in a good relationship develop a bond that at critical times becomes more important than either individual alone.

If I care about you, I don't want to hurt you. I don't want you to spend one minute feeling insecure or doubting my commitment to you. I don't want you spending even one minute wondering if I can be trusted or feeling even a twinge of jealousy or fear. I want to get the message across in my actions that I care about you and care about us. That doesn't mean you get everything you want or demand, but it means I will be sensitive to your wishes and strive to develop a "win-win" solution.

However, a sense of entitlement that says, in essence, "I'm more important than you are," or "My feelings matter more than yours do" impedes the development of a positive relationship and increases the risk of depression. If parents are willing to ignore their kids because they interfere with partying, or employers are willing to fire longtime employees in order to avoid paying retirement benefits, or teens are willing to have "friends with privileges" because more committed relationships are too much hassle, then the message comes through all too clearly that other people only matter to the extent that they give you something you want.

I'm highlighting how important it is for your own mental health to develop an attitude of both respectfulness and protectiveness toward other people. When you strive to protect others from your bad moods, irritable complaining, or angry outbursts, you are doing a good thing. That doesn't mean you don't acknowledge or speak openly about what you're experiencing, but it means you place a limit on how much and how often you talk about it, and what your attitude is when you do talk about it.

Fun Is a Casualty in Depression

The ability to have fun with others is one of the first casualties of depression. To avoid or curtail rumination, focus on other things besides depression with your family and friends. Make the relationship about much more than your depression.

Evolving an attitude of protectiveness towards others means prioritizing their needs as much as you reasonably can:

- It means being at your child's school play or soccer game even if you don't feel like going because being there means more to them than being home moping around means to you. And, it means doing it with a smile, however much effort that may take to accomplish.
- It means having a "date night" with your spouse and making a point of keeping depression out of it. No complaints, no deep discussion of serious issues, just focusing on recapturing what you can remember about what's enjoyable about this relationship. Make a point of saying *sincerely* at least three kind and loving things to him or her during the date.
- It means inviting friends over for a game or a show or something that requires only lighthearted participation. It means organizing and mobilizing the means for staying connected to people even when you're feeling disconnected.

Integrating the skills of being attentive to others' needs, sensitive to their wishes, capable of setting problems aside long enough to have some easy and enjoyable time together, setting limits on how long potentially endless discussions of the burdens of life will go on, and so forth, are all ways of protecting intimate relationships from the toxic effects of depression. Relationships *can* survive depression, but not without employing good judgment and sound strategies.

You, me, *we.* Make a point of participating in the relationships you have with others and *protecting* them. That's how you will keep people caring about you long after your depression is gone.

CHAPTER 6

Self-Deception and Seeking the Truth:

Learn to Test Your Beliefs

Thinking that is so distorted that people can come to believe almost *any-thing* as long as it fits with their *need to believe* is called "magical thinking." The distortions can range from mild (such as having to wear your lucky socks in order to win your tennis match) to severe (such as the psychotic patient who believes he is God).

We human beings are capable of extraordinary degrees of self-decep-tion that serve deep personal needs. It's a basic part of being human. *We all deceive ourselves at times to some degree.* For some people, though, self-deception is a barrier to living effectively; they generate so many bad decisions based on their unrealistic perspectives that they can become depressed when things go awry, which they frequently do.

Two For the Road

- Marcy's face is still bruised from the punch. Jay said, just as he has too many times before, "I'm really sorry . . . but you had it coming. Don't ever bring that sore subject up again, do you hear me?" Marcy only hears the words, "I'm really sorry," though, and concludes Jay feels bad and therefore is unlikely to ever hit her again.
- Jim knows Tina isn't happy with him. She has made it clear that if it weren't for the sake of their two kids, she'd have left him long ago. She is barely civil towards him, rolls her eyes with obvious disdain when he speaks, finds excuses to be anywhere in the house he isn't, and cuts him off instantly if he tries to talk to her about what obviously needs to be

talked about. Jim believes Tina is "just going through a mid-life crisis a little early, but eventually she'll come around and I'll still be here when she does." He finds some condoms in her purse while looking for a key, but somehow they don't even register in his awareness because he'd had a vasectomy years ago.

Both Marcy and Jim are reasonably intelligent people. They are well-educated, articulate, and even insightful at times. Yet both are terribly misguided in their thinking about such vitally important areas of their lives as their personal safety, intimate relationships, and the future of their primary relationships.

Marcy's magical thinking is that her abusive partner is "magically" going to stop being violent because she loves him and believes that, deep down, he loves her, too. Perhaps he does. But, by focusing on her love for him as the most important thing, she manages to totally ignore the fact that Jay justifies his violence by blaming her for bringing up what he considers to be a sore subject. In his view, she deserves to be hit. Realistically, why would Jay change his behavior if he believes his use of violence is both reasonable and justified?

Jim's magical thinking is that a woman who has made it clear she has no feelings for him, who openly displays contempt for him, will somehow "magically" fall back into love with him one day. In his view, the marriage isn't over as long as his sense of hope exists. Jim "magically" doesn't even notice condoms in his wife's purse, much less think about why his wife might need them. *Why would Jim leave his awful marriage when he thinks of it as simply going through a "bad phase?"*

Your beliefs about other people and the meanings you ascribe to their behavior can influence how you become depressed, especially if you've interpreted their behavior and motives from your own limited and possibly distorted perspective. The goal is to be clear about other people as much as you realistically can so that you are neither holding out hope for what is hopeless nor feeling unnecessarily pessimistic about the possibilities.

Pause and Reflect: You and Magical Thinking

Do you believe in astrology, past lives, UFO abductions, the "secret" that if you believe it will happen it really will, or any other such examples of beliefs that may be attractive but can't be proved or disproved? If you do, how do you rationalize (i.e., justify to yourself or others) holding such beliefs when you know they are unprovable and involve at least some magical thinking? More to the point, have you had episodes of magical thinking about other people ("He won't hit me again" or "She'll come back to me") that made you feel better but had no basis in reality? How might this affect your vulnerability to depression?

When we desperately want an answer but there are no facts, we are more vulnerable to believing anything that seems to explain things. People mistake "possible" for true, and they mistake "plausible" for true. People have earnestly believed many things throughout history that turned out to be entirely wrong, from the sun moving around the earth to the belief that if your cause is just, then you will prevail. People can be easily manipulated by their need to believe.

It's Natural—But Hazardous—to Theorize

You can't always read people easily, and sometimes they act in mystifying, unreasonable ways. It is natural to want to try to figure out their feelings and motives, and depressed people are no different in this regard. They theorize, too, about why people do what they do. Unfortunately, their theories tend to differ in one important way from those of people who aren't depressed: The theories and the conclusions they form tend to be self-damaging.

Jeff applied for a job he wanted badly, the kind of job he'd hoped for all his life. He was sure he had the right credentials—the right academic degree, the right kinds of experience, the right kind of resume. He carefully prepared for the interview, and felt afterward he had conducted himself quite well. But when too much time had passed and no one offered him the job, he knew in his gut that he didn't get it. As he replayed the interview over and over again in his mind trying to pinpoint what must have gone wrong, he became sure it was because the interviewer just didn't like him. He convinced himself that he had presented himself badly and then remembered in excruciating detail every other time he'd applied for a job he didn't get. Jeff decided he was kidding himself to think he'd ever get a good job when it was clear no one would take him seriously. He stayed in bed for three days before he could muster the energy to shave and shower again. Jeff would never know that he had done just fine in the interview, that the interviewer thought he was wonderful—and that the undeserving nephew of one of the company's most powerful board members got hired instead.

Jeff faced the uncertainty of no obvious reason why he didn't get the job. He started theorizing about what went wrong, trying to make sense of what happened. By convincing himself he had done badly, when in fact he had done well, and then filtering his history to look for further examples to support his theory, Jeff built an incorrect, self-damaging, negative evaluation of his merit as a person and of his future chances of *ever* succeeding.

Some of the errors in Jeff's thinking include his unrealistic expectations, a lack of actual information about the interviewer, global (overgeneral) thinking, and his use of uninformed but believed-in perceptions as a reference point. Jeff deceived himself into thinking he knew more than he really did, and he used that information to hurt himself emotionally. This is a pattern typical of people who are either already depressed or are vulnerable to depression.

Pause and Reflect: How Much Is Enough Information to Make a Good Decision?

Your "gut feelings" are not necessarily the right ones to go with in making a decision. People often make disastrous decisions on an impulse, suffering remorse over missed opportunities or for inappropriate actions. Do you know when you have enough information to make a sound decision or when you are jumping to conclusions on the basis of too little evidence? In what area(s) of your life are you most likely to make poor decisions based on too little information? Your family? Your job? Your friendships? Finances?

In studies of people who make good intuitive decisions, only the people with lots of training and experience (some say 10,000 hours worth) tend to make satisfactory "gut decisions." Thus, while some tout the advantages of "following your guts," the evidence is much greater that the best decisions are made, especially in relationships, according to a deliberate strategy of gathering, weighing, and using as much objective information as possible.

The Capacity to Deceive Yourself: Vulnerabilities in Thinking

It is comforting to think there is an order to things, a *reason* that can explain even the worst things that happen to us. It is natural to ask why, especially when we are suffering the pain or distress associated with some hurtful occurrence. *The meanings you assign to life experiences can cause you emotional harm.* Asking why something happens is the launch point for a search for meaning, an exploration into the possible significance of what has happened. How you conduct this exploration, how far you go in your search, and how attached you become to the explanation you eventually settle on are all factors that strongly influence your vulnerability to depression. Just as Jeff concluded he'd blown the interview and never knew that he lost the job to a board member's nephew, you may settle on interpretations for things that happen in your life that just aren't true.

Learn by Doing:
The Meanings in Your Life

Make a list of the things in your life that most occupy your time during the course of a typical week. That might include your job, running the household, volunteering, partying, reading, exercising, shopping, gossiping, whatever you spend your time doing. How you use your time makes a strong statement about what you think is important and what you consider to be meaningful. For each of the things on your list, make a statement about it that crystallizes the meaning that activity gives your life. If you volunteer, for example, you might say, "It gives my life meaning to be able to help people who are less fortunate than I am." Do you discover any discrepancies between what you think is meaningful in life and what you're spending time doing? If so, this is an opportunity for you to consider redistributing your time to be more in line with what you think is meaningful. You can be the one to give your life meaning through the choices you make.

Why We Strive to Make Meaning

As you learned previously, there is a danger in thinking *too* deeply. For all of human history, people have responded to the biggest questions of life by *making up answers*, because we want answers, we want to know (or, at least, think we know). Unfortunately, our quality of thinking is sometimes so poor that we accept things as true with no evidence, or even despite evidence to the contrary. That says something about how instinctive it is for humans to need something to believe. Our beliefs tell us how to react and what to do, and they provide us with some small measure of certainty in an uncertain world. How strongly you need that small measure of certainty will determine how quickly and forcefully you jump to conclusions that satisfy you even if more careful consideration would lead you to recognize your conclusion is without evidence.

What someone believes is important, of course, but *how* someone comes to believe it is even more important. When do you have enough evidence in order to believe something? Do you want to know what the scientific research says and to have information that is testable, researchable, and either provable or disprovable? Or, are you the kind of person who says, in essence, "I believe it and that's all there is to it!"?

Either style of thought has its vulnerabilities. Some important things in life simply can't be researched and proved or disproved: The strength of human spirit, love, and compassion are beyond the realm of science. Likewise, people can come to believe things that are clearly arbitrary and disempower themselves or others; they make their lives worse by *not* challenging these beliefs and demanding proof.

Filling in the Blanks . . . Dangerously

In the early to mid 1990s, psychotherapists were swept up by the compelling idea that the symptoms people presented (such as anxiety and relationship problems) *must* have their origins in some negative or even traumatic experiences in early life that would account for them. Many noncritical therapists believed that their clients had most likely been sexually abused as children. Even clients who claimed to have no such history of abuse, therapists believed, were repressing the memories, which *must* have been so horrific they were "split off" from awareness and "buried" somewhere in the person's unconscious.

As a result, many thousands of people who went into therapy for help with a variety of issues came out of therapy believing they had been sexually abused by loved ones. Lawsuits were filed against alleged perpetrators and courts across the country were hearing cases established on the basis of the memories recovered in therapy through a variety of questionable means. The mental health profession was deeply divided over the reality of these memories, and families splintered over allegations of terrible abuse that surfaced in therapy. Therapists didn't realize that the very techniques they were using to try to dig up the buried memories were capable of creating such memories. Fortunately, cooler heads prevailed and this sort of practice has all but stopped, although similar cases crop up on occasion.

I wrote the first of many books which eventually addressed this subject, a book published in 1994 called *Suggestions of Abuse*. In it I documented clinicians' responses to survey questions I posed about the workings of memory, the phenomenon of human suggestibility, and the relationship between suggestibility and memory. To my amazement, but not to my surprise, clinicians revealed their erroneous beliefs and range of misinformation that misguided their treatment of therapy clients by justifying the search for the memories they assumed *must* be buried somewhere.

This explosive issue showed that even well educated, well intentioned therapists were capable of deceiving themselves by discounting the need for proving an arbitrary belief. Their willingness to jump on the "repressed memories of abuse" hypothesis justified all kinds of behavior that was appalling by more objective clinical standards. As you could predict from your growing knowledge of the principle of cognitive dissonance, these therapists vigorously defended their beliefs and actions. Some of them did so by developing ever more elaborate additions to the theory to counter criticism of it. Others viciously attacked anyone who might question them rather than presenting data to support their hazardous views. Some professionals eventually allowed reason to return and even had the integrity to apologize for their bad judgment and behavior, but many others simply went on as if nothing had ever happened, even after being chastised by courts and licensing boards.

People adopt beliefs, and they act on those beliefs. They resist feedback that suggests their beliefs may be wrong, and they fight against those they think are trying to discredit them. People will hold onto their beliefs even in the face of evidence to the contrary, and they will ignore, discount, or trivialize such evidence.

If you have a human brain, these lessons apply to you. If you have thoughts, your thoughts may or may not be correct. If you have beliefs, they may or may not be provable. If you have feelings, they may or may not distort how you view information. Your need to believe can lead you to adopt perspectives that may or may not work in your favor. Every time you "fill in the blanks" by interpreting the meaning of what you observe in yourself or others, you run the risk that your ideas and perspectives will fuel your depression. And, just like the theory of repressed memories that spread contagiously through the mental health profession, your depressing inaccurate beliefs can be acquired through and transmitted by other people.

The solution is evident in the subtitle of this chapter: *Learn to test your beliefs.* Before you can do that successfully and regularly, you have to acknowledge that believing something doesn't necessarily make it true.

Learn by Doing:
Develop Flexibility in Your Thinking

Pick three events a day every day for at least one month that are impossible to interpret definitively. For example, you call someone and leave a message asking her to call you back, but you don't get a return call. What does this mean? If you are depressed now or are prone to depression, then your first, reflexive interpretation is likely to be negative, such as "People are irresponsible" or "She doesn't like me." These are called negative attributions—explanations that make you feel bad. To overcome such reflexive negative interpretations of neutral events, push your thinking a little by striving to generate at least three or four possible interpretations that aren't negative. "Perhaps my message was lost," or "Perhaps she was out sick and couldn't call back," or "Perhaps something else came up that prevented her from calling back." The more possible explanations you can generate that fit the same fact pattern, the more flexible your thinking will become. Then go the next step and ask what evidence there is for any of the possible explanations. When you discover you usually don't know why someone did or didn't do something, it will make it much easier for you to avoid getting trapped in the upset of negative interpretations for which there is no evidence. Mastering the skill of saying "I don't know why" will save you lots of hurt and despair.

The Costs and Benefits of Self-Deception

When you're depressed, thinking is hard work. Your thoughts are typically unfocused and scattered. It's hard to be decisive when you're filled with self-doubts from second-guessing yourself a lot, and it's stressful to be wracked with indecision. Difficulties in thinking straight, combined with the very human tendencies to follow the lead of your emotions as well as the path of least resistance, almost guarantee that you will jump to a conclusion that justifies your reactions and behavior. Very smart people fall into this same foolish trap; none of us is immune to these potential mistakes.

There are countless ways to deceive yourself into getting into and even staying in relationships that can hurt you: convincing yourself someone can be trusted who robs you blind, ignoring someone's history of violence because he says "You're different and I'd never hurt you," excusing someone's deception by saying, "Oh, well, everyone makes mistakes," feeling sorry for someone who keeps getting dumped by "all those mean and insensitive women out there," believing the gossip who says so reassuringly, "I'll keep your secret," and so on. As I explained earlier about assessing others, I'm not encouraging you to be paranoid, just cautious. I'm not encouraging you to believe or disbelieve, but to look for evidence in words and deeds that suggests how close you allow people to get to you. *Wanting to believe people is the start of distorting information about them to fit with your hopes.*

The price of self-deception is high. Believing that perhaps it's time to quit fooling around and get married when you still really like fooling around is a big step in the direction of divorce. Believing you are ready to have kids because the biological clock is ticking when you have neither the temperament nor the means for raising them is a big step in the direction of family dysfunction. Believing you are ready for *anything* when you haven't seriously made a realistic appraisal of yourself and your circumstances is extremely hazardous. This goes for anyone you tie your life to as well: How does that person know whether he or she is really ready for marriage, a family, or any relationship that requires commitment and skill? This alone can help explain why divorces happen so quickly: One or both members of a new marriage discover the hard way that they really didn't grasp how poor the fit was between what the relationship required and what they as individuals could bring to it. No one wants to think of himself or herself as immature, selfish, lacking good judgment, short-sighted, superficial, or anything else that isn't particularly flattering. So, if you find these traits in someone, it *won't* be because he or she drew your attention to them!

Strangely enough, self-deception allows us to preserve our self-esteem, for better or worse. People who fail miserably at marriage or parenthood brush the failure aside with the excuse: "Well, I guess it just wasn't the right time." Or, if they're a little meaner about it, "How was I supposed to know he/she was going to turn out to be the partner from hell?" Self-deception allows us to avoid the unpleasant realization that someone isn't who we thought, when we desperately want this person to be a certain way.

Perhaps you saw the movie, *A Few Good Men*, in which Tom Cruise plays a military prosecuting attorney who goes after a powerful Marine colonel, played by Jack Nicholson, who is accused of giving an illegal order that led to a soldier's death. At the height of an emotional shouting match between them in the courtroom, Cruise demands to know the truth as to what happened and Nicholson responds, with contempt, *"You can't handle the truth!"* It is an intense, dramatic moment that draws attention to the idea that one person can decide for another what he or she needs to know and is capable of handling. If you don't dig deeper for information, if you don't strive to find out what's really going on, you are giving validity to Nicholson's statement. You're saying, in essence, you can't handle the truth. This is how people disempower themselves and treat themselves as if too fragile to know and act on the truth.

Styles and Patterns of Self-Deception

When people are engaging in distorted thinking, *they don't realize it*, which is how they become trapped in their own thoughts, incorrectly and unwittingly assuming they're accurate. "Cognitive distortions" is the term used to describe patterned errors in thinking, meaning they are repetitive and reflexive. Here I want to emphasize the *social* side of these distortions, specifically how cognitive distortions and self-deception play out in hurtful and depressing relationships. Here are some of the key patterns of self-deception and distorted thinking that get in the way of healthy relationships.

Internal Orientation

As discussed in depth earlier, an internal orientation is using your feelings, values, expectations, or beliefs as the indicator of what's true, how things "should" be, and as the framework for making decisions. It includes making projections (interpretations) about the meaning of things and then believing them. The dangers are in ignoring facts that don't fit with your beliefs and thinking you know more than you actually do when what you don't know can hurt you. An internal orientation can also lead you to seem (and even be) self-absorbed or emotionally unavailable to others. You're either too preoccupied or you overreact or you take things personally that really are not personal.

Minimizing the Positive/Maximizing the Negative

When you have a hard time believing anything good about yourself, you distort your thoughts. For example, if you ignore or minimize positive feedback you receive from others, you eventually discourage them from trying to relate to you in a positive way and you may create the very circumstances of negativity and rejection you feared in the first place. When people say nice things to you, they don't want to have to expend energy trying to convince you of their sincerity. *Your self-esteem doesn't determine other people's level of sincerity.* If some people want to think you're wonderful, *let them.*

Another aspect of maximizing the negative is a pattern called "catastrophizing," where you anticipate all the worst that can possibly happen and then react as if it is inevitable that the worst *will* happen. It's self-deception to think there is nothing to be done to influence what happens and therefore catastrophe is unavoidable.

Minimizing the Negative/Maximizing the Positive

When you only see or believe the things that make you feel good, you're vulnerable to distorted thinking. You end up missing information that could be useful in helping you to make better, more realistic decisions. For example, if you assume someone with a bad history (such as Jay and his violence) won't repeat it with you, that is optimistic, but it's also *hazardous*. Yes, people can change, but they can also be manipulative and self-serving while seeming quite sincere. The danger is in giving someone the benefit of the doubt for no good reason or convincing yourself it's okay if things blow up later because you're caught up in strong feelings right *now*.

Taking the Victim Position

As soon as you get into an interaction with another human being, you are *at most* half of the relationship. Not all relationships are equal, though, and so your half many not be an equal half. For example, you are not an equal with your mom or dad, your boss, or your professor. Even in such unequal relationships, though, you are by no means powerless: You can say and do things that directly influence the course of what happens.

In most relationships, such as dating, friendships, and committed intimate relationships, you *are* fully half of the relationship. You have some power to shape the relationship in order to help make it a good one. *Your half is influenced by and influences the other half.* People define themselves as victims when they don't use this capacity for influence. Learning to use your power in relationships skillfully is ultimately what this whole book is about.

Perfectionism

When people set standards for themselves or others that reflect intolerance for mistakes or imperfections, they set themselves and others up to be unhappy. The relationship between perfectionism and depression is a strong one; predictably, when the standard of perfection isn't achieved, arbitrarily defined as it usually is, the flood of self-criticism or other-criticism begins. Typically, perfectionism isn't viewed as perfectionism. Instead, it's framed as "high standards," painfully unrealistic as they may be. In relationships in particular, there are few things one can say to another person that are more consistently demotivating and hurtful than some variation of, "You're not good enough." It reflects an extreme "all-or-none" style of thinking that suggests if it isn't perfect, it's no good. It is self-deception to think perfection is an ongoing possibility where imperfect humans are involved. The danger is in never realizing that what you have, though imperfect, can still be *superb*.

Global Thinking

Global thinking leads you to form overgeneralizations, beliefs and statements that are so broad in scope that they are overinclusive. If you find yourself using words such as "all" (as in "*all* men are bad news"), "never" (as in "you *never* think about anyone but yourself"), and "always" (as in "you *always* criticize me"), that's a good clue that you're engaging in global thinking in that moment. It helps counter global thinking to look for exceptions. Are there *some* times your perception *isn't* true? If you get hurt in a relationship and conclude that "people can't be trusted," you're overgeneralizing incorrectly because some people *can* be trusted. Global thinking also leads people to have poorly defined goals ("I just want to be married"), inadequate information before they make important decisions ("Gee, how can this home loan be so cheap? Let's grab it!"), and a marked tendency towards overreacting to things ("My son doesn't like sports! Where did I go wrong?").

Making Unreasonable and Excessive Demands for Support

Asking other people for special considerations, making excuses for why you can't fulfill your obligations, seeking constant reassurances from others that they still find you attractive, interesting, or whatever, or being "high maintenance" in any other way is a reliable way to make other people withdraw from you in order to keep themselves from "burning out" around you. Whatever insecurities you might have, it's okay to ask loved ones for some occasional reassurance, but putting someone else in the position of having to bolster your self-esteem or support you when you don't feel like living up to your part of the commitment is self-deception when you think you deserve it "just because."

Ignoring or Never Seeking Alternative Viewpoints

Getting locked into a point of view is the mark of a closed mind. It involves a pattern called "selective perception" and leads people to jump to conclusions with no evidence to support that conclusion. When you get locked into a view that is beneficial to you, it's much less a concern. But when you get locked into a point of view that hurts you, keeps you helpless, hopeless, and depressed, a rigid attachment to that point of view is obviously terribly detrimental. The importance of questioning yourself (and others) on a regular basis can be both life affirming and life saving. Ask yourself routinely, "How do I know if this is true?" *before* you evaluate whether it's either true or useful enough to accept and act on. People who are afraid to consider other points of view feel fragile about their beliefs. When they cut off discussion by dismissing any other position as having no merit, it tells you how desperately they want and even need to believe, and how poorly they tolerate uncertainty.

The need to believe sets you up to believe other peoples' lies, or even just your own. It stops you from looking for, much less finding, what's really true. If you simply believe someone who promises you the moon, it will never occur to you to try to find out whether the moon is theirs to give.

Is Reality Really Real?

Given the ways you can distort information and deceive yourself, it may now be clearer to you than ever before just how easy it is to get lost in your thinking or lost in your views of yourself, others, and *life*. This point has led some philosophers, some rather extreme ones in my opinion, to declare that "there is no such thing as reality, there is only illusion." Extreme as this perspective seems, it's not difficult to understand how someone might actually see things that way.

We don't need to deal with *all* of "reality" right now (or *ever*, for that matter!). All we really need is a system in place that serves as "checks and balances" in specific situations so we don't just react blindly and ineffectively. To respond realistically and skillfully, you must exercise impulse control and frustration tolerance, gather information, weigh options, consider consequences, and evaluate the message of the other person's behavior *before* you act. You can avoid, overcome, and even prevent depression when you handle the most difficult situations with forethought, clarity, and deliberateness. You become more in control of your life, rather than feeling like a helpless victim.

To do these things, you first have to learn to suspend your judgments and reflexive reactions in key situations, which you now know as "impulse control." The advanced skill that impulse control makes possible is called "reality testing." Reality testing means going outside yourself, beyond your own thoughts and perceptions, in order to gather information from other, hopefully more objective, sources that can help you have a better grasp of what's *really* going on so you can respond more realistically and effectively.

Let's go back to Marcy's situation from the beginning of this chapter.

When Marcy only heard the words, "I'm really sorry," she concluded that Jay feels bad and so is unlikely to hit her again.

Now, let's throw in some reality testing: Marcy caught herself reflexively thinking that Jay felt bad and so was unlikely to hit her again, but in the very next moment, she thought, "That's exactly what I thought the last time . . . and the time before that, and the time before that." She cried and told herself that although she loves Jay very much, she can't keep living in fear that he's going to kill her one day for who knows what reason. Marcy was confused: Should she forgive him and believe he loves her and is sorry and won't hurt her again? Should she accept her belief that "all men get violent sometimes, just like dad did," and stay with Jay because "better the devil you know than the one you don't know"? Should she get away from him and try to get by without him, maybe try to build a better life for herself somewhere else with someone else?

In her confusion, Marcy realized she didn't know how to answer any of these questions. She decided to get help from someone who could understand and help her with her dilemma. She discreetly asked around (her doctor, then a trusted neighbor, and then a woman she knew and liked who went through something similar a couple of years ago) and was referred to a psychotherapist, a woman named Marion who came highly recommended. She called, scheduled an appointment, and mustered the courage to actually go. She thought Marion would probably judge her negatively for staying in this relationship with Jay, but instead of making judgments, Marion let Marcy tell the tale her way, without interruption.

After Marcy told Marion her story, Marion simply asked her how she knew what Jay was capable of in terms of hurting her in the future. Marcy thought awhile, then replied, "I honestly don't know what he's capable of doing." When Marion asked her if she thought Jay was capable of changing, Marcy said, "I'm not sure." Marion asked her under what conditions Jay might be able to change. Marcy took some time before answering, "If he really knew what he did was wrong." Marion asked, "Does he know that what he did was wrong?" Instantly, it became clear to Marcy that she had to leave Jay, scary as that seemed. She answered, "No, he doesn't. He's sure I deserved it. And that means he'll do it again whenever he thinks I deserve it again." She began to cry, and said, "I'm so scared . . . but I can't stay with him. I can't. Oh, God, what am I going to do? What am I going to do?" Marion answered softly, "We'll think carefully and decide together, but whatever it is, it means you'll be safe and that's what matters the most. I'll be there helping you. You won't be alone."

Marcy's courageous step to go outside herself and talk to someone who could help her focus on the bigger picture of what matters, not just what she feels or thinks, is one example of reality testing. When you're not sure what to do, when your mind is swimming with fears and doubts, when you know the situation is too important for you, your kids, your marriage, your family, your career, your relationship, or your future, *information matters more than feelings*. Talk to people who can be objective (a therapist, an accountant, an attorney); consider the opinions of sensible people who have relevant experience; and go to objective sources (a trip to the library to do some research) when you need facts more than you need opinions.

Weighing and Using Information to Make Good Decisions

Getting information or perspective is one thing; using it is another. Everyone who smokes cigarettes has the information that smoking kills, but the information doesn't mean much when smokers manage to distort that information in order to continue smoking. They may say, "Well, I only smoke a few. Most people smoke much more than I do." Some say, "Well, you gotta die of something, might as well be something I like." Others say, "Heck, I don't believe they're that bad for you. I think it's just those nicotine patch companies trying to scare people into quitting so they can make some money." People can deceive themselves in all kinds of ways, with all kinds of lame excuses.

When there are multiple ways of interpreting something, or multiple ways of viewing some issue, how do you decide which interpretation or which view to go with? When you face uncertainty, how do you decide on a plan to follow? The first step, a difficult one because it requires you to be honest with yourself, is to explain what you want. In the examples above regarding smoking, the honest though unhealthy goal is to dismiss any perspective that would interfere with the desire to keep on smoking. To cut through the silly excuses and say directly, "I want to keep on smoking," is important but hard to say because it creates cognitive dissonance: "I think I'm a smart person, yet I want to continue doing something foolish that I know is very bad for my health." But, that's the kind of honesty that can lead someone to jump to a higher level and ask, "Is that *really* what I want?"

Consider Jim from this chapter's opening vignette. His wife, Tina, can't stand him and has made it clear she'd prefer to divorce him if it weren't for the kids. The condoms in her purse suggest there's good reason to suspect she's already in a sexual relationship with someone else. What does Jim want? He'd likely say, "I want to maintain my marriage no matter what, no matter how much my wife can't stand me and no matter whom else she might be sleeping with." Hearing himself say that, he might well jump to a higher level and ask, "Who am I kidding? This isn't a marriage. It's an endurance contest."

Only by speaking the painful truth can Jim face the confusion directly about what to do next. He can consult an attorney, and he can consult a therapist, together figuring out how to do what needs to be done in the least painful way possible for all involved. He may not avoid the pain of dealing with the breakup of his family, but he can move through the process skillfully and eventually end up in a better place as a result.

Bear in mind, I'm using Jim as an example of points I've made about distorted thinking and problem solving. I'm not encouraging anyone to get a divorce without much greater consideration than what little I'm offering here. A decision to divorce is one of the most serious decisions one can make in a lifetime and should be approached with caution and respect, especially when depression can distort one's thinking. I highly recommend two books for dealing with this issue realistically. The first is called *Divorce Busting*, written by psychotherapist Michele Weiner-Davis. The other is called *Should You Leave?*, written by psychiatrist Peter Kramer. Both are helpful in making one of life's toughest decisions.

When you're honest with yourself about what you truly want, especially when you want something that can hurt you, you can better evaluate the information available to you. You can weigh information more objectively and determine how you are minimizing or maximizing details to fit with what you want. You can distinguish between what's real and what's magical thinking, recognizing that some information is more significant than other information. Facts aren't all equal. Yes, nicotine patch companies make money by encouraging people to quit smoking using their product. That's a fact. But, it's also a fact that the nicotine patch companies don't make or sell the cigarettes that cause disease or profit directly from people becoming addicted to cigarettes. So, to continue smoking because you don't want nicotine patch companies profiting off you is a misguided conclusion that attaches too much weight to profit motives and too little weight to the actual dangers of smoking.

There is a dilemma associated with issues such as these: *Would you rather feel good, or would you rather know the truth?* When Marcy would rather excuse Jay's violence so she can stay with him and when Jim would rather ignore Tina's contempt for him so he can stay with her, they'd rather feel good (as good as possible when avoiding hurtful things they don't want to face) than face the truth about their circumstances. This is the most common way people trap themselves in circumstances that depress them: They ignore reality to their own detriment.

Pause and Reflect:
Can *You* Handle the Truth?

Are there any situations in your life that at least some part of you knows you are deceiving yourself about? Are you minimizing some hurtful situation rather than facing it squarely and skillfully moving through it? If so, what do you tell yourself that lets you do this? If you were going to handle it, would you know what to do but you're simply afraid to do it? Or do you have no clue about how to handle things well?

Sometimes people get "stuck" because they don't really know what their options are or what specific steps to take to handle a painful situation. That's when talking to someone trustworthy and knowledgeable can be invaluable. Other times, though, people know what the options are and just don't like any of them. So, they take no action and, naturally, things get worse. Not surprisingly, their depression does, too.

Depression: Misled by Our Moods

As I stated earlier, our thoughts affect our feelings and mood states, but *our moods affect our thoughts and feelings, as well.* Plenty of research shows that feeling depressed affects the rate and quality of your thinking. It takes longer to solve even relatively simple problems, and it takes longer to understand the implications of facts you are given. When people are angry, they are more likely to make reckless decisions, and when they are anxious or fearful they are more likely to make more cautious, conservative decisions. In regard to memory, it is especially interesting that studies show consistently that, when people are depressed, they are more likely to recall bad things that have happened to them than good ones.

William, age forty-four, is a successful attorney running a well-regarded legal practice. Historically, he has been a positive kind of guy whom other people enjoy. In the last six months, however, he has had a very difficult time both personally and professionally, overwhelmed with tough personal stuff to deal with, and he was starting to sink into despair pretty quickly. First, his beloved partner in the law practice, a very good man named Thomas, was diagnosed with pancreatic cancer and not expected to live much longer. Then, his wife, Billie, told him she was having "grave doubts" about their marriage of six years. She said she was sure she loved him, but was also sure she wasn't "in love" with him. She wasn't sure what that meant for their future, but William took the hint that it didn't bode well. And, to make matters even worse, William's mom was diagnosed with Alzheimer's and needed more care and attention now than ever before, a need that would only grow over time. On top of all of this, his son from his first marriage, now fifteen, was suspended from school when he was found to be a small-time pot dealer, selling marijuana to his classmates. William was enraged—and disappointed—beyond words.

When William went to see a psychologist to get help, he acknowledged the stresses of the last six months and heard himself say for the first time out loud, "I think I'm depressed." Then, he went further than he should have when he declared, "I don't know how I've managed to fool myself and everyone else all these years. But, I think I've been depressed my whole life. I can remember always feeling like I'm so different from everyone else, never quite fitting in. I can remember always wishing people would notice me and feeling like nobody ever would because I was a nobody. I'm forty-four, and I have nothing and I'm still a nobody. Even my wife thinks I'm a nobody . . . And now, I guess, it's time I face the truth about myself . . ."

This is the sound of depression talking: William *isn't* a "nobody." Until now he's been content with his life and is highly regarded by his peers and community. But now that he has entered a terribly difficult phase of his life, he isn't just limiting his problems to this time period. He is (globally) extending his bad feelings across his lifespan, re-writing his personal history from a depressed vantage point.

William illustrates well how a depressed mood acts as a memory "filter," leading him to unwittingly but actively select negative memories to justify his current depressed feelings. Instead of his problems becoming smaller and more manageable, they now become bigger and overwhelming.

Rewriting history in this way is another form of self-deception that you want to recognize and guard against. Think of the implications: When someone goes into therapy feeling bad, and tells a life story of hurt and misery, should the therapist believe her and accept as true that her *whole life* was terrible? When your previously good marriage hits hard times and both of you are unhappy and perhaps contemplating divorce, should you believe yourself (or each other) when you say, "We *never* had a good marriage—it was *always* a sham?" When you get into a fight with a sibling you've gotten along perfectly well with for years, do you really have good reason now to think twice when you say, "We were *never* close, anyway?"

Learn by Doing:
Mood as a Filter

Take a piece of paper and create two columns. In the first column, describe a series of perceptions or judgments you'd likely make about someone's behavior if you were in a good mood. In the second column, take that same person's behavior and write down how you'd judge it if you were in a bad mood. For example, if you're in a good mood, you'll say someone is "thrifty." If you're in a bad mood, you'd say he's "cheap." If you're in a good mood, you might call a person childlike. If you're in a bad mood, you'd say he is "childish." You may find that the behavior isn't really any different from column one to column two, just the value judgment you make about it depending on your mood.

Mood filters decision making, thinking, information processing, and memory. Mood also filters our perceptions of other people. Consider how your mood influences your judgments of others with just these few simple examples:

- When you're in a good mood, you think your child is wonderfully and happily energetic. When you're in a bad mood, you think, "Gotta get him some Ritalin."
- When you're in a good mood, you think your partner's cynicism is insightful. When you're in a bad mood, he or she is "always so negative."
- When you're in a good mood, the joke is funny. When you're in a bad mood, it's dumb.
- When you're in a good mood, she is "thoughtful." When you're in a bad mood, she is "too sensitive."
- When you're in a good mood, other people are "interesting." When you're in a bad mood, other people are "a drain."

Depression distorts perceptions, whether they are perceptions of yourself, your history, your future, or your relationships. *Before you let your depression decide what's true, learn to test your beliefs.*

CHAPTER 7

Drawing the Lines:

Protect Your Personal Boundaries

One of the ways depressed people unintentionally build depression right into their relationships with others is by not defining what they consider appropriate behavior. This leaves them vulnerable to mistreatment in a variety of ways that can easily culminate in depression. By "drawing the lines," I refer to where people place their boundaries in relationship to another person in a particular context.

She Thinks They Should Make Her a Grandma

Tammy and Mitch had been dating for only a few months, but their relationship got pretty intense pretty quickly, and they had been together almost every day. There was a hungry passion for each other, but they also talked a lot and savored the process of really getting to know each other. Something was different about this relationship from previous ones, and both found themselves secretly daring to think that "This is the special relationship I've been waiting for all my life."

Mitch invited Tammy to a dinner to meet his family. He was confident Tammy would really enjoy his sister, Alexis, but he wasn't so sure how well she'd do with his parents, who had always been overprotective of Mitch, and were sure there wasn't a girl on the planet good enough for him. He warned his parents to treat Tammy well or there'd be hell to pay later. His mom smiled sweetly and said, "Well, of course we'll be nice to her, dear! She's our guest and your new girlfriend."

Mitch's folks were on their best behavior, polite, friendly, pleasant and curious, and the evening went without a hitch until almost the last minute. Sitting together out on the patio, Mitch's mom casually asked Tammy what she saw herself doing five years from now, and Tammy responded she thought she'd be a few steps further into her demanding career. When Mitch's mom asked her about her intention regarding having children, Tammy answered honestly that she didn't plan to have any. Mitch's mom immediately turned to Mitch and asked him how he could possibly date a woman who had no intention of making her a grandmother.

Mitch paused and gave her the same kind of utterly detached look one might give an object of curiosity in a museum before he finally said, "It's not your decision, now, is it?" There was an awkward, uncomfortable moment before Alexis jumped in and asked, "Who wants some more coffee?" before suggesting, "Why don't we all go into the living room where we'll be more comfortable?" Tammy made eye contact with Alexis that clearly said, "Thank you!" and then flashed a look at Mitch that clearly said, "Nicely done. The going may get tough, but we'll be fine."

Mitch's mom feels she can pressure him to choose a woman according to standards that matter to *her*, not necessarily to Mitch. Should Mitch's mom have the right to attempt to impose her will on Mitch? How far can she go in expressing her feelings about wanting grandchildren before she has crossed the line and gone from simply expressing her feelings to being unreasonably demanding? Mitch's well-considered reply to his mom "hit the boundary nail on the head" by making it clear that any decision about his having children was for him to make, not her.

What Are Boundaries and Why Do They Matter?

Boundaries define a relationship: what you can and can't say, what you can and can't do in relation to someone else. Your boundaries help determine the quality of your relationships: obvious boundaries define a person as your boss, friend, or cousin. Other more subtle boundaries may define you as easy to intimidate, easy to manipulate in order to comply with other people's wishes, and reluctant to say what you think or want from others. Whenever you draw the line with people and say, in essence, "This is as far as I go with you on this issue," you are establishing a boundary.

Drawing the line with others is a necessary step for giving healthy definition to a relationship, but the greater task is holding the line once you've drawn it. Wherever you draw a line, you are guaranteed to inconvenience someone: But that's not enough reason to compromise the line you've drawn. If Mitch and Tammy in the vignette above stay together and eventually marry, assuming they are both clear and in agreement with each other that they don't want to have kids, that's a perfectly reasonable line to draw for themselves as a married couple. They can and must decide for themselves what they want their relationship to be about, and if having kids isn't what they want, so be it. Mitch's mom may attempt to get them to change their minds and may cross their boundaries again. Tammy and Mitch will likely need to develop a variety of ways to hold their line so they don't get pushed into doing something they really don't want to do just to make his mom happy. You can only imagine what kind of parents they'd be if they were pushed into parenthood out of guilt rather than having chosen it freely.

Knowing when and where to "draw the lines" allows you to assert yourself as a full partner in your relationships in order to build them in healthy ways that bring mutual satisfaction. But, if you're afraid to draw lines, you can easily become victimized, subservient to others' will and unable to assert your own. Then other people will seem hurtful and controlling. If you don't learn how to draw and hold the line with them, you may only find relief by withdrawing from them. Depressed people often blow up at others and then isolate themselves for these reasons.

How do you know if you have difficulties with boundary issues? Here are some consequences of **poor boundaries:**

- An inability to say "no" to controlling people or to set limits on others' hurtful behavior.
- An inability to say "no" to one's own destructive impulses.
- An inability to hear "no" from others and respect their stated boundaries.
- An inability to delay gratification and accomplish goals and tasks.
- Taking responsibility (especially blame) for other people's decisions.
- Struggles with intimacy and fearing a "loss of self" to someone else.
- An inability to be honest with those we are close to.
- An inability to confront others' transgressions and resolve conflicts constructively.

- Experiencing life as a victim of other people's mistreatment.
- An inability to "move on" when it's appropriate to do so.

Learn by Doing:
Evaluate Your Boundaries

Before you get any further in reading this chapter, take another look at the above list of negative consequences of poor boundaries. Write down as many examples of things you can point to in your life that reflect possible boundary issues you might have. Then, ask yourself: Do these issues tend to surface in one particular type of situation? Or with one particular person or, perhaps, a type of person? What allows these situations to occur? Do you fear confronting someone and facing his anger, or do you worry about hurting someone's feelings, or . . . what? It will help you to develop a strategy for strengthening yourself in your dealings with others if you know what specifically you seem to have a hard time dealing with.

Boundary Violations are Contagious

In this age of unprecedented openness, where seemingly normal people go on television or the Internet and reveal deeply personal things we usually wish they didn't, and where celebrities shamelessly sell their "tell all" stories that embarrass themselves and whomever else they were involved with, the positive trait of discretion is rarely on display anymore. (Perhaps you've used the popular acronym, "TMI," at those awkward times when someone gives you "too much information" of a personal nature that you really don't want.)

Our culture now discourages people from using discretion, perhaps the most visible indicator of someone with good boundaries. We have encouraged people to be *too* open in order to satisfy our unabashed desire to be "emotional voyeurs." We want to see people reveal their dirty secrets, watch the private celebrity sex film that mysteriously went public, and hear the sordid details about who did what to whom. The media are relentless about digging up and, if necessary, even *creating* stories (for example, the paparazzi who deliberately provokes a celebrity into an angry confrontation that gets recorded then sold to the highest media bidder) to feed our apparently insatiable appetite for trashy gossip. There is no discretion and there are no boundaries.

We have become accustomed to such continuous displays of invading people's privacy and even rationalize them by saying, "It's the price they pay for being a celebrity." Really? And if your kids ask you details about your sex life, is that "just the price of being a parent?" Or if your boss asks you what you do with the money you're paid, is that "just the price of being an employee?" No! There are boundaries that define what is appropriate to ask and, likewise, what is appropriate to reveal. If someone shows poor judgment and asks a question that is inappropriate, you can show the good judgment to deflect it.

Pause and Reflect:
Dealing with Inappropriate Questions

Can you think of some examples of when people asked you questions you felt uncomfortable answering? Were the questions too personal? Were they setups to make you look bad or foolish in some way? How did you respond? Did you answer the question even though it made you uncomfortable, or did you refuse to answer? If you answered it, why do you think you did so when you were uncomfortable about it? If you didn't answer it, how did you avoid doing so? Learning how to deal with such situations is vitally important to protecting your own self-esteem.

Having at least two or three different strategies of effective things to say ("I'm sorry, but I prefer not to discuss that") that you can use in an instant when someone is coming at you can save you from saying things you may regret later. You know someone is going to ask you something inappropriate sometime, you just don't know when exactly. Have ready some possible responses so you can offer one on the spot.

Inappropriate self-disclosures in the media provide yet another social mechanism that helps contribute to the spread of depression. When people are regularly exposed to things that initially are shocking, they become used to them. They even accept them as normal. This is a process psychologists call "desensitization," where we become less and less reactive to things that used to be considered quite emotionally charged. So, we become used to the war being beamed into our living rooms each night until the latest roadside bombing and casualty report barely stir a reaction. We get used to the latest political scandal as just another one. We get used to the metal detectors and armed guards in our high schools and to taking off our shoes and coats for airport security screenings. And, we get used to seeing private people's lives all over news and entertainment programs as well as on *YouTube* and *MySpace*. People reveal themselves willingly for attention, and the lines between public and private all but disappear.

There is a price to pay for losing a sense of what's decent and appropriate, and it manifests in poorer decision making (it's not a good idea to make videos of yourself having sex unless their ending up in the wrong hands is part of your plan), poorer self-esteem, poorer social skills, and increased depression resulting from the negative consequences.

Where Are Your Boundaries Supposed To Be?

How do you know where your boundaries are? Think of boundaries as the rules of conduct in your relationships, including your relationship with yourself. Like the rules of a game, these rules are there to ensure honest and fair play. There are rules for what happens when someone breaks the rules and, in healthy relationships, there are even rules for how to revise the rules.

The rules come from your own value system, your strongly held beliefs about what matters, what you consider good and bad, right and wrong, normal and not normal. You base your judgments, reactions, and behavior on your values. Valuing *money* more than *relationships*, for example, will allow you to take advantage of people for your own financial gain and feel perfectly fine about doing so. When you value *power* more than *people*, then hurting people to get your way won't bother you in the least. (You want to know how some ruthless politicians and business executives sleep at night? Now you know.) When you value being *right* more than you value being *effective*, you will stick to your way of doing things even when another way is shown to be at least as effective, and you'll likely devalue it in the process. When you value *profits or personal comfort* over *protecting the environment*, then it really won't matter to you how much old-growth forest gets cut down or whether you drive a gas guzzler. Your values define your perspectives and shape the actions you live by.

Learn by Doing:
Define Your Values

What are your values? Write them down: What matters to you? How do you know? Quietly explore your feelings and beliefs to answer these questions. Or, you can explore yourself from the outside in: As you read newspaper and magazine articles, watch TV shows, and have talks with other people, listen to what they care about and notice what you find yourself reacting to. Notice what you find yourself agreeing and disagreeing with, what you find yourself making positive and negative judgments about, what you accept as true and dismiss as untrue. It is very different to have a value system that says, for example, people are to blame for their poverty than it is to say, "we need to do something to help these unfortunate people." Every day, you are exposed to a great deal of information as well as the "spin" on that information. You have lots of opportunities to discover trends in your viewpoints and reactions, and these reflect your values.

Boundaries in Building Relationships

You are the one who decides what is important to you. You also decide whether to trust someone else by learning the values he or she holds. If you value being polite and respectful in your interactions with others and strive to be so, then being around someone who doesn't particularly care whether she is offensive to others may intrigue you at first, but will tend to get really old, really fast. If you want someone who can actually be aware of his feelings and express them appropriately, especially when angry, then being around someone who wouldn't know a feeling if it bit him in the behind and who yells and hits isn't going to make you happy. If you want someone to make your relationship a priority and spend time with you, then being around someone who puts work or hobbies ahead of everything else is always going to make you feel like you're second rate.

To know what other people value, you have to assess them realistically. When you say, in essence, "This is what matters to me and I'd like you to respect it even if you don't necessarily agree with it," you will learn whether that person feels it is more important to accept or change you. Every relationship faces the challenge of how to bridge value differences. You can bridge some through acceptance or compromise, but some value differences you cannot. Sometimes, all good communication does is show you how far apart you are. For example, if either Tammy or Mitch from this chapter's opening vignette changes his or her mind about having kids a couple of years into their marriage, this is an irreconcilable difference. You either have kids or you don't—there are no halfway solutions. There aren't any compromises either on loyalty, compassion, respect, and honesty in healthy relationships.

You must decide whether your boundary is firm and unyielding, or whether there is some room for compromise. That's a decision to be made on a case-by-case basis. You'll have to decide whether you're being flexible or "wishy-washy." (Hint: If you cave in to avoid conflict, compromise a value you genuinely believe in, and like yourself less for doing so, it's "wishy-washy.")

Will *You* Respect Someone Else's Boundary?

When someone tells you, "Here's my line, please respect it," are you likely to do so, or are you likely to strive to get him to change it because you're not happy with it? Having good boundaries means respecting your own as well as *other* peoples' boundaries. When Mitch in the opening vignette said to his mom, "It's not your decision, now, is it?" in response to her rudeness to Tammy and pointed comment about wanting grandchildren, his boundaries are clear. A mom with clear boundaries accepts that she can't push her son or daughter into a demanding, lifelong commitment of parenthood for her own personal satisfaction. Accepting other peoples' decisions with grace when those decisions are unfavorable to you is one of the clearest signs of a mature person.

Here's another example: If you notice I'm being grumpy today and ask me what's wrong, I can view your question on a continuum that ranges from caring at one end to intrusive at the other. If I tell you there's nothing wrong, or more honestly say, "Yes, I *am* in a bad mood today but I don't care to discuss it," will you accept that and stop asking me about it? Or, will you intensify your probing by saying, "C'mon, you can tell me what's wrong"? If you decide it's more important to satisfy your curiosity about what's wrong (or your desire to help me be fulfilled) than it is to respect the line I've drawn, then you'll intensify your probing. If you decide it's for me to disclose what I choose to, then you'll still be curious but respect my wishes and drop it. If I'm wise, though, I can do something to help you reduce your curiosity or desire to know if you might have done something to contribute to my grumpiness: I can give you the assurance that *my grumpiness isn't about you.*

This is a wonderful strategy for protecting your relationships with others: Let them know, honestly of course, that they need not wonder or worry that your emotional state has something to do with them. This is especially important in your relationship with your spouse or partner, and even more so in your relationships with your kids. Younger children are especially prone to thinking it's personal and that if you're acting grumpy around them, it's because they must have done something to displease you. *Protect others from that self-blaming, hurtful thinking whenever you possibly can.*

People Want What They Want

What do people want from you? Different people will want different things, of course, but the following are some of the most common things people strive to get from each other:

- Love
- Attention
- Approval
- Commitment
- Expertise or advice
- Money
- Sex
- Emotional support
- Professional support
- Economic support
- An apology
- Obedience

If you can name whatever it is that people in your life want from you, then you can more easily go to the next step and understand why they would want this from you. All you have to do is recognize how it benefits that person, how it is in his best self-interest, to get what you have.

Sometimes it may be confusing because the person denies it's in his best self-interest and insists it's for *your* benefit. (Can't you just hear Mitch's mom from the opening vignette saying, "It's not that I have to be a grandmother. I just don't want you to miss out on the joys of being a parent. I just know you'll regret it one day!") And, *it may genuinely be for your benefit*, so you do have to consider that possibility.

Someone pushing you to stop smoking or lose weight, or make some similar healthful change, is doing so clearly for *your* benefit, not hers. But more often than not, other people want what they want from us because it serves them, not us. *If you care to be generous, and it doesn't hurt you, the other person, or the longer term health of the relationship to comply with his wishes, then go ahead.* That's the normal "give and take" of relationships. But, when you are clear that what serves that person best hurts you and hurts the relationship, then you must be careful about where to draw the line and how to hold it.

It is your responsibility to protect yourself from attempts to exploit you. You can't stop people from going after what they want, and if you happen to have what they want, they will almost surely go after it. That is human nature and you won't be able to change it. Letting someone hurt you for his personal gain, either directly or by getting you to hurt yourself when you beat up on yourself for having given in to something you don't feel good about, is abusive. It leads to sharp self-criticism and a loss of self-respect, and it inadvertently reinforces further violations of your boundaries by having given in. People will continue to do what you reward them for doing, whether the reward is intentional or otherwise.

Avoid Conflict . . . and Harm the Relationship

In studies of depressed people's styles of social interaction, a clear pattern of "conflict avoidance" is evident. This means that when they routinely interact with others in cases that need simple clarifications or where even mild confrontation is necessary, they find the possibility of conflict so aversive they'd rather avoid interactions altogether and simply suffer the consequences.

Do you strive to avoid conflicts with people because getting into scrapes with others is so distasteful to you? Believe it or not, that's perfectly normal. It doesn't mean you're a wimp. With the exception of a few obnoxious talk show hosts who make a living by stirring things up, most people would rather have calm and harmonious interactions with other people. The reasons are sensible enough: We like to feel good, and arguing, bickering, fighting, feeling attacked or devalued simply doesn't feel good. We also like to feel safe, and conflict can lead people to say terrible things and possibly even lead to violence. At first glance, avoiding conflict seems a smart thing to do. But, it isn't.

Pause and Reflect: The Merits of Conflict

Can you think of any positive value conflict might have in a healthy relationship?

No matter how much you and someone else might agree on things, there will inevitably be times when you don't. You can't be afraid of disagreeing, if you are to be honest with each other. If someone does something that is thoughtless or hurts you, or vice versa, you have to acknowledge it and learn to do something different in order to correct the mistake and allow the relationship to continue in a positive direction. Conflict is a means of keeping a relationship "on track," and in that sense is vital for a relationship's well-being.

Anger and Self-Justification: "He Had It Coming!"

Conflict isn't easy. It requires considerable effort to handle well. If you simply don't care about the future of the relationship, and you don't care if you hurt someone, then you can pretty much say anything you want and make no effort to keep it either civil or constructive. Unfortunately, people make this choice all too often; they destroy the relationship rather than strive to resolve the situation respectfully. They say terrible things that cannot be unsaid, they do awful things that cannot be undone, and the relationship ends with a crash. They do this with family members, friends, co-workers, people they're dating, anyone and everyone they want to hurt when they're angry. After their hot heads cool a little, they may have some regret about what they've done, but it can quickly be masked by the self-justification, "They deserved it." Well, maybe the other person *did* do something wrong, perhaps even terribly wrong, but how you handle the problem is important. Do you really want to establish yourself as someone who viciously "goes off" on someone? Or do you want to act with grace under pressure?

A person who is explosively angry has no boundaries containing the anger in order to express it appropriately or respectfully. He or she has some very predictable patterns: rigid and usually unrealistic expectations for how things "should" be, low frustration tolerance (difficulty handling it when efforts don't immediately succeed or when things don't go the way you think they should), poor impulse control (difficulty containing your immediate feelings or reactions long enough to coolly evaluate options), and an external orientation (blaming others when upset).

The people who are most prone to explosive rage and even violence typically believe that their anger is justified and there's no reason for them to hold back. Many even believe that it is *healthy* to vent their anger. Unfortunately, the mental health profession itself is partly to blame for encouraging this perspective. It became very common practice years ago to encourage people to "get in touch with their anger" and "vent their anger" as ways, presumably, of reducing that anger. As social psychologist Carol Tavris described in her illuminating book, *Anger: The Misunderstood Emotion*, the research on such methods shows that the opposite has happened: Venting anger didn't reduce it, it actually *magnified* its intensity. As you have learned, when you focus on something, you amplify it. Focusing on anger made angry people angrier, *not better*. Telling someone to pound a pillow or pound the wall may give them some temporary relief, but it doesn't teach the more important skills of anger management, such as recognizing when expectations are unrealistic, catching yourself when you're only irritated well *before* you become enraged, and learning *what* to express as well as *when* and *how* to express it.

You don't have the right to dump your anger on people because you think they deserve it or because it makes you feel better to do so. Neither does anyone else. You have to have respectful boundaries in your interactions with others, lines you won't cross even if you're hopping mad. Good boundaries allow you to contain your feelings (impulse control) while you decide what your next *constructive* move is.

Avoiding Conflict and the Depressing Demise of Relationships

Earlier I said that avoiding conflict seems like a good idea . . . but *isn't*. Conflict avoidance all but guarantees problems:

- The relationship can't be honest (it's more important to avoid upsetting someone than to tell him or her the truth).
- The person who is less afraid of confrontation or is more comfortable with aggression will control the relationship, making someone a "winner" in arguments, and by default, someone else a "loser."
- The relationship develops no means of "course correction" if it starts to drift in unhelpful directions.
- It sends the message that you don't believe in yourself (your values, your preferences) enough to be willing to stand up for yourself.
- In families, it models to the children that it's more important to get along with people, seeking their approval, than it is to be yourself and learn to deal with the fact that no matter who you are or what you do, someone isn't going to like you.

How much do you value individual rights? What happens when someone else's expression of his or her individual rights interferes with your own? This is what makes the issue so difficult: How much should I give up of my own wishes or preferences in order to be accepted or liked by you? If I give up too much of myself so you'll like me, I may lose myself in the process. If I give up too little of myself and attempt to impose my will on you, then I may lose you in the process. This is the issue at the heart of conflict. Each person wants others to do as he wishes, each person thinks he's right, and each person wants what he wants. People clash over who is going to get their way. And some people will stoop to despicable behavior in order to get their way. Their lack of boundaries makes it easier, perhaps even easy, to say and do things to other people that someone with integrity and a conscience would *never* say or do. Your boundaries define who you are in so many important ways.

Learn by Doing:
How Do *You* Do Anger?

It may seem a strange question, but how do you know when you're angry? What are the cues you notice that tell you you're angry? Does your anger explode suddenly, or are you the slow-to-anger type? How angry do you have to be before you recognize you're angry? Some people are in touch with lesser precursors, such as feeling annoyed or irritated, well before their anger becomes full blown. When you're angry, do you say and do things you'll regret later?

Create a flow chart of how your anger generally starts, builds, surfaces in your awareness, how you express it, what happens in the aftermath, and how long it takes to subside. What do you discover about your particular sequence for experiencing and expressing anger? Is there anything about it you'd like to change?

There will always be a potential for conflict where there is a free exchange of ideas and perspectives between people free to express their points of view. *The goal isn't to prevent conflict: The goal is to learn to manage conflict with skill.*

Developing any skill involves a learning curve. First, you have to have a reason to learn, a motivation. I hope I'm giving you the motivation to learn to overcome conflict avoidance by pointing out that conflict is inevitable and that there are some hazards to your relationships and mental health when you strive to avoid conflicts and thereby adopt a position of being a victim to someone else's will. *No one overcomes depression by declaring himself or herself a victim.*

The actual skill of managing conflict well can be broken down into several core components, the first of which is the ability to know your own boundaries well enough to know when someone is starting to come over the line, attempting to influence you in some way. *You need to know when someone is demanding or expecting something of you in order to know whether you prefer to comply or refuse.* If you're okay to give this person what he or she wants, that's fine. But the next step is critical: *Determine the "message value" of your response.* In other words, decide what you are telling the person in your reply.

> Dan asks Linda out on a date. She doesn't know anything about Dan beyond the pleasant sense of humor he displays in her brief interactions with him when she shops in his store. She agrees to go out with him and Dan says he'll pick her up Friday evening at 8:00. Friday night comes around, and Dan shows up at Linda's at 8:30. He strolls in nonchalantly, with no apology or explanation for his late arrival. Linda silently debates whether she should say something to Dan about the slow burn she's been doing while waiting for him, or whether she should just let it pass without comment.

Should Linda say something to Dan about his arriving late? If she doesn't, she is sending him the wrong message that, "It's okay to be late." If she sends him that self-defeating message, she may unintentionally build Dan's lack of consideration for her time right into their relationship from the very beginning. But maybe she shouldn't say anything to Dan because it's only a first date and they really don't have a relationship yet. *If* she decides to go out with him again *then* she can tell him she would like the courtesy of a phone call if he's running late.

As you can appreciate, now we're talking about *when* to set a limit, not *whether* to set a limit. I hope we're agreed that Linda will need to set a limit *sooner*, not later. And, just because she says, "I'd appreciate you being on time when we make plans to do something together," doesn't mean he'll accept the limit. He could easily turn on her and defend his bad behavior by attacking her: "Hey, it's only thirty minutes, what's the big deal? You're too uptight! Why don't you lighten up and just go with the flow?" If his reply to her limit (requesting he be punctual) is to attack her, he's making it clear that things have to be his way, he's unwilling to adapt, and he's willing to justify his irresponsibility by blaming her. If Linda is smart, this first date will be the *only* date. She's learned all she needs to know about Dan in one very important interaction.

The message value of behavior is inevitable. *Everything you do says something, and the artistry of living with integrity is making sure that what you say through your behavior is what you intend to say.* If you refuse to voice an opinion because you're afraid you might get a negative reaction, what are you saying? If you let someone abuse you in some way without either fighting back or walking away (assuming you're an adult and have the power to do so), then what are you saying? If you feel depressed and don't know what to do to get over it, and you do nothing to seek help, then what are you saying? What is someone saying when he refuses to vote? When he doesn't reciprocate dinner with someone who had him over for dinner? When she doesn't share in the housework? There are endless examples of people sending others some pretty poor messages. The faster you can identify the message in a specific behavior whether yours or someone else's, the faster you can determine whether that message is or is not acceptable.

Learn by Doing: What is the Message?

Please review the questions in the preceding paragraph and write down your answers to them. Putting into words the message you're sending someone when you take some position is great practice for helping speed up how quickly you recognize what the message is you want to put forth and then how to do so effectively. Generate at least half a dozen more examples of interactions in your own life and sift out the message value of the position you take in each of them.

What allows people to endure confrontations with others is knowing they would be sending the wrong message if they didn't make a deliberate point of sending the right one. Self-respect demands no less. *Conflict is necessary, even desirable, for transforming wrong messages into right ones as soon as possible.*

Boundaries and Building Good Relationships

The whole idea of building good relationships is to surround yourself with people who will respect your limits, just as you strive to respect theirs. You can't choose your family or your co-workers the way you can choose your friends or romantic partners, but *you can certainly strive to teach people how you want to be treated.* You can only do that, though, when you're willing to correct people, respectfully confronting whatever they're doing that is hurtful to you or damaging to the relationship. People who are willing to consider and even adjust to your preferences, and you to theirs, are "keepers." Walk away from people who are willing to hurt you for their own personal gain, who are indifferent to your attempts to make the relationship more comfortable or effective for you both. It's not that people have to do as you wish—but they have to show you enough courtesy to be willing to consider your wishes and deal with them respectfully, even if their answer happens to be "no." Here's yet another opportunity for you to be able to walk away from an interaction saying to yourself, "I like the way I handled that."

Handling Manipulative Tactics
in Ways You Can Feel Good About

By building relationships that allow us to thrive, even when our history might be a terrible one, we can create what psychologist Mary Pipher called *The Shelter of Each Other* in her wonderful book by that name. Yet many of the depressed people I have treated over the years have come pretty close to selling their souls in order to give someone else what he or she wanted. They end up with no self-respect, and they end up losing the very affection they crave because the other person doesn't respect them, either.

How people go after the things they want defines their integrity in relationships. Depressed people, and those most vulnerable to depression, are often victimized by self-serving people using abusive tactics. When they're caught off guard, even shocked, by a someone who intrusively demands something unexpected, they are unable to find the effective words they need to defend themselves. They are easily manipulated.

My goal here is to help you recognize other peoples' tactics for attempting to manipulate you and to help you develop effective ways of responding to their tactics without caving in and feeling victimized by them, then being angry with yourself for caving. Some tactics can be truly brutal. Most are not. All are fairly transparent and easy to stay a step ahead of *if* you know what the other person wants. After all, the tactic is meant to get something from you. If you get lost in how the tactic makes you feel and thereby lose sight of the other person's agenda and what your most effective response should be, then the tactic is far more likely to work. The other person gets what he or she wants, you feel bad, and you're left wondering what just happened.

Buy Yourself Some Time to Think: Master the Delayed Response

Knowing what the other person wants is essential in preventing yourself from getting manipulated. Most of the time, what the person wants from you is pretty obvious, if you take the time to think about it *before* you react. (When he saunters over, delivers a clever opening line and wants to buy you a drink or "take you to an island as beautiful as you are," it's not too difficult to figure out what he wants.) But, sometimes, the person's goal *isn't* obvious, what's commonly called a "hidden agenda." You may sense the person's hook dangling in front of your nose, yet still be unclear what he or she is fishing for. Or, you may be entirely clear what this person wants (examples: they want you to work their shift for them, lend them money, reveal a secret someone told you, lie to someone else on their behalf, join them in some behavior you don't care to engage in) and you know you don't want to comply but you're afraid of (anxious about) his or her disapproval, criticism, or rejection.

When you start to feel pushed by someone, your first priority is to handle things in a way you'll feel good about later. If you're not sure what the best response is, the first tactic for you to master and employ is the "delayed response." Instead of giving an immediate reply you're not sure you'll be happy with later, make a point of taking some extra time to consider what you want to say and how you want to say it. Say something such as, "I need some time to think about this. I'll get back to you tomorrow (or next week, or later today)." If the person pushes back hard and says, "Not okay. I need an answer from you *right now!*" you can say, "If you need an immediate answer, then I'm afraid it's no. I don't want to be pressured to agree to something I may not feel good about later. If I had time to really consider it, maybe my answer would change. But if you need an answer right now, the answer is no. Sorry." Most people have enough sense of courtesy to know "I need some time to think about this" is a cue for them to back off. It won't satisfy their wish for an immediate answer, but comforting them with an instant answer at your own expense will fill you with regret, anger, and self-criticism. A delay tactic can prevent all that.

Intimidation Tactics:
The Nuclear Bomb of Depressed Relationships

Unfortunately, intimidation as a tactic often works all too well. The bully at school gets the weakling's lunch money, the overbearing manager gets his anxious employee's cooperation, and the raging husband gets his wife's meek compliance. People who threaten and even perpetrate violence in order to get their way are scary, dehumanizing, demoralizing, and make you feel weak and controlled.

Consider this on global and political levels first: How much has life in the United States, indeed the world, changed as a result of the ongoing threats of terrorism? For example, travel isn't nearly as easy or fun as it used to be because the extra security measures make it so much more burdensome. The fact that such measures are necessary is what's so sad: The harsh reality is that there are people who are willing to kill others to make a statement, and most of us don't even know what the statement is. The extra security at government buildings, post offices, sporting events, *all over*, forces us into making concessions in order to prevent our own harm. It raises anxiety, fear, suspicion, and polarizes people in arguments about whether safety matters more than freedom. What a shame to have to make such a choice *ever*, much less every day.

In your life, are *you* threatened by someone who intimidates you? Is your physical or emotional safety at risk in some way? If so, feeling trapped and helpless in such a painful relationship is an obvious pathway into depression. Getting out of such a hurtful relationship, particularly if you are dependent in some way, is exceedingly difficult to do without some outside support and guidance, and I'd encourage you to get some help right away. Don't try to adjust yourself to terrible circumstances and then think you can be okay anyway. That's an unrealistic expectation, and it shows cognitive dissonance at work—a self-justification for staying trapped and depressed because no other option seems possible.

You have other options, to be sure, but you won't discover them huddling in fear somewhere. You can call a mental health association, a domestic violence shelter, a doctor . . . just call *somebody*. Set aside your fear and doubts for a moment and keep your eye on the goal: to get your life back. Simply telling someone to stop using intimidation tactics is unlikely to help much. The people who are willing to threaten others to get their way aren't usually the sensitive, flexible types. They're the types who are willing to hurt you in one way or another in order to get what they want. *Controlling you is more important to them than looking out for your well-being.*

Threats of violence aren't the only forms of intimidation. Someone can threaten your reputation, threaten to leave you, threaten to kill themselves, threaten to sue you, threaten to fire you, threaten to reveal something delicate said in confidence, and threaten you in all kinds of other ways, too. Any threat to harm you in some way is an intimidation tactic. Getting away from someone who is intimidating may not be possible for one reason or another, but you still have to respond in some way that takes you out of the victim role. You may have to suffer through the pain such people inflict (respond to the lawsuit, get another job), but it helps a great deal to get someone else's support to help keep you on the track of getting out from under the pressure of such tactics. It may be a psychotherapist, or an attorney, or both. But, getting as much advice for your circumstances as you possibly can as early as you can may well help you cope with adversity and come out stronger than ever. Giving in to intimidation and living in fear, being controlled by someone who is willing to hurt you is depressing. To learn what to do and what to say to get out of the victim position, get the advice of an expert. It's a relatively small cost for getting your life back.

Guilt: How Can You Do That to Me After All I've Done for You?

Guilt is a powerful manipulation, but only if you allow it to be. Guilt makes you feel as though you have done something terribly wrong simply because someone else stated or implied their disapproval. It's one thing if you actually *did* do something to injure someone else and you feel bad about it—then guilt *can* be appropriate, the evidence of having a conscience and wanting to do the right thing. Too many people, though, make mistakes and *don't* take responsibility for them. They blame someone else.

Guilt presupposes responsibility: If you don't feel responsible for it, then you won't feel guilty about it. Hence, the problem; people who are depressed or vulnerable to depression typically have difficulty sorting out what they are and are not responsible for in their relationships with other people. So, if someone blames you for something, and you're not clear where the true responsibility belongs, you may well accept that blame and feel bad unnecessarily. Guilt mongerers are great at telling you what they want and making you feel like it's your responsibility to fulfill their wishes. They make it clear how hurt, disappointed, unhappy, or traumatized they'll be if you don't do as they expect. They make you feel responsible for how they feel or for fulfilling their expectations so that they can get what they want from you. They're satisfied, and you're miserable. What's wrong with this picture?

You have to be able to endure conflict in order to address guilt effectively. I prefer a straightforward approach to training a guilt mongerer to stop manipulating me by saying something such as, "Can't you just ask me without trying to guilt me into doing what you want?" Sometimes humor can be a good way to make this point, too: "Pack your bags, we're going on a guilt trip."

Praise, Flattery, and Love Bombing

While intimidation and guilt are negative ways of getting people to comply with one's wishes, another self-serving manipulation—praise, flattery, and affection—on the surface seems so positive that you can miss how controlling it can be. Praise doesn't hurt the way intimidating threats do. People like to be praised and flattered, noticed and complimented. Social psychologists have demonstrated in many ingenious experiments on interpersonal attraction that we like those people who make us feel liked. We strive to please them and we go to extraordinary lengths to get more and more of their approval. The hungrier you are for someone's approval, the further you may go to get it. Pay attention to your boundaries when you're trying to get someone's approval. Will you have sex with someone to get approval? Will you look the other way and let someone (or even let yourself) do something illegal or hurtful to someone else for approval? Will you work ridiculous hours, give away time or money you don't have, miss opportunities that would benefit you, or do other such things for approval?

When people give up themselves—their values or beliefs—in order to "fit in" or "get along," their need for approval outweighs their need to assert their individuality. At the extreme, this is how people get swept up in cults or gangs. Cult members hang around train stations and bus stations looking for people who look lost and without someplace they belong. Cult members (and pimps and sex traffickers) approach such people and begin the "love bombing"—they show interest in them in a nonthreatening way, engaging them in casual conversation. They seem nice, attentive, warm, and welcoming. When they offer the lost soul someplace to stay for awhile ("Hey, you should check out our farm—we live with a bunch of really nice folks and you'd fit right in!"), the answer is, "Well, why not?" The lost soul goes with them, meets a bunch of really nice, complimentary, interested people. No one has said a word about religion or beliefs. As the new arrival gets more and more comfortable, soaking up all the positive attention, the attachment to these nice people grows. When they finally start to share their common beliefs, whatever defines them as a cult, the cognitive dissonance strikes: "These are great people, and they all believe XYZ, so believing XYZ must be okay."

I'm not telling you about "love bombing" because I'm worried you'll join a cult, but to show you how vulnerable people, desperate for a kind word or deed, can become slaves to their needs. When people are depressed, they can also be particularly vulnerable to promises, flattery, and attention. Someone can promise them the moon, but when they end up with only some emotional craters, their depression gets *worse*.

The human need for attention, acknowledgment, affection, touch, and love make us all vulnerable to one degree or another. But your boundaries and integrity become especially important to protect when someone is striving to get what he wants from you to your own detriment, armed with nothing more than a dazzling smile and lots of kind words.

Rigid and Flexible Boundaries

Some boundaries that you establish never will and never should change. At no time should you *ever* allow someone to abuse you sexually, physically, or emotionally. Those boundaries must stay rigidly protected all your life.

Pause and Reflect: Changeable Boundaries

Think of limits you've set with others that you have modified over the years, and some to which you have firmly adhered. Are there specific cues you rely on to tell you that you'd better adhere to a standard with someone or that it is time to revise an established boundary? Identify these cues and consider how they can guide you through different interactions.

Where you draw the line with someone will need to be revisited from time to time, especially if it's an ongoing relationship where time changes people (kids grow up and need less parental controls) or where conditions change the requirements (an economic downturn results in a layoff and the need to rewrite a job description). What doesn't change, though, is the boundary that demands people deal with each other respectfully rather than through exploitive, damaging tactics.

You'll need to continually adjust some boundaries over the course of your lifetime. Saying no to your six-year-old about crossing the street makes sense, but not to your sixteen-year-old. Relationships change, and as they do, some (but not all) of the boundaries will likely need changing, too. Treating your adult child as though she's still a teen is one way to make sure you're in conflict with each other a lot. Treating your grandchild as though he is *your* child, bypassing his parents, is another example of a boundary needing redefinition.

Every relationship inevitably has boundaries. Be aware of where you place them. The most important guideline to keep in mind whenever you are dealing with boundary issues is: What am I telling this person, what message will he or she get, if I draw, or *don't* draw, the line *here*? Staying out of depression depends on keeping "on message" about what's important to you.

CHAPTER 8

Marriage Can Save Your Life:

How to Keep Yours Healthy

Positive and healthy relationships are important to feeling good and avoiding and overcoming depression. Some of the strongest evidence that close relationships help to insulate people against depression comes from epidemiological research regarding marriage and depression and it shows quite clearly that *the people who describe themselves as happily married have a much lower incidence of depression than the general population.* Just as clearly, research shows that people who describe themselves as unhappy in their marriage are *much* more likely to meet the criteria for being diagnosed as depressed.

For Better or Worse: A Shared Approach

From across the room, Graham watched Veronica sitting at her computer. She was gazing at the screen, but Graham had his doubts she was really seeing anything on it. For what seemed an eternity Veronica had been unfocused, detached, and clearly unhappy. Married eight years, Graham knew his wife better than anyone else, but this woman wasn't the Veronica he knew. He was deeply worried about her, but every time he asked what was wrong, she would blow up and tell him to back off and give her some space. Space for what? The lack of communication was not only worrying him, but angering him, too. She had become untouchable, physically and emotionally, and wouldn't, or perhaps couldn't, tell him why.

Graham had had enough. Mustering some courage, he approached Veronica and gently asked if he could speak to her. She rolled her eyes and, just as before, started to tell him to leave her alone. Something in his eyes

stopped her from finishing her sentence, though, and she suddenly realized that the man she most loved in the whole world was right in front of
her, expressing his love and concern for her, and she was about to push
him away. After a long moment, while Graham wondered what was coming next, Veronica jumped up, hugged him, and began to sob uncontrollably. He held her, let her cry, and simply said, "I love you, and whatever
is going on with you, we'll work it out." When Veronica was finally able
to talk with Graham about how depressed she had been feeling, he said
he knew that already, but just didn't know what she was depressed
about or what to do to help. Veronica confessed that she didn't know,
either. Together they decided to go for professional help. To their credit,
because they both faced Veronica's depression as a shared problem affecting their marriage, Veronica and Graham have a new level of understanding and stability in their marriage that reinforces how important a good
relationship is to recovering from and even preventing depressive episodes.

Depression can harm a marriage, but there are ways to minimize the
potential damage—and even *improve* the relationship. How you handle
issues in your marriage helps determine whether you are more or less
likely to suffer depression. If you're depressed and married (or in a long-
term, committed relationship), *how you deal with your depression helps
determine whether your marriage is likely to survive your depression.*

Although I will use the term marriage throughout this chapter, I'm
actually addressing *any* relationship that involves two people living
together in the context of an intimate, loving, exclusive, committed relationship. Gay or straight, living together as an unmarried couple, *whatever* form your commitment to each other might take, you need to
recognize that *depression doesn't just affect one partner—it affects that individual's spouse or partner, too.* This chapter will help you recognize how
depression has affected the most important relationship in your life. If you
are not currently in such a relationship, but eventually hope to be, you
can still learn how to prevent depression from negatively affecting your
choice of partners and how you build the relationship together.

The Relationship Between Marriage and Depression

Up until relatively recently, the relationship between marriage and depression wasn't examined very carefully and therapists focused on only the

individual person who was depressed: his or her symptoms, as well as issues such as physical health, medical history, family and personal history, personality and emotional makeup, cognitive style, diet, coping style, and so on. Until I wrote *Hand-Me-Down Blues: How to Stop Depression from Spreading in Families*, surprisingly little had been written about the effects of depression on marriages and families. Since then, researchers in marriage and family therapy have learned a lot more.

A good marriage promotes a better quality of life. People in good marriages have been shown to:

- Be happier overall and suffer fewer mood problems
- Have better physical health and suffer fewer serious illnesses
- Have a better rate and quality of recovery from illness
- Have a more satisfying family life
- Have a better rate and quality of recovery from traumas

Indeed, married Americans are about 70 percent more likely to report being "very happy" than those who have never married. Such tangible and measurable benefits to being in a good marriage provide compelling reasons to strive to build and live in one. Marriage *can* save lives.

On the other hand, people in distressed marriages are *at least ten times*, and perhaps as much as *twenty-five* times, more likely to suffer depression than other married people, depending which set of data you review. *An unhappy marriage actually serves as a predictor, a risk factor, for eventual depression.* Interestingly, the research also shows that, of those individuals who seek help for depression who are married, at least half report suffering marital distress. And, of those couples who seek marital therapy for their strained relationship, at least half have at least one depressed partner in the marriage.

In sum:

- There is a measurable link between unhappy marriages and developing depression.
- An unhappy marriage predicts an increased vulnerability to depression in its members.
- An unhappy marriage can cause depression.
- Depression can cause an unhappy marriage.
- Marital therapy can improve distressed marriages and reduce depression.

Pause and Reflect:
Who Is Happily Married?

Is it marriage itself that can make people happy or is it something about the person who is capable of sustaining a good relationship with another person?

Marriage isn't a "thing." It's dynamic and ever changing, just as the people who build and maintain it are also changing over time. People who can set aside hurts from small disagreements do better. The people who can put someone else's needs ahead of their own at times do better. The people who easily accept inevitable differences of opinion as well as changing opinions and interests do better. Actually, the same skills that allow you to enter into and maintain a long-term, committed, and close relationship with another person are the very characteristics that help you manage life well and insulate you against depression.

All marriages will face times of stress, but when a marriage is damaged by hostility and constant arguing, violence, hurtful manipulation, lies, and coldness or apathy, it is easy to appreciate how someone can feel "trapped in enemy territory." Feeling trapped in any negative circumstance elevates your risk for depression, but no circumstance affects as many aspects of your personal life as your marriage. It defines your physical space (where you live), your personal space (this person who is always there, even when he or she isn't home), and it regularly forces you to have to interact with and react to whatever this person happens to say or do.

But a marriage doesn't just turn bad in one fateful moment. In the same way that depression doesn't generally just "strike out of the blue" (because the risk factors had typically already been in place for years), a marriage can become distressed by factors that had been built right into the relationship all along. It is most important that, before you get married, you have a good grasp of the issues raised throughout this book. You'll need to know how both of you think, how you go about solving problems together, how much frustration tolerance and impulse control you both have, how well you can communicate together, and how well your expectations for yourselves and each other reflect your true capabilities. *It takes skill to build a marriage from the ground up so that it can withstand the challenges of life and thrive in the face of them.*

The percentage of people who marry has gradually dropped in recent years, but most still consider marriage desirable: Only 24 percent of Americans have never married. Even with relatively high rates of divorce (slightly more than one divorce for every two marriages), nearly 60 percent of Americans are currently married. This shows that people desire to be connected, to have a stable, loving, intimate relationship with another person. Having the desire, *the motivation—without ability—simply isn't enough.*

Ideally, before you marry, you date and spend time learning about each other, and you establish how this relationship is going to develop.

Dating takes time and requires deliberate choices that go beyond the heat of the moment. Every interaction requires clear communications about where your boundaries are and what your behavior when you're with each other means. When you choose simply to follow your heart and enjoy the thrill of a new relationship, all the things you're *not* paying attention to are likely to come back to hurt you. In a nutshell, this is how bad relationships become depressing traps.

Choosing a Partner

Relationships require effort and attention even when you have two positive, healthy people involved. Depression leads people to make bad relationship choices in a number of ways:

1. People who dislike themselves don't really expect anyone else to like them, either. So when someone shows them some of the positive attention they've been craving, they get captivated. (Remember how "love bombing" works?) By the time they realize they've been captivated by someone who is actually hurtful to them, they're already in too deep emotionally and feel powerless to get out.

2. They engage with the other person by training him or her to see them in the same way they see themselves. This is what's called "self-verification," a process of agreeing with (and thereby reinforcing) their partner only when their partner sees them in the same negative way they see themselves. If I see myself as stupid, then only when you call me stupid do I think you're telling me the truth; only then can I see your feedback as

credible because it confirms what I already believe about myself. This is a powerful but negative process for creating agreement in a relationship.

3. They choose to get involved with people who are at least as wounded as themselves. They may think it's evidence of tolerance or compassion to do so, but it's actually a too-comfortable familiarity with pain that lets them bring even more of it into their lives through someone else. Another facet of this is what's known as "family reenactment": You grow up in a family thinking "this is how marriages are" and so recreate what you know. A depressed marriage as a model gives rise to other depressed relationships.

4. They think that no one but another depressed person can understand them. They dismiss people who are happy as ignorant, "in denial," or superficial. For them, choosing to be around someone who is active, upbeat, and pleasant is undesirable.

5. Probably the most common reason that depressed people make bad relationship choices isn't because of any great need to suffer more than they already do, but because they reflexively follow their feelings. And when you're depressed, you're following *depressed* feelings. If you don't recognize that you have the power to shape the relationship, if you don't even know you're *supposed* to shape the relationship, you're going to make bad decisions to just "follow your heart" or "go with the flow."

Learn by Doing:
How Do *You* Choose Relationship Partners?

Review the five points above about how depressed people choose partners in ways that work against the health of the relationship. Do any (or all) of these reflect your experience? If so, how? If not, why not? Grab a sheet of paper and a pen and write down what factors most influenced your choice of partners. If you have had multiple marriages or committed relationships, then do this for each of them. How did the factors you considered, and also the ones you didn't, influence how the relationship played out?

No decision you make in your lifetime has more power to help or hurt you than who you decide to marry. Carefully assessing others *before* you get attached is incredibly important. You have to choose *a* right person and *be* a right person in order to have a long, healthy—and health-inspiring—marriage.

Similarities and Differences Between You

As a general principle, we like people who are like us: people with our values, interests, and outlook on life. We tend to like people who reinforce us, and when people see things the way we generally do, it's rewarding to have that kind of support. As it turns out, though, similarities may bring people together, but it's how people deal with their differences that most determines whether the relationship will grow or implode. When you're dating, consider how your partner deals with differences of opinion. Does he either state outright or simply imply that "if you had any sense, you'd see it my way?" Does she make value judgments that say, in essence, "You're wrong to feel that way?"

You will inevitably have differences between you, but if you don't establish a boundary early on in the relationship that makes it possible for both of you to maintain and demonstrate a respectful acceptance of differences of opinion, the relationship can turn judgmental, hostile, and even abusive over time.

Psychologist John Gottman has been studying marriages for more than a quarter century in his lab at the University of Washington and has developed an exceptionally clear view of why marriages do or don't endure. Gottman can predict, on the basis of just a small sample of a couple's behavior, whether they are likely to stay together or split. His predictions are accurate a whopping 91 percent of the time. In his book, *Why Marriages Succeed or Fail*, Gottman describes the poor relationship skills that harm a marriage and proposes specific remedies for them. He has identified four negative relational patterns that most predict a breakup, which he calls the "Four Horsemen of the Apocalypse." They are:

1. *Criticisms* in the form of character attacks
2. *Contempt* in the form of insults, name calling, sneering, mocking the person, and rolling your eyes with disgust
3. *Defensiveness* in the form of making excuses, justifying bad behavior that shouldn't be justified, and counterattacking rather than responding to the expressed concern
4. *Stonewalling* in the form of withdrawing from the relationship rather

than talking things through, walking away from the conversation, giving the "silent treatment," or answering in single syllables

These damaging patterns reflect the problems I've laid out previously, such as low frustration tolerance, inability to accept responsibility for one's actions, self-justification of bad behavior, negative and self-serving manipulations, and poor boundaries. Learning to be a better partner and striving to make your communications and interactions better is how a relationship gets healthier over time—and how to keep it from being depressing. As marital therapist Sue Johnson described in her wonderful guide to healthy relationships, *Hold Me Tight: Seven Conversations for a Lifetime of Love,* each of us needs to know that our partner can be counted on, that our emotional connection to that person will be protected. Getting past anger to respect and honor that need is a core component of her highly effective approach to treating relationships, called emotionally focused therapy, or EFT.

Kindness and Fun Are Casualties of Depression

Depressed people gradually lose their capacity for pleasure. The depressed person, or the one headed for depression, starts to withdraw from life a little at a time. Depressed people's attention turns inward (the "internal orientation," which you've learned to recognize as a major hazard). Their focus narrows to what's wrong as they ruminate about their problems and feelings, adding each hurt, real or imagined, to an ever-growing list of complaints. They stop noticing what's right in their life. An exercise that follows, the "Gratitude List," is helpful in stopping and reversing that inward focus. It has been well researched within positive psychology, as have many other such exercises to increase happiness that are offered in psychologist Sonja Lyubomirsky's helpful book, *The How of Happiness: A Scientific Approach to Getting the Life You Want.*

Learn by Doing:
A Marital Gratitude List

The Gratitude List is an exercise in deliberately noticing what's good, what's beautiful, what works, no matter how small it might seem. It might be a beautiful sunset, the smile of a stranger, the foam on a latte that tickles your lips, the feel of a comfy sweater, anything that reminds you that good things happen, too. As simple as this exercise sounds, when it is made a daily ritual it has been shown to be very effective in improving people's depression in enduring ways. I encourage you to do a general Gratitude List every day, and a marital Gratitude List, as well.

Notice at least three positive things your partner does, and write them down. Then, some time during the day, perhaps when just kicking back after dinner, share those things you're grateful for. Bring kindness and a generosity of spirit into the relationship again or, perhaps, for the first time.

You have to practice appreciation, pleasure, and kindness if they are to be stable aspects of a relationship. After all, even a relationship that *doesn't* have depression as a concern will still require deliberate effort to keep it healthy, fresh, and *fun*. Depression, however, adds an extra measure of difficulty to the relationship. *Before* depression gets worse, ideally when you feel your mood slipping, that's when you have to take steps to make sure it doesn't turn ugly for you as an individual or for the relationship.

When I'm conducting clinical trainings for my colleagues, I'll ask, "How many of you would describe yourself as happily married or happily involved in a committed relationship?" Most hands go up. Then I'll call on people and ask them about the role of fun in their relationship. Without exception, every single person who describes his relationship as a good one reports still having fun together with his partner. Not only do they still laugh at each other's crummy jokes, but they go out of their way to create relaxed, fun time together: "date nights" to get away from the kids and the bills for awhile; days to "go exploring" and see something new together even if it's just a mile away; book or movie discussions with friends; neighborhood walks; or fun classes together, like photography or creative writing or how to be a better flirt.

Whatever they do, they prioritize having fun and, in the process, put a "lid" on how much they focus on problems. What a difference to make problems your total focus versus making fun your focus at least some of the time. Your problems never go completely away: the tough issues in life will always be there. *Guarding a good relationship, keeping fun from draining away from it, is an ongoing task.* The same is true for close-ness, support, sexuality, kindness, politeness, and generosity.

Pause and Reflect:
Do You Know How to Have Fun?

Can you set aside time for having fun and then actually do so? What does it take for you to be able to get into the spirit of enjoying other peo-ple or doing enjoyable physical activities? How often do you do things that make you laugh? If it's easy for you to set aside everyday stressors and enjoy the pleasures of life, that's wonderful. But if it isn't so easy, then it is a worthwhile goal to learn to "lighten up" and enjoy more of what's best about life. Realistically, how are you supposed to feel good if you don't do the things that help you feel good—and do them often?

The "Wall of Health" Between You:
Compartmentalization Skills in Marriage

Protecting a relationship from decay, especially the decay of depression, is easier when you know it's an ongoing and equal responsibility for both partners. Easier, perhaps, but *not* easy. One particular skill above all oth-ers can help you maintain a healthy marriage. It's called "compartmental-ization."

Compartmentalization refers to the ability to set aside different compo-nents of some larger entity, as if they're in their own individual compart-ments separated by an imaginary wall. It's how you can focus on one part of an experience and thereby amplify it, and stop focusing on other parts of the same experience and thereby deemphasize them in your awareness.

Consider some examples:

- Do you like your job? If so, do you like *all* aspects of the job, or are there *some* aspects of the job you don't like very much? If there are parts of the job you don't like, then how can you still like the job?

- Do you have a favorite movie? If so, were there some parts of the movie that you didn't particularly care for, that were perhaps a little boring or where things happened you wish had not? If there were parts of this favorite movie you didn't care for, then how can it still be your favorite movie?
- Do you like keeping up to date with the news? If so, when there are news stories that anger you or upset you, why do you still like staying current with the news?

If you are able to enjoy the "whole" despite there being "parts" you don't like, then you are, much to your credit, demonstrating an ability to compartmentalize. You are able to set aside the parts you don't much care for and still appreciate the greater value of all the rest.

When I have a large audience at a presentation, I'll ask for a show of hands of people who are happily married or in a happily committed relationship. Lots of hands go up. I'll then call on half a dozen people and ask the question, "Are there things about your spouse that irritate the heck out of you?" Every single one, without exception, says yes. Then I ask, "How can you be happy with this person if he or she does things that irritate you so much?" Each one, without exception, answers with some variation of, "My love for him or her way outweighs the little stuff that annoys me." Yet the people with poor relationship histories always seem confused by that statement.

Think about this response for a moment: "The love I have for my spouse far outweighs the irritations." That seemingly simple response actually reveals a great deal about the sophisticated style of thought that goes into building and maintaining a loving relationship. It reveals:

- The person is not engaging in distorted "all or none" thinking; He or she is able to appreciate that someone is not either "perfect" or "no good."
- He demonstrates an ability to assess his partner realistically, identifying specific flaws as well as specific strengths.
- She demonstrates an ability to prioritize, to establish a hierarchy of what matters. She won't likely file for divorce by saying, "It drives me crazy that he squeezes the toothpaste tube in the middle."
- He demonstrates an ability to effectively set aside negatives, as if there is a dam between the positives and negatives so that the negatives

do not spill over and contaminate the positives. I refer to this dam as "the wall of health."

- She demonstrates both frustration tolerance and impulse control: She contains the feelings of irritation rather than badgering her spouse, controlling the impulse to want to blast him when he does something annoying. She recognizes it's not worth it to cause the needless harm that would result.

These are exceptionally important skills to have in order to build and maintain a healthy marriage. No one is perfect, everyone has quirks and annoying habits, including *you*, and this is how tolerance is put into practice. It's not a realistic goal to find the "perfect" partner nor is it realistic to try to *be* the "perfect" partner. The far more realistic goal is to build compartmentalization skills into the relationship from the very beginning, and put them to regular use. It's a skill that takes practice, but no relationship can succeed without it. Let's break compartmentalization down into its components and consider how to develop each one.

Global Thinking versus Compartmentalization

The more global someone is in her style of thought the less able she will be to compartmentalize. If you can only see the forest and not the trees, compartmentalization isn't going to happen. If you habitually see only a global "all" or "none," "perfect" or "lousy," and lose sight of the "gray" in between the black and white, then your very style of thought has most likely worked against you in relationships. It doesn't mean you're a "loser" or that "no one will ever love you" or that you must have some "unconscious fear of intimacy." As you've learned, the motivation to succeed doesn't mean much if the ability to do so isn't there. I suggest you reread the section on global thinking in chapter 6 and strive to train your thinking to go back and forth between the big picture and the details of that picture.

Assessing Someone Involves More Than How He or She Makes You Feel

As you become less global and more detailed in your thinking, you can identify specific characteristics of your partner. In clear language, what are his or her values, priorities, strengths, resources, and skills? What specifically do you admire, appreciate, or even wish you could have more of in your own personality? What defines these characteristics as valuable? How will they keep showing up in your interactions together?

> Hanna was attracted to how cool-headed and reasonable Keith was in his way of handling things. Sure, he'd get upset about whatever crummy thing happened at work that day, but he'd shrug it off and say, "And this, too, shall pass." Hanna admired how he'd think through and talk openly about what was bothering him. Keith focused on trying to figure out the best way to handle the issue, whatever the "issue du jour" happened to be.
>
> Months after they'd been dating and getting truly close, Hanna got really upset about something that happened with a good friend. True to form, Keith started weighing options about what to do to remedy things, and Hanna exploded, "I'm trying to tell you how I feel and you're trying to figure out what I should do! Why can't you stop being so level-headed in giving me advice for the moment and just listen to me?"

Should Hanna really have been surprised that Keith was going to want to problem-solve an issue she presented? It's what he does, it's how he operates. But Hanna saw it as a flaw *in that moment* because she wanted a different reaction from him. In the next moment of this important interaction, though, the boundary gets set, the precedent established for how upsets will be handled in this relationship. Hanna might back off and accept Keith's focus on problem solving or Keith might regroup, stop the problem solving, and simply listen to Hanna vent.

In the best of worlds, *both* of them will back up and regroup. *Both are right*, and both need to be validated: Hanna has a right to her feelings and to want to express them, and Keith has a right to want to help her develop a solution. The ability to step back in order to see *all* the points of view means more to the relationship than just how someone makes you feel in a given moment. Appreciating the positive intention behind someone's position can help you put aside whatever might be clumsy about it in that moment. A great deal of nasty conflict can be averted when you can see the person and appreciate his or her position even when you strongly disagree with it.

Prioritizing What Matters and Setting Aside the Rest

Jeremy and Beth had been married only two years when Beth's irritation with him began to grow. Jeremy was a good husband, in fact, the ideal husband: smart, sensitive, generous, and compassionate. Jeremy loved Beth deeply, was loyal and reliable, and also loved her friends and family. He was a "winner" in almost every way.

One of the ways he wasn't so much a winner, though, was in how he kept his home office, which was a chaotic, messy, take-your-life-into-your-hands-when-you go-in-there place. It didn't bother Jeremy in the slightest, but it drove Beth to the edge. They had arguments and discussions regularly, but no amount of haranguing by Beth motivated Jeremy to clean his office. Beth would yell, cajole, offer bribes, make threats, but Jeremy was maddeningly impervious to all of it.

Somewhere along the way, it occurred to Beth that despite her best efforts, it wasn't in her power to make Jeremy care about having a clean, orderly office. She also began to think that, given how exceptional Jeremy was in so many ways, maybe a messy office just wasn't worth battling over. It just wasn't that important when Jeremy was not only a good husband but a hard-working, responsible, and superb guy. With effort, Beth controlled the impulse to say something every time she caught a glimpse of Jeremy's office room. Instead she kept her attention on maintaining open communication between them and focusing on what's right with Jeremy rather than what was wrong. Beth's anxiety about Jeremy went down, Jeremy's comfort around her increased, life got better for everyone, all because priorities changed with Beth's decision that, of all the things to bug Jeremy about, how he kept his office was lower on the list.

Pause and Reflect:
Never Miss a Good Opportunity to Keep Quiet

How do you decide what's worth commenting on? What is worth criticizing? Compartmentalization involves being selective, exercising enough impulse control to pause and think through whether something is worth saying before saying it. Criticizing someone for something she can't control ("Why aren't you taller?") is an obvious error, but criticizing some-thing based on a value he has that you don't happen to share ("Why do you go to church on Sunday? What a waste of time!") is also an error.

Practice Tolerance, the Pinnacle of Compartmentalization

People today seem to feel entitled to whatever they want regardless of whether they can actually afford it. They buy homes they can't afford, charge things they want but don't need past the limits of their credit, and spend for now rather than investing for tomorrow. Too many people live by the risky principle of going with their feelings.

We don't get formal instruction regarding the boundaries of what feelings to express and which might be better to keep to ourselves. (We learn through observation and modeling, which is why I addressed the detriments of trashy talk shows earlier.) Compartmentalization means using the skills just mentioned: breaking experiences down into parts, assessing what matters more and what matters less, and developing discretion about what's worth saying and what's better left unsaid.

These skills can protect your marriage by building and maintaining a respectfulness and generosity of spirit within the relationship. By always feeling valued, even when you might clash over some issue, neither of you suffers the distress of being mistreated through humiliation, rejection, or abandonment. You can love and respect each other *for a lifetime* even when *today's* not so great.

Is There a Down Side to Compartmentalization?

There is no pattern I'm aware of that is *always* positive *everywhere*. Hope, for example, can be a good thing when someone is unrealistically hope-less. But, hope can be destructive when it leads people to underestimate and respond poorly to what they're dealing with. After all, every guy who walks into a casino is hopeful, but when he loses his paycheck, hope clearly worked against him.

Compartmentalization can be a great thing in relationships, but you can also compartmentalize in ways that work against you and your spouse.

When the allegations of sexual misconduct were first raised at a press conference with then President Bill Clinton, long before he admitted to his improper behavior, President Clinton was asked how he could possibly continue to function as president with the allegations of impropriety swirling around him. He replied with a dismissive attitude, "Those allegations? I just put them in a little box in the bottom drawer of my desk and push it to the back of the drawer." He offered a very concrete image of compartmentalization in that response. To his credit, his ability to compartmentalize in this way allowed him to function well as president during a tumultuous year of hostile impeachment proceedings and constant ridicule from all sides. But that same ability to compartmentalize is exactly what allowed him to cheat on his wife and justify it to himself.

People who are "in denial" effectively separate the truth from their motivation to minimize that truth. People who tolerate violence or abuse in their relationship are able to compartmentalize when they overlook the violence and excuse it by saying, "But I love him/her." Companies that are willing to poison a few people in order to increase their profits are compartmentalizing in order to ignore any sense of decency or social responsibility. People who minimize "this" inconvenient truth so they can engage in "that" bad behavior are using their ability to compartmentalize to justify their chosen actions.

Compartmentalization can bring out some of the best in people and, unfortunately, some of the worst. In your most important relationships, keep the focus on love and what's right more than on anger and what's wrong, especially when what's wrong may not objectively be all that important.

A Little Support Goes a Long Way . . .
But Maybe Not Far Enough

As a general principle, people who are connected to something greater than themselves do better in life on almost every measure. Are you connected to something greater than yourself? Your marriage, perhaps, or your family? A social cause, perhaps, or a philanthropic one?

Ask people what's more important than themselves, and too many will say, "nothing." They've grown up believing they are the center of the universe and that "self-love is the most important love of all." Unfortunately, self-love doesn't teach tolerance of other people, self-love doesn't teach empathy or compassion or frustration tolerance or impulse control. It does teach self-absorption, a pattern closely linked to depression. From within a self-focused framework, the ability to give and receive social support is diminished.

Being supported by and supporting others is a powerful way to have connections to people, which, as you learned in the first chapter, have emotional and physical consequences.

In a fascinating study of how positive social contact enhances physical health, while their brains were being scanned through functional magnetic resonance imaging (fMRI), married women were subjected to the threat of receiving electric shock while either holding their husband's hand, the hand of another man they didn't know, or no one else's hand at all. The fMRI measured how much neural activation of the brain's threat response was activated in each of the conditions. Threat response was greatest when there was no one's hand to hold, and least when holding the hand of their husband. Most telling, though not surprising, was the finding that the quality of their marriage predicted the magnitude of their threat response when holding their husband's hand: The better their marriage, the less their brain's activation of a threat response. A strong bond and the lending of a supportive hand can make tough times easier psychologically as well as physically, as modern neuroscience is demonstrating.

The type of support you share with your spouse or partner strongly influences the quality of your relationship. So often, people feel trapped in, victimized by, and depressed about their marriage when they do not feel supported by their spouse as they'd like to be.

What type or types of support do you want and expect in *your* marriage? *Instrumental support* is support vital to achieve some goal. An example is economic support so you can have a roof over your head and food on the table. Another form of instrumental support is support in parenting and sharing fairly the responsibilities in raising children together.

Informational support includes providing the information someone needs in order to make sensible decisions. You can't follow through on giving Billy his new medications unless you know that I took him to the doctor this morning.

Emotional support is the caring, affection, and reassurances found in a secure and trusting relationship. So often people just want to be heard: they want their feelings acknowledged; and they want their efforts and sacrifices acknowledged. Kind words of support go a very long way in good relationships.

A strange thing happens, though, when depression enters the relationship. The depressed person typically becomes more emotionally needy, more demanding of more support. The depressed person doesn't typically realize how much more demanding she has become, and tends to perceive that the support from others is available for the asking (generally an unexamined, possibly unrealistic expectation). For her spouse, the level of demand has gone up and now crosses the line into the range of being burdensome, leading to the stressful feeling of being overloaded. He communicates those feelings, hopefully delicately, and that's when things explode. Research on perceived support and perceived demands shows us that this is an area fraught with danger for depressed marriages. When depressed partners feel unsupported, they believe that their spouse is now judging them more negatively. This, understandably, leads them to want even *more* reassurance from them, which just increases the level of demand on the spouse, which further adds to his or her sense of burden. It's a "vicious cycle."

Worse, while a depressed partner is in this more emotionally needy frame of mind, he is much more likely to view other people *in general* (another danger of global thinking) as not being supportive, either. When in that needy state, behavior that almost any nondepressed person would say *was* helpful and supportive, a depressed person will dismiss as "too little, too late." *Depression increases the need for support, yet decreases awareness of and responsiveness to others' efforts to support them.*

One of the most reliable ways to drive your spouse and friends away from you when you're depressed is to ignore or minimize their attempts to be supportive. *It saps anyone's motivation when they have been trying and their efforts have either been trivialized or ignored altogether.* Should you respond to your emotional neediness by asking for more and more reassurance, or should you notice and praise the efforts your spouse is making to support you even if you feel it's not enough?

How you handle this type of issue in your marriage affects whether you will recover from depression, how long your marriage will survive, and how your physical health will fare. Keep one simple principle in mind:

People respond much better to praise than they do to criticism. Not very many people can live comfortably with the message that, no matter what they do, it isn't good enough. It may not be easy for you to find the positive in a response to your needs that seems inadequate to you, but here is another example of the importance of sometimes putting the desired response ahead of your feelings. After all, when your depression lifts, as it is most likely to do, you still want your spouse to be there.

When Your Partner Says You Need Help, You *Both* Do

It happens all too frequently that someone will be suffering through depression, and her spouse tries to be helpful but either doesn't really know what to do to help or tries to help but gets pushed back with an angry, "Leave me alone!" Eventually, the depressed person's spouse will again try to say "You need help. Please get help!" And again, the angry, "Leave me alone!" reply. The story of Graham and Veronica at the beginning of this chapter illustrates the resistance many people have to acknowledging and addressing depression. Fortunately, Veronica came to realize she needed help, and Graham recognized he needed to be part of that process.

Getting angry when it's suggested to you that you're not coping well and that your depression is getting worse is a pretty typical reaction. To some people, it's a clear sign they're failing themselves and others when their spouse tells them they need help. It makes them angry with themselves and everyone else, too. Then, avoidant coping kicks in, the feelings of genuinely not wanting to deal with any of it; so, instead of responding to the concerns of the spouse, they blow up angrily. This is the manipulative tactic of intimidation, using anger as a weapon, taking away the spouse's voice. It's a bad strategy: It keeps you, the depressed person, from getting help, it victimizes the spouse, and it makes things worse, not better. Too often, not dealing with depression directly and in a timely way culminates in a breakup or divorce that could have been prevented.

Put *being effective* ahead of your personal comfort, ahead of your fear and anxiety, ahead of *anything else* that can derail your efforts to get past your depression while still maintaining your most important relationships. As someone wise once said, "Obstacles are what you see when you take your eyes off the goal."

Learn by Doing:
Effectiveness Has a Price

In suggesting you strive to put being effective ahead of your comfort, I recognize I am pulling you out of your comfort zone. To want to be effective, you'd have to acknowledge that getting a particular result matters more, in some cases, than how you feel. For example, if you want people to be honest with you, you must be willing to listen to things you'd rather not hear. You need to set aside your anger and hold your tongue because you want to keep the communication going more than you want to blow off steam. It's not easy to hear other people's viewpoints, particularly if they're critical of you in some way, but by acknowledging the person's feelings (not necessarily agreeing with them), you'll go a long way toward keeping the relationship open. That's effective. And, believe it or not, you'll feel better about yourself for conducting the relationship with integrity.

When your spouse says you need help, even if you don't agree, how can you ignore her saying directly that she is feeling hurt in some way by what's going on with you? Why hurt her even more by ignoring her concerns simply because you don't *feel* like dealing with it? It is a courageous act of integrity to give your spouse a voice and then listen to what that voice says. It doesn't mean you're simply being blindly obedient or controlled by your spouse. It means you're listening and acknowledging her needs and points of view at an important time in your relationship. It may lead you into treatment in ways you didn't plan on initially, but the greater goal of staying connected during the hardest of times is what matters most.

Can Marital Therapy Help Depression?

Given the relationship consequences of depression, and, in many cases, even the relationship triggers for generating depression, it's logical to ask whether marital therapy can help as a form of treatment for depression. The short answer is yes.

Before considering marital therapy, first consider yet another limitation of antidepressant medication that surfaces in the relationship domain: negative sexual side effects are among the most common, perhaps *the* most common, side effects of many antidepressant medications. These include erectile dysfunction in men, diminished sex drive in both men and women, and delayed or absent orgasm in women. Negative sexual side effects are a leading reason that people who begin taking antidepressant medications soon discontinue them. The sexual difficulties make them feel even *worse*. Given how important a loving and healthy sexual relationship is in a marriage, and the complications that can arise in the relationship when sexuality is impaired, the use of antidepressant medications is not a treatment to choose without careful consideration.

When your marriage plays a large role in your depression for any of the reasons described in this chapter (or even for some I didn't describe), then it makes good sense to talk to a clinician who has an expertise both in treating depression and working with couples. Be aware of all the areas of difficulty in a marriage that depression can either cause or exacerbate: quality of life, how well the couple (or family) functions as an integrated unit, the marriage (or family) atmosphere (the emotional "feel" together), quality of support for each other, quality of communication, and more. Marital therapy addresses these issues, and the evidence is unambiguous that as the relationship improves, depression lifts.

Marriage and family therapists (MFTs) are professionals trained to develop an expertise in treating problems from a relationship perspective, including depression. The American Association for Marriage and Family Therapy (AAMFT) is the national organization for those psychotherapists licensed as MFTs. For information and local referrals, go to their website, aamft.org. Other specially trained psychotherapists (such as psychologists and social workers) can also have great expertise in treating depression within a marital framework. Contact the American Psychological Association (apa.org) or the National Association of Social Workers (socialworkers.org) for referrals in your area.

What can marital therapy do for depression? Here are just some of the possibilities:

- Give each marriage partner a voice to be heard and acknowledged and thereby provide emotional support.
- Provide a safe place to explore difficult issues and express feelings.

- Provide current, relevant, and helpful information.
- Create a means for identifying, *supportively* challenging, and clarifying individual points of view.
- Provide structured homework assignments to help new skills and perspectives develop and take firm hold in the marriage.

A good therapist can be worth his or her weight in *platinum*. When your depression is hurtful—even just to yourself—and you're at a loss as to what to do about it, it makes good sense to get professional help. When it's hurtful to more people than you alone, not only does it make good sense, it's the only socially responsible thing to do.

Marriage in Perspective

A good marriage doesn't just "happen." It is the product of many decisions made each day about what you will and won't say, what you will and won't do, and how you are able to build and protect the "we" of this most special of relationships.

Marriage is the foundation of the family; the quality of your marriage has a profound effect on the quality of your family life. That includes whether your family's interactions increase or decrease their own vulnerability to depression. As you will learn in the next chapter, parents can unwittingly pass along the risks for an increased vulnerability to depression to their children just by the way they go about living their lives. You can learn how to keep from passing along to your kids what I have come to call the "hand-me-down blues."

CHAPTER 9

Hand-Me-Down Blues:
Learn to Reduce Your Child's
"Depression Inheritance"

Children of depressed parents are at least three times more likely to develop depression than others, but there are early warning signals that help you spot depression developing and preventive steps to take to reduce a child's vulnerability.

People incorrectly assume that when a condition is elevated within a family, genes must be responsible. *The genetic research makes it clear that there is no single, specific gene that causes depression.* However, there is a genetic vulnerability, termed a "genetic predisposition," that increases some individuals' sensitivity to environmental influences, such as the quality of the family milieu. This so-called "genetic variance" accounts for anywhere from 30 to 40 percent of depression, reinforcing the conclusion that most of what contributes to depression is more than biology alone.

If a child's depression is not primarily the product of a parent's genes, then we must consider the way a parent, whether depressed or not, raises a child that increases his vulnerability to depression. If you are depressed and have children, especially younger children, I urge you to take active steps to help prevent your children from developing depression, and I'll help you recognize and treat it as early as possible to minimize its long-term effects. Every day that a child struggles with depression makes it more likely to become a chronic, pervasive factor that can cause lifelong harm. With children, recognizing the fact that depression is contagious is most important.

Depression for a Reason:
The Consequences of a Depressed Home

Bill and Sue are the parents of a twelve-year-old son, John. For the last year, they have been vigorously arguing every time they're in a room together for more than a minute. The tension in the house is palpable. Bill's job started going badly after he lost a promotion to a fellow he hates, and with it the salary increase he was counting on. Bill began to sit in front of the TV night after night, drinking too much. Sue would push Bill to "get over it" and rejoin the family, but Bill just couldn't. He was sullen, hostile, terrible to be around. Their conflicts escalated as Sue pushed Bill to get help. Bill resented Sue's criticism, and her suggestion that he needed attention from a mental health professional made him angry.

Initially, John had tried to be a peace maker, but the boy's noble efforts were dwarfed by the intensity of his parents' obvious hostility toward each other. Sue and Bill were so preoccupied with their own issues that neither noticed that John was growing more moody and with-drawn, gradually spending more time by himself than with his friends or playing sports the way he used to. He slept poorly, frequently com-plained of being tired, rarely smiled any more, and showed little enthu-siasm for anything. When Bill and Sue eventually noticed and asked him what was going on, John's standard reply was, "Nothing." As time went on, his concentration grew worse, his grades dropped, and he became even less communicative. His dad's struggles continued to preoccupy both his parents, which, unfortunately, is typical: often the person who suffers in silence, the one who needs the most help, is overlooked because others openly demand greater attention.

When Bill and Sue finally took John to a therapist, a young man to whom they hoped John would open up, the therapist quickly found out that John was feeling hopeless about ever having a normal home life again. He hated being at home, hated all the fighting, hated his parents, especially his father for starting it all, and hated his life. John had wanted to talk to someone about his feelings, but not his parents. He was glad to be seeing a therapist, and relieved to be able to tell somebody about all he'd bottled up inside. When the therapist told his parents what was troubling John, Sue cried and Bill got defensive and enraged. Fortu-nately, both quickly remembered this was John's crisis, not theirs. To their credit, they hugged him and reassured him that everything would

be okay, that they'd get back on track together as a family. John dared to believe them and felt the first glimmer of hope in a year.

With the guidance and support of a trained mental health professional, John will come to understand that he is not to blame nor responsible in any way for what has happened between his mom and dad, and he'll learn to appreciate that whatever happens between them isn't what defines him or his worth as a person. He'll likely emerge stronger, clearer, and better prepared for future challenges in life that will require him to do many of the things we've addressed, from assessing others carefully to creating and maintaining clear boundaries that he can defend in ways he couldn't when he was younger. *Everyone* needs to learn these skills, regardless of their history.

Bill and Sue are not bad people. They love John and try to do what they can to be there for him, but they were distracted with their own problems and, worse, didn't know how to communicate openly and honestly. When a family's social environment does not model and encourage supportive sharing of sensitive thoughts and feelings all along, children are unlikely to suddenly open up and share their feelings. Similarly, when parents haven't followed through consistently on what they say or promise to do, children will not trust them. Too many families learn the hard way that what goes missing in parental interactions (such as trust, honesty, responsibility, and respect) will generate problems later, especially when their children become adolescents who are missing these same important attributes.

Children are simply not equipped with the means to navigate the dangers of life. John was not and could not have been ready to cope with the family conflicts at such a young age. Thus, it is imperative that parents grasp the vulnerabilities of their kids and do their utmost to protect them and to teach them to protect themselves. *The greatest preventive tool you can teach a child is the ability to think critically.*

Pause and Reflect: Can You Distinguish Protective from Overprotective?

Today's world presents parents with challenges that did not exist when they were growing up. How much computer time is too much? At what age should a child post an entry on MySpace or Facebook? How much is reasonable to disclose on such sites and how much is too revealing? Which chat rooms are safe to enter and which ones have pedophiles lurking in them, and how can you tell? How much text messaging is okay and how much is too much? How do you prevent kids from seeing movies and video games that are violent and sexually explicit, and television that pushes the limits of discretion?

You can't change the world. These technological and social changes are now an inevitable part of all our lives, like it or not. But as a concerned parent, you can stay current, ask questions, be familiar with these things, keep connected through actual time spent with your kids (not through nannies and babysitters) all through their childhood. You can teach your child to think, not just react or try to fit in with others. We want to protect our kids to the extent that's possible, but there are many influences you simply can't protect your child from because you're not there when they present themselves. Trying to control your child's every movement is overprotective. Teaching your child to protect himself or herself through good judgment and a clear sense of cause and effect, is the best protection you can hope to offer.

The World of Children Is No Longer Fun and Innocent

Family life today presents difficult challenges for kids: high rates of divorce, hard-working and often physically and emotionally unavailable parents, single parents who have no interest in or intention of having a stable partner to help raise a child, parents who risk their very lives in the selfish pursuit of thrills in extreme sports, parents who are too depressed or substance-dependent to function, parents who are too self-absorbed to be there emotionally for their kids, parents who don't set limits with their kids or have the energy to tangle with them. With parents like these, kids are the big losers. They can only try to survive such bad, even hostile, environments without being damaged by them too much.

Children may have to deal with mom and dad's angry divorce; shared custody schedules in which every decision is a drawn-out negotiation; inconvenient or even terribly taxing visitation schedules; peer pressure to own costly clothes and computer games; intense parental and social pressure to perform in school at ever earlier ages; less face-to-face social time with friends and family and more text messaging and online chatting; safety threats at school that require the presence of metal detectors and armed security guards; and terrible cultural role models who emphasize some of the worst behavior imaginable. Being a kid these days is not easy. *Kids face lots of challenges they are simply not equipped to meet, socially based challenges that lead them to have higher rates of depression than any previous generation of kids.*

From Parent to Child:
Ways Depression Can Affect Your Parenting

The incidence of depression is greatest in the twenty-five to forty-five age group—adults who are in their prime childbearing years. This means that the *largest* group of depression sufferers is raising the *fastest growing* group of depression sufferers—their kids.

In the first study of its kind, epidemiologist Dr. Myrna Weissman from Columbia University followed three generations of high-risk families. The study took more than twenty years to complete. The findings are troubling, though not surprising: Most of the grandchildren who had depressed parents and depressed grandparents developed anxiety disorders *before* they hit puberty that developed into depression as they became adolescents. In another study, Dr. Weissman followed the offspring of moderately to severely depressed parents from age fifteen to thirty-five, and found that these children had a much higher probability of suffering anxiety disorders, depression, substance abuse, and social difficulties (such as shyness or fighting). As these children entered middle age, they had much higher rates of medical problems and even premature death. The risk to children of depressed parents is serious.

Parents provide physical, emotional, and social environments that teach their children about virtually every aspect of living. Let's consider just some of the effects of a depressed parent on a child's development.

Parents Are Emotional Catalysts for Brain Development and Gene Expression

In studies of infants of depressed and nondepressed parents, especially mothers, infants are modeling the parent's emotional displays from a surprisingly early age. Infants as young as three months old have been shown to detect their mother's mood and alter their responses as a result. When parents show a broad range of emotions, including laughter and enthusiasm, and when they engage a lot with their babies, the infants have a much better quality and rate of emotional and neurological development. *When a baby is neglected, or the parent is bland and emotionless, as when depressed, the baby's brain simply does not develop normally.* The baby's range of emotional expressions narrows and the smiling and laughing stop, as do eye contact and making sounds. When the emotional center of the brain is understimulated the genes necessary for normal brain development are not activated. Given how often a mother has to deal with postpartum depression and is emotionally distant and bland, the risk to an infant is painfully obvious.

Parents Are Social Role Models for Their Toddlers

In interactions with their toddlers, depressed mothers are less likely to get and stay connected through the course of an interaction. If the mother gets called away from her child (as in leaving to take a phone call), she is less likely to resume the interaction. *The child learns the interaction is less important than the distraction.* Depressed mothers are less likely to get the "rhythm" of interactions with their child, and they end up stimulating the child when he or she is tired and ignoring the child when he or she wants stimulation. Coordinating with a child requires learning that child's rhythm and style, but too often depressed parents are so inwardly focused on their depression that they miss the child's cues. Toddlers of depressed parents typically show more out-of-control behavior, more sad facial expressions, and poorer social exchanges with peers.

Depressed Parents' Negative Effects on Their Children

Symptoms of depression may impair and even prevent good parenting. A child notices a parent's depression and finds it distressing, and the child's life is made more stressful by having a depressed parent. Depressed parents are more likely to be inconsistent in the way they interact with their kids at a time when consistency is crucial, especially in enforcing discipline. Depressed parents are more likely to either blow up angrily or retreat when they encounter difficulties with their kids. They are more likely to take it personally when a child tests the parent's limits. They are less likely to engage and talk with their kids, and when they do, they are much more likely to be criticizing, complaining, and negative in tone. They are more likely to overreact to relatively mild challenges; for example, they are twice as likely to take their child to the doctor for a stomach ache as a nondepressed parent. The children of depressed parents are more likely to come to see the world as dangerous and other people as unpredictable and scary. Their ability to solve problems develops poorly.

Depressed Parents' Negative Effects on Their Teens

Depressed parents are more negative, unsupportive, and intrusive with their teens compared to nondepressed parents. They are also more likely to have difficulty maintaining boundaries with their kids. In a revealing survey of randomly interviewed twelve-to seventeen-year-olds, for example, kids expect to have to ask parents an average of *nine* times for something they want before their parents finally give in to their nagging. Yet parents' giving in reinforces the nagging and makes the child seem even more difficult to manage. Giving in is an example of conflict avoidance that rewards children for being obnoxiously persistent and teaches them that *what they have matters more than who they are.* Depressed parents find their teens more difficult to manage than nondepressed parents, and the way they communicate their negative views about their children to their children is quite likely to be recognized and absorbed by the teen. *Kids tend to know when they are wanted and loved and appreciated, and when they're not.*

Early Warning Signs to Watch For

The following clues can suggest depression in children:

- A change in personality, especially from relatively positive to negative, from light to heavy in attitude
- Lethargy, little energy to do things
- Frequent somatic complaints (such as stomach aches, headaches, backaches)
- Loss of interest in the things that usually interest him or her, including socializing with friends or engaging in enjoyable activities
- Extreme and global self-condemnation ("I'm stupid, I'm ugly, everybody hates me")

- Difficulty concentrating, anxiety, easily distractible
- Low frustration tolerance, gives up easily in the face of even small obstacles or challenges
- Appetite problems
- Sleep problems

None of these signs alone necessarily means the child is depressed, but the presence of any one or several certainly suggests the need for a closer look.

I want to focus in greater depth on two key diagnostic clues that a child is depressed that also have implications for treatment.

Anxiety

Anxiety in kids is a key early warning sign of emotional difficulties that can easily mushroom into eventually suffering anxiety and depression together. In fact, in the majority of adults, depression and anxiety coexist, but they don't have the same age of onset. Typically, anxiety precedes depression by many years; the anxious child is much more likely to become an anxious and depressed, or "comorbid," adult.

The most common form of anxiety is *social* anxiety. When a child is fearful of other kids and avoids interacting with them (stays in the classroom at recess instead of going out and playing, for example), there is good reason to be concerned. As children get older and the more they don't fit in with other kids, the more they accumulate negative feedback from other kids; they are made fun of, they experience more rejection and their feelings get hurt, which further raises their anxiety about being around others. As time goes on, they become increasingly shy and quite likely lonely, as well. Shyness, loneliness, and depression are related. All are associated with higher levels of anxiety, greater scanning for and detecting negative reactions in other people, and more internal focus (higher levels of rumination) on negative feelings. Shyness leads to more social avoidance, and as you've learned, avoidance increases a sense of victimhood and depression.

Loneliness doesn't just hurt emotionally, it hurts physically, too. Feeling lonely can make you more vulnerable to illness, and new research in the area of genetics suggests why. A study at UCLA revealed that people who described themselves as the loneliest on loneliness scales exhibited increased gene activity associated with inflammation and reduced gene activity for antibody production and antiviral responses. Chronic loneliness changes gene activity.

This relationship between inflammation and depression is currently being studied in many places. Medical research has shown that higher levels of inflammation may play a role in a number of disorders, including heart disease, cancer, and diabetes, all of which have been associated with depression. According to a recent study by researchers at Emory School of Medicine, individuals with major depression have an exaggerated inflammatory response to psychological stress compared to those who do not suffer from depression.

If your child is socially anxious, the psychological stress can affect her in emotional and physical ways. To counter the social anxiety, the most important thing you can do is help her to develop coping and social skills. Every day this child doesn't get along with others, she gets negative feedback that can cause bad feelings early in life, and lead those bad feelings to be an enduring *way* of life. Learning how to begin and end friendly interactions, how to keep a nice conversation going, how to be easy to be around, how to "read" others, how to be smart about what to disclose and when, and many other such skills are best encouraged early on. Being trapped in a world with billions of other people with whom you don't know how to interact skillfully assures a much more difficult life.

Helping children to learn how to think about people, how to recognize their character strengths and talents, as well as their motivations and how to manage their manipulations, is most easily done by helping them learn about their own such patterns. Talking with kids about important interactions they have with teachers and other students, encouraging the child to think through what was said and what the impact was or is likely to be is the kind of conversation that can start relatively early in life. Asking questions such as, "Why do you think the teacher said that to Billy?" and, "How do you think Billy was feeling when the teacher said that to him in front of the whole class?" or, "What would you have done if the teacher said that to you?" are questions that stimulate conversation and encourage the child to be observant, thoughtful, empathetic, and deliberate. Be especially careful not to make global statements about people, such as "The other kids act that way because they're *all* jealous of you" or "They're *all* spoiled rotten." *Global thinking discourages critical thinking.*

Asking kids, "What if?" is a good technique for learning to manage anxiety. "What if something happened to me, what would you do? What if another kid did such-and-such, what do you think you would do?" Anxious children (and adults, too) tend to ask themselves "what if?" questions regularly, which scares the heck out of them because they don't have answers: What if I get lost and mom can't find me? What if my parents divorce? What if my daddy dies?

The anxiety that comes from asking such frightening questions is normal. The key to learning to manage the anxiety and empower yourself in the process to trust your own judgment is to *answer the question*. It would be unpleasant to face the circumstances in the "what if?" question—unpleasant but *manageable*. In dealing with your child, help him answer the question. Let the child learn to be a problem solver instead of a worrier. Help your child learn to calm himself with self-soothing techniques like slow, deep breathing, and relaxation or self-hypnosis techniques when facing stressful situations. These techniques will help prepare your child for a lifetime of challenges.

Learn by Doing:
Creating a Calm Space

When you were a kid, did you have "quiet time" in school, when all the kids in class would lie on their floor mats and take twenty minutes just to relax and be still? Today, there is no quiet time for most kids anymore. They are revved up from the time they wake up to the time they go to bed. It would be a great thing for you and your child to create a quiet time each day. You don't have to say a word to each other, just share the experience of listening to some soothing music, or listening to a relaxation CD. Even better, though, is if you take turns guiding each other through such an experience: Talk gently in an "imagination exercise" in detail about a trip you took or some other positive experience you shared together. The next time it's your child's turn to do the same for you. Learning to deliberately create a calm space inside yourself is empowering and reinforces the recognition that you can manage how you feel.

Rigidity and Flexibility in Children's Problem Solving

Rigidity means doing what doesn't work and then, instead of adapting in more beneficial ways, doing more of the same. To help a child deal with many different challenges, we need to encourage her to be flexible in her thinking, to generate other possible ways of handling some difficulty she isn't handling very well. If she can't generate other options, don't just give them to her or she will not learn frustration tolerance. Make it a joint session in problem solving so that you model focusing on the problem as well as focusing on feelings. First, clearly define the problem, then generate possibilities, then think through the different options—what's likely to help and what isn't—then consider how and when to implement the solution you chose, and finally, how to adjust based on new feedback as the solution gets implemented.

Here's an example of the process: Your kid complains he doesn't understand his math assignment. Together, you sit down and begin the discussion by acknowledging his feelings ("You seem pretty upset about not understanding your math assignment").

- **Step 1:** Define the problem ("What about the assignment don't you understand? Do you need help with how to do it, or is it that you don't have enough time to do it properly, or is there something else upsetting you?").
- **Step 2:** Generate possibilities of what to do ("How can you get the help you need in order to complete the assignment? Do you need to send an email to your teacher? Call your cousin who has explained this kind of material to you before? What do *you* think would be a good solution?").
- **Step 3:** Think through the different options: thinking through each possibility takes a little time but teaches important skills for being deliberate in one's approach.
- **Step 4:** Implement the solution ("That sounds good. Your teacher said it was okay to e-mail her, so do it now before it gets too late.").
- **Step 5:** Make adjustments ("If you don't hear back from your teacher in a couple of hours, then you could call your cousin for help. Why don't you do some other homework while you're waiting?"). This is how problem-solving skills evolve.

Depression is most dangerous to a child when he faces some situation that is stressful and difficult, and simply freezes and gives up. The hopelessness and helplessness that define depression are immediately evident. When someone of *any* age freezes and has no idea what to do next, yet knows something effective needs to be done, the self-doubt, self-criticism, and fear all intensify to almost excruciating proportions. It is vitally important that, when someone has no idea what to do next, he learns how to be a problem solver instead of spinning off into indecision, anxiety, and depression: Who can I consult? Who has the experience or expertise I need? Who would know someone with the experience or expertise I need if I can't think of anybody myself? The importance of developing solutions instead of giving up cannot be overstated. But the solutions have to be realistic for the circumstances— they have to be viable. *Telling the kid to take his medication on time isn't how children learn frustration tolerance or problem-solving skills.*

Not every problem has a solution, of course. A child can't do anything about mom and dad's decision to divorce, for example, but, he can learn enough skill to avoid self-blame for the divorce. He can learn how to make use of supportive friendships and even ask for supportive therapy, if so inclined. He can strive to keep the divorce from contaminating his view of people and relationships. He can make his feelings known and, even if they are ignored, then feel comfortable the communication problems aren't for a lack of trying on his part. In short, there's a lot a child trained to be a good problem solver can do to keep from getting overwhelmed by the many challenges of life.

As a parent, you can't teach a child what you don't know. Are you a good problem solver? Do you bear down and gather information and weigh options and implement solutions, or do you get overloaded and give up easily? Do you avoid problems, using obvious avoidance strategies like drugs or alcohol or sex to get by? You are the model for behavior that your children follow, so your goal is to model the best ways to live well without succumbing to depression when things go badly, which they do at times for everyone.

Depression Raises Questions
about the Decision to Be a Parent

In June 2008, one of the major news stories that had the airwaves buzzing was about the extraordinarily high rate of pregnancies at a high school in Gloucester, Massachusetts. Most years, three or four girls in the high school would get pregnant, presumably the unintended outcome of unprotected sex. But in 2007, the number of such pregnancies more than *quadrupled*. Many of these young girls had been repeatedly asking for pregnancy tests from the school nurse, and if these came back negative, the girls weren't relieved as one might expect. In fact, they were obviously disappointed. When the tests eventually came back positive, apparently there were congratulatory "high fives" for each other.

Gloucester's mayor and school superintendent said that these sophomore girls were apparently deliberately trying to get pregnant and had formed some sort of pact with each other about getting pregnant together and then raising the babies together. The girls have denied such a pact ever existed, yet there is good reason to doubt their denial.

Whether the pact existed or not, however, the result was seventeen new babies born to girls ages fifteen and sixteen who are unmarried, uneducated, emotionally immature, impulsive, and uncaring about the very serious implications of their foolhardiness for both themselves and their babies, who have now placed huge additional burdens on their families which they may or may not be able to manage well.

The reasons why someone decides to have a child or, conversely, chooses *not* to have one, are highly personal and reflect his or her deepest values. Who you are as a person, and how well you function in your relationship with the partner you may want to have children with are the foundation on which the decisions are built. There are people who are in loving, stable, committed relationships and who have the maturity, wisdom, and resources to have and raise a child in a healthy, positive environment that will maximize the chances to live a good life. But, unfortunately, babies are born to people who have little actual interest in raising one and no realistic concept of what it actually takes to raise a child well. When I talk about this in my clinical trainings for mental health professionals, I talk about *all those people who wanted to have children . . . but who just didn't want to be parents*. The gasp from the audience is always audible.

People get wrapped up in the concept of parenting, but not in the realistic details of what they will need to give of themselves. They love the idea of having a baby, but they manage to ignore the fact that, barring tragedy, this cute baby will grow into an unruly teenager. Parenting well under the best of conditions is hard. Parenting well when disabled by depression, or conditions even worse, is close to impossible if you want to have healthy, happy kids, but more likely when you are able to focus on the skills of good parenting rather than getting lost in the depression. As Dr. Constance Hammen, a distinguished researcher at UCLA who has done brilliant work on the intergenerational transmission of depression, summarized, "Being a good parent certainly means putting a lot of time and effort into listening and talking, being good and consistent role models of good values and effective social problem-solving." All the relationship skills I have presented in this book can make for strong marriages, which can also make strong families.

Pause and Reflect:
Reasons to Become a Parent

Do you believe someone needs to have a good reason, a justification of some sort, for bringing a child into this world? Or, is it a good enough reason to simply say, "Because I want to?" Do you believe someone can have good and healthy reasons for choosing not to have children? Or do you consider not wanting children a defect of some sort?

How you answer these seemingly simple questions will reveal some of your core values that will powerfully influence your view and style of parenting. The quality of your parenting can either increase or decrease your child's vulnerability to depression. The right to have children goes universally unquestioned, but I don't think anyone would advocate, and I certainly don't, that people have children who don't want or value them. This is the most irreversible of decisions. To make it solely on the basis of simply "wanting to have a kid" without any deeper thought about one's capacity for being a good parent is how children are born to people who don't have the temperament, skills, or financial resources to meet the complex demands of being a good parent in today's world. Someone may well choose not to have children for sensible reasons, particularly when he or she could be an effective parent but simply doesn't want the lifestyle that having children engenders.

Each person must decide for him or herself how to address this value-laden issue meaningfully. No one would dispute, though, that having a child is a huge decision that must be approached sensitively and with clarity regarding the implications of one's decision, whatever it might be.

Clear Signs That Someone Isn't Ready for Parenthood

If you already have children, this section is irrelevant. Readers who think of having kids as a religious or moral obligation might well be offended by this discussion. If you think that having kids is "just something you do," without thought or reason, you may be offended that I would question your belief. I hope you'll appreciate, though, that in more than thirty years of clinical practice and teaching to and consulting with organizations all over the world, I am driven by having repeatedly observed how miserable a child's life can be when born into a family that sees no inherent value in its members or responsibility to them.

It is devastating to witness how badly kids can be neglected and abused simply because their lives matter so little to their parents. It is also devastating to see kids absorb their parents' depression, not because of blatant abuse, but simply because the adults were too depressed to function as effective parents, unable to create a loving and supportive environment. The family is the ultimate social unit that can protect its members from depression when that family takes its responsibilities seriously and develops the skills to carry out those responsibilities. *Depression doesn't have to be contagious.*

Here are ten clear signs that an individual or couple is not ready to have kids, and that lack of readiness increases the likelihood that a child will be raised poorly and suffer as a result:

- If you can't put someone else's needs first, even temporarily; if you live your life according to the belief that it's all about *you*, then you're not ready.
- If you can't make your child your enduring priority, rather than something you just squeeze in between other stuff, then you're not ready.
- If you can't openly express love, affection, approval, respect, or caring because it somehow makes you uncomfortable, or because you're too depressed to say positive things, then you're not ready.

- If you think of kids as just small adults, then you're not ready.
- If you think your partner should do most of the parenting while you pursue other interests or concerns, then you're not ready.
- If you're concerned that having a kid will adversely affect your partying and painfully limit your freedom to do whatever you wish, then you're not ready.
- If you don't want to be a role model and you don't like the pressure of having to be your best in handling things for the welfare of others, then you're not ready.
- If you think you can break promises or make up for the time you don't spend with your kid by simply buying him or her more stuff, then you're not ready.
- If you think it's okay to lie to your kid, throw tantrums when you're angry, give up on or avoid dealing with things you just don't feel like dealing with, use your kid as an ally or weapon in arguments with your partner, and sulk when you don't get your way, then you're not ready.
- If you don't know how to take responsibility for your actions and apologize when they are hurtful to others, then you're not ready.

Depression is about more than bad parenting, or *any* one factor, of course, but there is no greater force than the power of the family to insulate its members from a vulnerability to depression.

Being Ready: What *Can* a Family Do to Protect Its Members?

A couple can do many things to be ready for the responsibilities of parenthood, and many things can be built into family interaction that can teach the skills known to help reduce the likelihood and the suffering of depression in children. All of them start with the powerful realization that every interaction you have from the moment your baby is born has the potential to model behavior and teach specific skills. The goal is to model *good* behavior and teach *effective* skills.

Amy and Shawn are a well educated couple in their late twenties, professionally successful, financially fairly comfortable; they came to therapy to attempt to answer whether they should have kids together. They have been married six years, and the relationship has been good, though not easy, because Shawn has suffered depression for much of his life. When he got depressed he would withdraw from others, become humorless, say little, and be difficult to have a regular conversation with.

Fortunately, however, he rarely has episodes these days. Through Amy, a perpetual optimist with a very forceful personality, Shawn has learned the value of having someone else around he can confide in, discuss problems with, and do so with someone who interprets the issues and sees the challenges of life in an entirely different way than he does. Amy's practical, down-to-earth way of handling life's difficulties, however small or big, has touched Shawn in ways he would never have predicted when he was single. Through Amy, Shawn has learned all kinds of little tricks for staying out of the "mental quicksand" he used to regularly fall into. Therapy has also been a big help to Shawn.

The concern, though, belongs to both Amy and Shawn. Shawn begins the session by saying, "I have a history of suffering depression. I used to have some terrible, terrible times. In recent years, thanks to Amy and to therapy, too, I hardly ever feel depressed, and even when I do I know how to keep myself from sliding down that slippery slope."

Amy jumps in and says, "He really is a different person these days. It's great. But, the question we both have is, if we have a child, is that child going to be depressed like Shawn was?"

Shawn jumps back in and says, "I couldn't bear to have my kid go through what I went through. I just don't want to have a kid knowing he or she will be depressed when I could have made the decision not to have a kid and saved a kid from a life of suffering."

What would *you* tell Amy and Shawn?

If you have a history of depression, that doesn't mean you shouldn't have kids. It does mean, however, that you will need to *take extra steps to minimize the likelihood of passing this particular "inheritance" on to them.* That includes taking the time to learn your particular vulnerabilities, your particular triggers for depressive episodes. It means learning to recognize when your mood is slipping and taking active steps to stop the slide before it becomes a full blown episode. If you notice changes in your sleep, for example, that can be an early warning signal. If you find yourself irritable and starting to withdraw, that is another signal. One way you'll know you're ready is when you know the signs and symptoms of starting to slide and have a means for catching and responding to them early on.

It will save you lots of grief if you can *be realistic in your expectations about parenting*. Understand that when you bring a life into this world, it isn't *yours*. Your child will learn to think and will learn to discover his or her own preferences, values, and uniqueness. He or she may end up deeply interested in things you are not. As in *any* good relationship, the differences between you are far less important than how lovingly and respectfully those differences are managed.

It is vitally important for you to *be careful and deliberate about what you model through your behavior*. That's much easier said than done. No one wants to be on display all the time, yet kids pick up what parents model even when the parent doesn't know the child is watching. Kids also pick up on what parents do much more than what they say. Telling a kid not to smoke while you puff away, telling a kid to stop to think when you are prone to tantrums, telling a kid to be nice to other kids when you're trashing the neighbors, well, you get the idea. Showing a child *how* to do something counts for more than simply telling a child *what* to do.

The language you use teaches concepts, which in turn teach perspective. *Be deliberate in using language that teaches clear thinking and good problem solving*. Blaming others for mistakes you make, globally condemning others ("That guy is useless") or life ("Life is so unfair"), modeling helplessness ("There's nothing I can do") and hopelessness ("Why bother?"), and giving up when things get tough ("I just can't deal with this") send the wrong messages.

Talking to each other counts for a lot. *Learn to ask open-ended questions of your kids instead of closed ones*. "Tell me about your day" will get you a better reply than will asking, "How was your day?" Acknowledging your child's feelings is important to help a child learn to recognize and manage them. Acknowledging their hurt or anger is a way of connecting to where the child is emotionally, even if the goal is to help move him or her through the feelings to some new learning or resolution. Along those lines, you'll know you're ready to parent when you recognize the value of teaching your child to be intentional. Asking a child in anger, "Why did you do that?" invites excuses and justifications for what happened. Asking, "What was your goal here? What did you want to have happen?" helps the child learn to build the bridge between first developing goals and then developing ways of reaching them. That's how kids can become creative and effective problem solvers, skills that will serve them for a lifetime.

Learn by Doing:
Recognizing Your Risky Patterns

Recognizing that depressed parents pose a strong risk for raising depressed kids, you also need to know what it is about your individual way of looking at things or doing things that may pose risks to your kids. What are your strengths as a parent, and how can you continue to expand them? What are the things you don't manage very well that, by modeling them to your child, increase his or her vulnerability to depression? It would be very helpful if you could develop a journal, or a manual, where you keep a written record of significant interactions you have each day that highlight what you do well as well as what you could learn to do better. The goal, of course, is for you to take active steps to develop good problem-solving skills, critical thinking, good social skills, and a consistency between what you want and expect from your child and what you model in your own behavior. Developing such a manual is a great way of organizing your thoughts and observations in such a way that you are actually able to learn progressively from your own experience.

It helps to know that plenty of research indicates that, when depressed parents receive help and apply new skills they learn in their interactions with their kids, *both* benefit greatly. (Other resources to help with the challenges of parenting well and preparing kids for the challenges they will inevitably face are included in the Notes section at the end of this book.)

Medicating Kids for Depression

As I write this, the issues associated with the use of antidepressant medications for children have never been more complicated, confusing, and controversial. Professionals cannot agree that the drugs for young people are effective and safe, so it is no wonder that parents wanting to help their depressed children in the best way possible are confused about what to do.

Currently, only one antidepressant medication is specifically approved by the U.S. Food and Drug Administration (FDA) for use by children (ages 7–17) for treating depression. That drug is Prozac. Despite this being the only one approved, millions of children are regularly prescribed antidepressants, and not just Prozac. The demand for antidepressants is high, and "off label" prescribing means doctors can use their judgment to prescribe drugs even for uses other than those approved by the FDA. The problem is obvious: These drugs have not been adequately tested for their effectiveness for children, or their safety, or the dosage adjustments necessary for smaller bodies, so relying on one person's clinical judgment can be scary. After all, some people's judgment is considerably better than others. It is most telling that a survey of North Carolina pediatricians revealed that 72 percent of them had prescribed antidepressants to children under eighteen, but only 8 percent of them said they felt they had adequate training to prescribe them.

There just aren't enough good studies to make it clear that antidepressants are effective for children. As for adults, the reports are mixed: Anecdotally, there are some who say, "That medication saved my life," and they mean it. Conversely, there are others who say, "That medication made me worse," and they mean it. The research is just as mixed, with some studies being favorable (and more likely to be published), and other studies being unfavorable (and less likely to be published). Thus, medicating children has to be considered an experiment; medication's effectiveness is uncertain. We don't know how these drugs will affect developing minds, nor developing bodies. We don't know how they will affect developing self-images and how they will affect relationships with family and friends. We simply don't know what the long-term effects will be of kids getting on, much less staying on, these medications.

The safety issue is huge. On one side, you have expert proponents of drugs declaring them safe and that whatever risks they may pose are outweighed by their benefits. On the other side, you have expert opponents of these drugs expressing their concerns that the opposite is true: the risks outweigh the benefits.

One issue in particular has polarized the profession: There is an increased risk for suicidal thoughts and behaviors in young people being given antidepressants. Psychiatrists are divided, but the FDA initially recommended so-called "black box" warnings, the strongest warning possible, be placed on antidepressant packaging materials about the increased potential for suicidality in children up to age eighteen. Yet in the April 18, 2007 issue of the *Journal of the American Medical Association,* researchers claimed that the suicide threat from SSRIs, the most commonly prescribed class of antidepressants for young people, was exaggerated and recommended that the "black box" warning be lifted.

On May 2, 2007, just two weeks later, the U.S. FDA required drug manufacturers to *expand* their black box warnings of increased suicidal thoughts and behavior on their product labels and warnings in their medication guides for patients. The original warning was for children and adolescents up to age eighteen. It is now for young adults up to age twenty-four as well.

Pause and Reflect:
Conflicting Information Causes Confusion

How much more contradictory can it get than some experts saying there really is no problem and other experts saying there is a big problem with placing kids on antidepressants? It's confusing for everyone to hear similar contradictions such as these: The drugs are safe to take during pregnancy, except they may cause potential harm to the fetus; the drugs aren't addictive, but there are troublesome side effects to getting off them.

Such contradictions should tell you that you can get expert opinions about what to do with your child, but you will have to make the final decision after reviewing the evidence and weighing it according to the needs of your child. You might well decide to pursue medications, but as long as you do so on an informed basis and not just because your neighbor's kid takes them, you will greatly increase the probability of making a good decision.

We don't know a lot about these drugs—including how they work (*if* and when they do)—but we do know that they are powerful and have lots of side effects. What's more, *we know these drugs can't teach any of the social skills that are known to reduce depression.*

If your child is depressed, it can help to know that you have more choices than only deciding whether to medicate. The fact that psychotherapy has a treatment success rate that matches that of medication *without the side effects and with a lower relapse rate,* can provide comfort. Most important, kids can learn the skills that will help them get through whatever is going on right now, and will provide them the skills they'll need and be glad to have in the future.

CHAPTER 10

Afterword

When I first began studying depression more than thirty years ago, there was very, very little in the way of effective treatment available. The newer medications with fewer, less extreme side effects didn't exist yet, and most psychotherapists were still only talking to their patients about their childhood, their nightly dreams, or both, rather than teaching focused and specific skills as they are far more likely to do now. The importance of developing key skills in order to better handle the complicated demands of life as a means of managing depression effectively was simply not understood.

Now, all these years later, there are good psychotherapies available that help the majority of people who receive treatment by empowering them to think more clearly, behave more effectively, and relate to others more skillfully. The fact that these therapies can match the success rates of antidepressant medications and can even exceed their effectiveness in key areas (such as by reducing the vulnerability to relapse) has great significance. I know many depressed people won't seek therapy, though, and so I hope this book will provide some comfort and help. For those who do seek help, I hope this book serves as a useful adjunct to treatment.

The Next Steps

By reading this book, you've come to recognize that depression affects everyone directly and indirectly. With that education comes a responsibility to yourself and to others to build high-quality relationships that can better insulate you and those you care about from depression. The relationships you build predict and even provide a direct measure of how likely you are to feel good. So, while people have been taught to strive to improve their own self-esteem and focus on themselves, the net effect has been to make people more distant from each other and unhappier as a result.

In the Introduction, I mentioned the growing emphasis in the mental health field on a positive psychology, a scientific approach (finally!) to studying people who are happy and effective. We have a great deal to learn from such people. After all, they, too, suffer the pain of people they love dying, the enormous stresses of their jobs disappearing, the scares of their health deteriorating, and all the other things that happen in life that can easily cause us to sink into despair. How do people manage to be happy in the face of loss, rejection, humiliation, abuse, and all the rest?

You've now learned at least *some* of the answers to that question. You've learned how arbitrary points of view can be and that *how* you think is even more important than *what* you think. You don't have to *believe* something simply because you *think* it. You've come to understand that no one experience, good *or* bad, defines you or your life. You're more than your feelings and you're more than your history. And you've learned that the happiest people get that way by serving others. They openly express affection to others, they are grateful for the everyday things (the sunsets, the courtesy of having a door opened for them, the smile of a stranger), and they are deliberate in offering their gratitude to others. This may or may not come easily to you, but you now know that it is learnable and doable. You can be the person you want to be, generous in spirit and positive in action. You can recognize the opportunities that are on the other side of challenges.

You Can *Live* a Positive Psychology

The strengths of happy and effective people are strengths you have, too. You already have the ability to speak the truth, even when others are lying. You have the capacity right now to do kind things each day, things that make other peoples' lives, even those of perfect strangers, easier. You have the potential to love people, despite the risks of caring and possibly getting hurt by caring. You have the immediate power to take the lead in redefining how your relationships work, and you get to choose what desirable characteristics you'll reinforce in each other.

One final story to make the point:

It rained and rained, and then rained some more, as if the sky had opened up and an ocean of rain fell to the earth. As the flood waters began to rise, the Holy Man looked all around him and wondered if the rains were a sign from God. He felt sure that even if they were, as a man of God, he was safe. He stood at his door, and as the water began to spill into his house, a man in a boat rowed up to him and said, "Holy Man, save yourself! Get into my rowboat." The Holy Man replied, "I am a man of God, and I have faith God will not let me drown. Give the place in your rowboat to some other deserving soul." The man rowed on.

The flood waters continued to rise above his home's first level, and so the Holy Man went up to his second-floor bedroom and waited and watched, hoping for an end to the rain. But the rain continued. Soon, another man in a rowboat floated up to his window and said, "Holy Man, you are in danger. The water is still rising and if you don't leave, you will surely drown." The Holy Man once again declined the offer of help, and said, "I have faith God will not let me drown. I am His servant, His voice. Give the place in your boat to someone else who is worthy of saving." The man paddled on.

The rains continued, and the rising water level soon forced the Holy Man onto his roof. As the waters began to cover his home, he climbed onto the chimney. Soon, a helicopter approached and hovered over him. A booming voice coming over a loudspeaker said, "Holy Man, I will drop a rope to you and pull you from your chimney into the helicopter. Grab the rope tightly and save yourself." The Holy Man shouted back, "God will not let me drown. Fly on and rescue someone else needing your help." The helicopter flew on.

The rains continued, the waters rose, and . . . the Holy Man drowned.

When he came before God in Heaven, he asked, "God, how could you let me drown? Have I not served you faithfully all my life? Did I not devote my entire life to your greatness and bring others to know your glory? I don't understand. Why did you let me drown?"

And God replied, "What more could I do? I sent you two rowboats and a helicopter!"

More often than not, there are solutions right in front of us, if only we would recognize them. But, it's easy to miss what's available to us when we get locked into a viewpoint that blinds us to the possibilities. It's easy to overlook what's right when we get too focused on what's wrong.

I hope this book provides you with the rowboats, helicopters, and other means you need to save yourself from the rain of life challenges that you face. Without the rain, of course, you'd never have a chance to see a rainbow—the strengths you develop by facing and overcoming hard times.

Notes

Foreword

Polster, E. (1987). *Every Person's Life is Worth a Novel.* Highland, NY: The Gestalt Journal Press.

Polster, E. (2006). *Uncommon Ground: Harmonizing Psychotherapy and Community to Enhance Everyday Living.* Phoenix, AZ: Zeig, Tucker & Theisen.

Siegel, D. (1999). *The Developing Mind.* New York: Guilford Press.

Introduction

xiii *According to the World Health Organization:* World Health Organization (2002). *The world health report 2002: Reducing risks, promoting healthy life.* Geneva, Switzerland: Author.

xiii *This is not simply because:* Kessler, R. Berglund, P., Demler, O. et al. (2003). The epidemiology of major depressive disorder: Results from the National Comorbidity Survey Replication (NCS-R). *Journal of the American Medical Association, 289,* 3095–3105.

xiv *Known as positive psychology:* Seligman, M. & Csikszentmihalyi, M. (2000). Positive psychology: An introduction. *American Psychologist, 55,* 1, 5–14.

xiv *Unlike the well-known psychiatric manual:* American Psychiatric Association (APA). (2000). *Diagnostic and statistical manual* (4th ed. revised). Washington, DC: Author.

xiv *a new manual called:* Peterson, C. & Seligman, M. (2004). *Character strengths and virtues: A handbook and classification.* New York: Oxford University Press.

xv *Even a cursory review:* U.S. Census Data, available online: http://www.census.gov/

xv *For over half a century:* Uchino, B. (2006). Social support and health: A review of physiological processes potentially underlying links to disease outcomes. *Journal of Behavioral Medicine, 29,* 377–387.; Reblin, M. & Uchino, B. (2008). Social and emotional support and its implication for health. *Current Opinions in Psychiatry, 21*(2), 201–205.

xvi *New research makes it clear:* Joiner, T. & Coyne, J. (Eds.)(1999). *The interactional nature of depression.* Washington, DC: American Psychological Association.

xvi *For every depressed person:* U.S. Preventive Services Task Force (2002). Screening for depression in adults. *Annals of Internal Medicine, 136,* 765–776; Goodman, S. & Gotlib, I. (Eds.) (2002). *Children of depressed parents: Mechanisms of risk and implications for treatment.* Washington, DC: American Psychological Association.

xvii *Depression has a huge financial impact:* Greenberg, P., Kessler, R., Birnbaum, H. et al. (2003). The economic burden of depression in the United States: How did it change between 1990 and 2000? *Journal of Clinical Psychiatry, 64*(12), 1465–75.

xvii *Hence, a biopsychosocial model:* Dubovsky, S. (1997). *Mind-body deceptions: The psychosomatics of everyday life.* New York: Norton.

xvii *A young field called:* Damasio, A, Grabowski, T., Bechara, A. et al. (2000). Subcortical and cortical brain activity during the feeling of self-generated emotions. *Nature Neuroscience,*

3, 1049–1056; Davidson, R. & Irwin, W. (1999). The functional neuroanatomy of emotion and affective style. *Trends in Cognitive Sciences, 3*, 11–21.

xviii *This is primarily because the drug industry:* Lacasse, J. & Leo, J. (2005). Serotonin and depression: A disconnect between the advertisements and the scientific literature. *PLoS Medicine*, 2(12): e392.

xx *How effective medications truly are:* Healy, D. (2004). *Let them eat Prozac: The unhealthy relationship between the pharmaceutical companies and depression.* New York: New York University; Moncrieff, J. & Kirsch, I. (2005). Efficacy of antidepressants in adults. *British Medical Journal, 331*, 155–157.

Chapter 1 Depression Doesn't Arise in a Social Vacuum

1 *But our brains also change:* Cozolino, L. (2006). *The neuroscience of human relationships: Attachment and the developing social brain.* New York: Norton; Siegel, D. (2006). An interpersonal neurobiology approach to psychotherapy. *Psychiatric Annals, 36*(4), 248–256.

2 *Our brains evolved:* Siegel, D. (1999). *The developing mind.* New York: Guilford.

2 *Perhaps the most telling discovery:* Rizzolatti, G. & Craighero, L. (2004). The mirror-neuron system. *Annual Review of Neuroscience, 27*, 169–192; Rizzolatti, G., Fogassi, L. & Gallese, V. (2001). Neurophysiological mechanisms underlying the understanding and the imitation of action. *National Review of Neuroscience, 2*, 661–670.

2 *Some experts in neuroscience:* Gazzaniga, M. (1985). *The social brain: Discovering the networks of the mind.* New York: Basic Books; Iacoboni, M. (2008). *Mirroring people: The new neuroscience of how we connect with others.* New York: Farrar, Straus and Giroux.

2 *In one recent study:* Marci, C., Ham, J., Moran, E. et al. (2007). Physiologic correlates of perceived therapist empathy and social-emotional process during psychotherapy. *Journal of Nervous and Mental Diseases, 195*(2), 103–111.

3 *Cutting edge research suggests:* Thomas, R. & Peterson, D. (2003). A neurogenic theory of depression gains momentum. *Molecular Interventions, 3*, 441–444.

4 *A remarkable study at UCLA's Neuropsychiatric Institute:* Hunter, A., Leuchter, A., Morgan, M. et al. (2006). Changes in brain function (Quantitative EEG cordance) during placebo lead-in and treatment outcomes in clinical trials for major depression. *American Journal of Psychiatry, 163*, 1426–1432.

4 *In a classic set of experiments:* Schachter, S. & Singer, J. (1962). Cognitive, social and physiological determinants of emotional state. *Psychological Review, 69*, 379–399.

5 *The NBC Nightly News:* Story reported on *NBC Nightly News with Brian Williams* on December 14, 2007.

6 *I'll mention just a few:* Ohayon, M. (2007). Epidemiology of depression and its treatment in the general population. *Journal of Psychiatric Research, 41*(3–4), 207–213; Pickering, T. (2000). Depression, race, hypertension, and the heart. *Journal of Clinical Hypertension, 2*(6), 410–412; Garland, A., Hough, R., McCabe, K. et al. (2001). Prevalence of psychiatric disorders in youths across five sectors of care. *Journal of the American Academy of Child and Adolescent Psychiatry, 40*(4), 409–418.

6 *Doctors are influenced by the ads, too:* Kravitz, R., Epstein, R., Feldman, D. et al. (2005). Influence of patients' requests for direct-to-consumer advertised antidepressants. *Journal of the American Medical Association, 293*, 1995–2002; Zimmerman, M., Posternak, M. Friedman, M. et al. (2004). Which factors influence psychiatrists' selection of antidepressants? *American Journal of Psychiatry, 161*(7), 1285–9.

7 *The American Medical Association:* 2005 Report: Pharmaceutical Research and Manufacturers of America; Barber, C. (2008). *Comfortably numb: How psychiatry is medicating a nation.* New York: Pantheon.

7 *In January 2008:* Turner, E., Matthews, A., Linardatos, E. et al. (2008). Selective publication of antidepressant trials and its influence on apparent efficacy. *The New England Journal of Medicine, 358*, 252–260.

7 *In February 2008, researchers reported:* Kirsch, I., Deacon, B., Huedo-Medina, T. et al. (2008). Initial severity and antidepressant benefits: A meta-analysis of data submitted to the Food and Drug Administration. *PLoS Medicine, 5*(2), e45.

7 *Just days earlier:* Barbui, C., Furukawa, T., & Cipriani, A. (2008). Effectiveness of parox-etine in the treatment of acute major depression in adults: A systematic re-examination of published and unpublished data from randomized trials. *Canadian Medical Association Journal, 178*(3), 261–262.

8 *In April 2008, two explosive articles:* Ross, J., Hill, K., Egilman, D. et al. (2008). Guest authorship and ghostwriting in publications related to Rofecoxib: A case study of indus-try documents from Rofecoxib litigation. *Journal of the American Medical Association, 299*(15), 1800–1812; Psaty, B. & Kronmal (2008). Reporting mortality findings in tri-als of Rofecoxib for Alzheimer disease or cognitive impairment: A case study based on documents from Rofecoxib litigation. *Journal of the American Medical Association, 299*(15), 1813–1817.

8 *In a blistering editorial:* DeAngelis, C. (2008). Impugning the integrity of medical science: The adverse effects of industry influence. *Journal of the American Medical Association, 299*(15), 1833–1835.

10 *As two researchers pointed out:* Buchwald, A. & Rudick-Davis, D. (1993). The symptoms of major depression. *Journal of Abnormal Psychology, 102*, 197–205.

10 *Depression affects physical health:* Penninx, B., Beekman, A., Honig, A. et al. (2001). Depression and cardiac mortality: Results from a community-based longitudinal study. *Archives of General Psychiatry, 58*, 221–227; Kanner, A. & Palac, S. (2000). Depression in epilepsy: A common but often unrecognized comorbid malady. *Epilepsy & Behavior, 1*(1), 37–51; Salaycik, K., Kelly-Hayes, M., Beisen, A. et al. (2007). Depressive symptoms and risk of stroke. *Stroke, 38*(1), 16–21; Egede, L., Nietert, P. & Zheng, D. (2005). Depres-sion and all-cause and coronary heart disease mortality among adults with and without diabetes. *Diabetes Care, 28*, 1339–1345.

11 *Depression affects thought (cognitive) processes:* Gotlib, I. (Ed.) (1997). *The cognitive psychol-ogy of depression.* East Sussex, UK: Psychology Press.

11 *Depression affects productivity:* Seligman, M. (1990). *Learned optimism.* New York: Alfred Knopf; Stewart, W., Ricci, J., Chee, E. et al. (2003). Cost of lost productive work time among US workers with depression. *Journal of the American Medical Association, 289* (23), 3135–3144.

11 *The antisocial effects:* Abraham, H. & Fava, M. (1999). Order of onset of substance abuse and depression in a sample of depressed outpatients. *Comprehensive Psychiatry, 40*(1), 44–50; Dozois, D. & Dobson, K. (2004). *The prevention of anxiety and depression.* Washington, DC: American Psychological Association; Joiner, T. & Coyne, J. (1999). *The interactional nature of depression.* Washington, DC: American Psychological Association; Yapko, M. (1999). *Hand-me down blues: How to stop depression from spreading in families.* New York: St. Martins.

16 *Physical exercise has been shown:* Tkachuk, G & Martin, G. (1999). Exercise therapy for patients with psychiatric disorders: research and clinical implications. *Professional Psychol-ogy: Research and Practice, 30*, 275–282.

17 *In fact, in a study done at Stanford University:* Nie, N. & Erbring, L. (2000). Internet and society: A preliminary report. Stanford, CA: Stanford Institute for the Quantitative study of Society. Retrieved November 30, 2008: www.stanford.edu/group/siqss/Press_Release/Preliminary_Report.pdf

22 *Depressed people tend to have:* Keltner, D. & Kring, A. (1998). Emotion, social function and psychopathology. *Review of General Psychology, 2*(3), 320–342.

Chapter 2 Other People Are NOT Just Like You

25 *The quality of your relationships:* Goleman, D. (2006). *Social intelligence: The new science of human relationships.* New York: Bantam.

27 *Recently, studies from a variety of fields:* Robles, T. & Kiecolt-Glaser, L. (2003). The physiology of marriage: Pathways to health. *Physiology & Behavior, 79,* 409–416.

33 *In chapter 1, I spoke about:* Twenge, J. (2006). *Generation me: Why today's young Americans are more confident, assertive, entitled—and more miserable than ever before.* New York: The Free Press.

37 *Depressed people tend to see themselves:* Beck, A. (1976). *Cognitive therapy and the emotional disorders.* New York: International Universities Press.

37 *You have to regularly challenge:* O'Connor, R. (2001). *Active treatment of depression.* New York: Norton.

37 *Psychologists call this stubborn mechanism:* Festinger, L. (1957). *A theory of cognitive dissonance.* Stanford, CA: Stanford University Press.

41 *On the other side, therapists think that:* Hayes, S. (2004). Acceptance and commitment therapy: Relational frame theory and the third wave of behavior therapy. *Behavior Therapy, 35,* 639–665.

41 *One of the most valuable techniques:* Kabat-Zinn, J. (2003). *Coming to our senses: Healing ourselves and the world through mindfulness.* New York: Hyperion; Siegel, D. (2007). *The mindful brain: Reflection and attunement in the cultivation of well-being.* New York: Norton.

42 *There are plenty of people:* Seligman, M. (1995). *The optimistic child.* New York: Houghton Mifflin.

44 *Psychologists refer to this as an absence of "mindisight":* Baron-Cohen, S. (2003). *The essential difference: Men, women and the extreme male brain.* London: Allen Lane.

Chapter 3 Expectations and Relationship Satisfaction

45 *What single factor most influences:* Gottman, J. (1995). *Why marriages succeed or fail . . . and how you can make yours last.* New York: Simon & Schuster.

45 *Your expectations for how others will see or respond to you:* Dill, J. & Anderson, C. (1999). Loneliness, shyness and depression: The etiology and interrelationships of everyday problems in living. In Joiner, T. & Coyne, J. (Eds.)(1999). *The interactional nature of depression.* Washington, DC: American Psychological Association.

60 *The deepest core dimension of a person:* Massey, M. (1979). *The people puzzle.; Understanding yourself and others.* Reston, VA: Reston Publishing; Rokeach, M. (1973). *The nature of human values.* New York: The Free Press.

61 *We generally are attracted:* Bordens, K. & Horowitz, I. (2002). *Social psychology* (2nd ed.). Mahwah, NJ: Lawrence Erlbaum.

Chapter 4 Thinking Too Much and Too Deeply

70 *Research on rumination shows:* Nolen-Hoeksema, S. & Davis, C. (1999). Thanks for sharing that: Ruminators and their social support networks. *Journal of Personality and Social Psychology, 77*(4), 801–814.

71 *Rumination is a style of coping:* Nolen-Hoeksema, S. (2000). The role of rumination in depressive disorders and mixed anxiety/depressive symptoms. *Journal of Abnormal Psychology, 109,* 504–511.

74 *Reflexively, as soon as people who engage:* Lyubomirsky, S., Tucker, K., Caldwell, N. et al. (1999). Why ruminators are poor problem solvers: Clues from the phenomenology of dysphoric rumination. *Journal of Personality and Social Psychology, 77,* 1041–1060.

74 *The research shows quite clearly:* Mor, N. & Winquist, J. (2002). Self-focused attention and affect: A meta-analysis. *Psychological Bulletin, 128,* 638–662.

75 *Rumination increases self-doubt:* Muris, P., Roelofs, J., Rassin, E. (2005). Mediating effects of rumination and worry on the links between neuroticism, anxiety and depression. *Personality and Individual Differences, 39,* 1105–1111.

75 *The most common complaint:* Szuba, M. (2001). The psychobiology of sleep and major depression. *Depression and Anxiety, 14*(1), 1–2; Thase, M. (2000). Treatment issues related to sleep and depression. *Journal of Clinical Psychiatry, 61*(Suppl. 11), 46–50.

75 *As you contemplate whatever is bothering you:* Harvey, A. (2000). Pre-sleep cognitive activity: A comparison of sleep-onset insomniacs and good sleepers. *British Journal of Psychology, 39*(3), 275–286.

77 *It isn't clear, however:* Papageorgiou, C. & Wells, A. (2004). *Depressive rumination: Nature, theory and treatment.* New York: Wiley.

77 *The therapies that have the highest treatment success rates:* Martell, C., Addis, M. & Jacobson, N. (2001). *Depression in context: Strategies for guided action.* New York: Norton.

78 *In the United States, the rate of depression is almost double:* Nolen-Hoeksema, S. (1990). *Sex differences in depression.* Stanford, CA: Stanford University Press; Piccinelli, M. & Wilkinson, G. (2000). Gender differences in depression. *British Journal of Psychiatry, 177,* 486–492.

78 *Perhaps the greatest factor, though:* Nolen-Hoeksema, S. (1990). *Sex differences in depression.* Stanford, CA: Stanford University Press.

80 *Numerous research studies consistently show:* Nolen-Hoeksema, S. & Morrow, J. (1993) Effects of rumination and distraction on naturally occurring depressed mood. *Cognition and Emotion, 7,* 561–570; Nolen-Hoeksema, S., Wisco, B. & Lyubomirsky, S. (in press). Rethinking rumination. *Perspectives on Psychological Science.*

80 *Researchers in positive psychology:* Lyubomirsky, S. (2008). *The how of happiness: A scientific approach to getting the life you want.* New York: Penguin.

82 *Physical exercise has been shown repeatedly:* Blumenthal, J., Babyak, M. Moore, K. et al. (1999). Effects of exercise training in older patients with major depression. *Archives of Internal Medicine, 159,* 2319–2356.

83 *Mindful meditation, described earlier:* Williams, M., Teasdale, J., Segal, Z. et al. (2007). *The mindful way through depression: Freeing yourself from chronic unhappiness.* New York: Guilford.

83 *People in hypnosis are highly attentive:* Yapko, M. (2003). *Trancework: An introduction to the practice of clinical hypnosis* (3rd ed.). New York: Routledge.

84 *Doing exercises in mindfulness and hypnosis:* Siegel, D. (2007). *The mindful brain.* New York: Norton.

Chapter 5 Don't Bring Others Down with You

90 *People generally want to be around people:* Taylor, S., Peplau, L. & Sears, D. (2005). *Social psychology* (12th ed.). New York: Prentice Hall.

93 *There's a peculiar form of self-righteousness:* Wilson, E. (2008). *Against happiness: In praise of melancholy.* New York: Farrar, Straus and Giroux; Kramer, P. (2006). *Against depression.* New York: Penguin.

95 *Perhaps you've decided you'd be better off:* Kramer, P. (1999). *Should you leave: A psychiatrist explores intimacy and autonomy—and the nature of advice.* New York: Penguin.

96 *There are some who grow up:* Timberg, B. (2002). *Television talk: A history of the TV talk show.* Austin: University of Texas Press.

99 *The mental health profession got this one wrong:* Seligman, M. (1995). *The optimistic child.* New York: Houghton Mifflin.

99 *We've raised a younger generation to believe:* Twenge, J. (2006). *Generation me: Why today's young Americans are more confident, assertive, entitled—and more miserable than ever before.* New York: The Free Press.

102 *A relatively young field called "affective neuroscience":* Panksepp, J. (2004). *Affective neuro-*

science: The foundations of human and animal emotions. New York: Oxford University Press.

102 *When I'm working with couples or families:* Papp, P. (1997). Listening to the system. *Family Therapy Networker, 21*(1), 52–58.

103 *All of us are affected:* Katon, W. (2003). Clinical and health services relationships between major depression, depressive symptoms, and general medical illness. *Biological Psychiatry, 54*(3), 216–226.

Chapter 6 Self-Deception and Seeking the Truth

112 *Thinking that is so distorted:* Serban, G. (1982). *The tyranny of magical thinking.* New York: Dutton.

114 *They theorize, too, about why people:* Yapko, M. (1997). *Breaking the patterns of depression.* New York: Random House Doubleday.

117 *For all of human history:* Ornstein, R. (1991). *The evolution of consciousness.* New York: Prentice Hall Press.

118 *In the early to mid-1990s:* Yapko, M. (1994). *Suggestions of abuse: True and false memories of childhood sexual trauma.* New York: Simon & Schuster.

122 *"Cognitive distortions" is the term used:* Burns, D. (1999). *Feeling good: The new mood therapy revised and updated.* New York: Harper.

130 *Plenty of research shows that:* Kyubomirsky, S., Tucker, K., Caldwell, N. et al. (1999). Why ruminators are poor problem solvers: Clues from the phenomenology of dysphoric rumination. *Journal of Personality and Social Psychology, 77,* 1041–1060; Watkins, E. & Teasdale, J. (2001). Rumination and overgeneral memory in depression: Effects of self-focus and analytic thinking. *Journal of Abnormal Psychology, 110,* 353–357; Watkins, E. & Moulds, M. (2005). Distinct modes of ruminative self-focus: Impact of abstract versus concrete rumination on problem-solving in depression. *Emotion, 5,* 319–328.

131 *Rewriting history in this way:* Barry, E., Naus, M. & Rehm, L. (2004). Depression and implicit memory: Understanding mood congruent memory bias. *Cognitive Therapy and Research, 28*(3), 387–414.

Chapter 7 Drawing the Lines

134 *Your boundaries help determine:* Katherine, A. (2000). *Where to draw the line: How to set healthy boundaries every day.* New York: Fireside.

137 *When people are regularly exposed:* Bordens, K. & Horowitz, I. (2002). *Social psychology* (2nd ed.). Mahwah, NJ: Lawrence Erlbaum.

142 *In studies of depressed people's styles:* Pettit, J. & Joiner, T. (2006). *Chronic depression: Interpersonal sources, therapeutic solutions.* Washington, DC: American Psychological Association.

Chapter 8 Marriage Can Save Your Life

156 *Some of the strongest evidence:* Lamb, K., Lee, G. & DeMaris, A. (2003). Union formation and depression: Selection and relationship effects. *Journal of Marriage and Family, 65,* 953–962; Simon, R. (2002). Revisiting the relationships among gender, marital status, and mental health. *American Journal of Sociology, 4,* 1065–1096.

158 *A good marriage promotes:* Diener, E. & Seligman, M. (2001). Very happy people. *Psychological Science, 13,* 81–84; Seligman, M. (2002). *Authentic happiness: Using the new positive psychology to realize your potential for lasting fulfillment.* New York: The Free Press.

158 *On the other hand, people in distressed marriages:* Weissman, M. (1987). Advances in psychiatric epidemiology. *American Journal of Public Health, 77,* 445–451.

158 *In sum:* Anderson, P., Beach, S. & Kaslow, N. (1999). Marital discord and depression: The

potential of attachment theory to guide integrative clinical intervention. In Joiner, T. & Coyne, J. (Eds.) *The interactional nature of depression* (pp. 271–297): Washington, DC: American Psychological Association.

160 *Only 24 percent of Americans:* U.S. Census Bureau, Housing and Household Economic Statistics Division, Fertility & Family Statistics Branch, 2007.

160 *Depression leads people to make bad relationship choices:* Ambady, N. & Gray, H. (2002). On being sad and mistaken: Mood effects on the accuracy of thin-slice judgments. *Journal of Personality and Social Psychology, 83*(4), 947–961.

162 *As a general principle, we like people:* Bordens, K. & Horowitz, I. (2002). *Social psychology* (2nd ed.). Mahwah, NJ: Lawrence Erlbaum.

167 *The more global someone is:* Philippot, P., Baeyens, C. & Douilliez, C. (2006). Specifying emotional information: Regulation of emotional intensity via executive processes. *Emotion, 6*(4), 560–571.

172 *Being supported by and supporting others:* Baumeister, R. & Leary, M. (1995). The need to belong: Desire for interpersonal attachments as a fundamental human motivation. *Psychological Bulletin, 117*, 497–529.

172 *In a fascinating study of how positive social contact:* Coan, J., Schaefer, H. & Davidson, R. (2006). Lending a hand: Social regulation of the neural response to threat. *Psychological Science, 17*(12), 1032–1039.

173 *Research on perceived support:* Maher, M., Mora, P. & Leventhal, H. (2006). Depression as a predictor of perceived social support and demand: A componential approach using a prospective sample of older adults. *Emotion, 6*(3), 450–458.

176 *Before considering marital therapy:* Montejo, A., Llorca, G., Izquierdo, J. et al. (2001). Incidence of sexual dysfunction associated with antidepressant agents: A prospective multicenter study of 1022 outpatients. *Journal of Clinical Psychiatry, 62*(Suppl.3), 10–21.

176 *When your marriage plays a large role:* Mead, D. (2002). Marital distress, co-occurring depression, and marital therapy. *Journal of Marital and Family Therapy, 28*(3), 299–314.

Chapter 9 Hand-Me-Down Blues

178 *Children of depressed parents:* Goodman, S. & Gotlib, I. (Eds.) (2002). *Children of depressed parents: Mechanisms of risk and implications for treatment.* Washington, DC: American Psychological Association.

178 *The genetic research makes it clear:* Plomin, R. & McGuffin, P. (2003). Psychopathology in the post genomic era. *Annual Review of Psychology, 54*, 205–228.

180 *The greatest preventive tool you can teach a child:* Goleman, D. (1995). *Emotional intelligence: Why it can matter more than IQ.* New York: Bantam; Hockey, K. (2003). *Raising depression-free children.* Center City, MN: Hazelden; Seligman, M. (1995). *The optimistic child.* New York: Houghton Mifflin.

182 *Kids face lots of challenges:* Coontz, S. (1997). *The way we really are: Coming to terms with America's changing families.* New York: Basic Books.

182 *In the first study of its kind:* Weissman, M. (2005). Families at high and low risk for depression: A 3 generation study. *Archives of General Psychiatry, 62*(1), 29–36.

182 *In studies of infants:* Field, T. (2002). Prenatal effects of maternal depression. In Goodman, S. & Gotlib, I. (Eds.) (2002). *Children of depressed parents: Mechanisms of risk and implications for treatment* (pp. 59–88). Washington, DC: American Psychological Association; Carver, L. & Vaccaro, B. (2007). 12-month-old infants allocate increased neural resources to stimuli associated with negative adult emotion. *Developmental Psychology, 43*(1), 54–69.

183 *When the emotional center of the brain:* Ashman, S. & Dawson, G. (2002). Maternal depression, infant psychobiological development, and the risk for depression. In Goodman, S. & Gotlib, I. (Eds.) (2002). *Children of depressed parents: Mechanisms of risk and implications for treatment* (pp. 37–58). Washington, DC: American Psychological Association.

183 *Depressed mothers are less likely to get the "rhythm":* Field, T. Healy, B., Goldstein, S. et al. (1990). Behavior state matching and synchrony in mother-infant interactions of nonde-pressed versus depressed dyads. *Developmental Psychology, 26,* 7–14.

183 *Toddlers of depressed parents:* Zahn-Wexler, C., Iannotti, R., Cummings, E. et al. (1990). Antecedents of problem behaviors in children of depressed mothers. *Development and Psychopathology, 2,* 271–291.

183 *Symptoms of depression may impair and even prevent:* Radke-Yarrow, M. (1993). *Risk and protective factors in the development of psychopathology.* Cambridge: Cambridge University Press.

184 *They are more likely to overreact:* Levy, R., Langer, S. Walker, L. et al. (2006). Relationship between the decision to take a child to the clinic for abdominal pain and maternal psychological distress. *Archives of Pediatrics & Adolescent Medicine, 160*(9), 961–965.

184 *Depressed parents are more negative, unsupportive:* Cummings, E & Davies, P. (1999). Depressed parents and family functioning: Interpersonal effects and children's functioning and development. In Joiner, T. & Coyne, J. (Eds.), *The interactional nature of depression* (pp. 299–328). Washington, DC: American Psychological Association.

184 *In a revealing survey of twelve-to-seventeen-year-olds:* Schor, J. (2005). *Born to buy: The commercialized child and the new consumer culture.* New York: Scribner.

185 *Typically, anxiety precedes depression:* Wittchen, H., Kessler, R., Pfister, H. et al. (2000). Why do people with anxiety disorders become depressed? A prospective longitudinal community study. *Acta Psychiatrica Scandinavica, 102*(Suppl. 406), 14–23.

185 *Shyness, loneliness, and depression are related:* Dill, J. & Anderson, C. (1999). Loneliness, shyness, and depression: The etiology and interrelationships of everyday problems in living. In Joiner, T. & Coyne, J. (Eds.), *The interactional nature of depression* (pp.93–126). Washington, DC: American Psychological Association.

185 *Loneliness doesn't just hurt emotionally:* Cole, S., Hawkley, L., Arevalo J., et al. (2007). Social regulation of gene expression in human leukocytes. *Genome Biology,* 8(9), R189.

186 *According to a recent study by researchers at Emory:* Pace, T., Mletzko, T., Alagbe, O. et al. (2006). Increased stress-induced inflammatory responses in male patients with major depression and increased early life stress. *American Journal of Psychiatry, 163*(9), 1630–1633.

186 *Helping children learn how to think about people:* Gottman, J. (1997). *Raising an emotionally intelligent child.* New York: Fireside.

191 *As Dr. Constance Hammen, a distinguished researcher:* Personal communication. December 20, 2007.

197 *It is most telling that a survey:* Rushton, J., Clark, S. & Freed, G. (2000). Pediatrician and family physicians prescription of selective serotonin reuptake inhibitors. *American Academy of Pediatrics, 105*(6), 1326–1327.

197 *Yet in the April 18, 2007, issue:* Bridge, J., Iyengar, S., Salary, C. et al. (2007). Clinical response and risk for reported suicidal ideation and suicide attempts in pediatric antidepressant treatment: A meta-analysis of randomized controlled trials. *Journal of the American Medical Association, 297*(15), 1683–1696.

198 *On May 2, 2007, just two weeks later:* Friedman, R. & Leon, A. (2007). Expanding the black box—depression, antidepressants, and the risk of suicide. *New England Journal of Medicine, 356*(23), 2343–2346.

APPENDIX A

Exercises to

Pause and Reflect and *Learn By Doing*

Self-Help Materials

It's an unfortunate fact that the majority of people who suffer depression do not seek the help of a mental health professional. So self-help becomes infinitely more valuable than getting no help at all. Even for those people who do participate in therapy, self-help as a means for reinforcing the skills and perspectives learned in therapy must realistically be considered essential. Thus, I have created a number of self-help programs that you can use to reinforce many of the key points presented in this book while also developing additional skills that can make a big difference in how you feel and how you approach the challenges in your life. **These are all available on my website, yapko.com.** There you will find additional details about the programs, as well as ordering information.

Focusing On Feeling Good:
A Self-Help Program for Depression

This innovative series of self-help experiential exercises for managing depression involves hypnotic methods of relaxing and focusing. The exercises teach you to create feelings of comfort while you actively build a positive frame of mind in order to deal effectively with some of the most common problems associated with depression. These exercises can help you focus better and think more clearly, take sensible and appropriate action, and thereby better accomplish your specific goals and resolve troublesome issues.

Each session provides a discussion of relevant information and perspectives, and all sessions but the first contain hypnosis and focusing exercises to help you get absorbed in positive and helpful ways of thinking and feeling regarding specific issues. The topics are listed below.

Session 1 Depression as the Problem: Hypnosis as a Solution (A discussion about how to manage depression)

Session 2 The Power of Vision (The importance of goals in overcoming past and present hurts)

Session 3 Try Again . . . But Do Something Different (The importance of developing the flexibility to learn new skills)

Session 4 Is It In Your Control? (Learning to better distinguish what is and is not controllable)

Session 5 You're the Border Patrol (Learning to build and maintain self-protective boundaries)

Session 6 Presumed Innocent But Feeling Guilty (Resolving feelings of guilt)

Session 7 Good Night . . . and Sleep Well (Slowing down your mind and body to get some sleep)

Session 8 Prevention Whenever Possible (Learning to think in terms of preventing depression)

Calm Down!
A Self-Help Program for Managing Anxiety

Everyone gets anxious from time to time, of course. But, if you find yourself worrying too often, thinking too much about how things may go wrong, spinning around the same thoughts over and over, avoiding situations that cause you discomfort, or regularly feel you might not be able to cope with life problems without getting overwhelmed, then anxiety is likely to be a bigger part of your life than it needs to be.

Calm Down! will help you manage—and even prevent—episodes of anxiety in your life. In *Calm Down!*, Dr. Yapko brings his substantial clinical expertise to teaching you many of the key skills that are known to reduce and even prevent anxious thoughts, feelings, and behaviors. These are skills for identifying and correcting the thoughts ("What if . . . ?") and perceptions ("I could never handle it if . . .") that lead to anxiety.

Calm Down! offers seven different hypnosis or focusing sessions that make skillful use of structured relaxation processes that not only allow you to feel physically comfortable, but also make it easier to learn new ways of thinking about yourself and the life issues you face that may contribute to your anxiety. The *Calm Down!* CD program contents are listed below.

Session 1   Anxiety: What It Is, Where It Comes From, and What Can Help (A discussion about how to better understand and manage anxiety skillfully)

Session 2   Change as a Process: From Fear to Acceptance Without Thinking Too Much (The importance of adapting to changes in life without overanalyzing them)

Session 3   Comfortable Familiarity and Seeking Out What's New (Sensible and positive ways of venturing outside your comfort zone)

Session 4   Thinking Globally But Acting Locally (The danger of thinking in overly general terms and missing helpful opportunities)

Session 5   Separate This from That (A divide-and-conquer strategy for rising above fear and self-doubt)

Session 6   Sleep Well (A soothing journey into a good quality sleep which has restorative benefits)

Session 7   It Seems Risky . . . or Am I Just Too Cautious? (A focus on assessing risks realistically and enhancing trust in yourself

Session 8   Looking Forward
(The importance of considering the future . . . but without the catastrophes)

Sleeping Soundly:
Enhancing Your Ability to Sleep Well

While there are many different medical and emotional factors that can cause or exacerbate sleep difficulties, one of the most common is the "spinning around and around" of anxiety-producing thoughts, a stressful pattern called "rumination." This specially structured hypnosis session can help you reduce rumination, naturally fall and stay asleep more easily, and thereby develop good quality, restorative sleep. The CD contains two tracks; the first is an overview of insomnia and its relationship to the way you think and problem-solve. The second track features a hypnosis session that provides you with an easy path to follow into a good night's sleep. NOTE: There is a sleep CD already contained in the *Focusing on Feeling Good* and *Calm Down!* programs, so there is no need to get this CD if you have the others.

Websites of Note

The amount of information available today is extraordinary, and the rate at which information is expanding can be nothing short of mind-boggling. Can one get too much information? The stress of "information overload" is a real phenomenon, not imaginary. Thus, despite the fact that there are literally millions of websites out there that can offer information and perspective, I here mention only a few of the ones in which I have a high level of confidence for their relevance and accuracy.

Depression-Related Websites: Information

WebMD: *webMD.com*
Medline: *medlineplus.gov*
National Institute for Mental Health: *nimh.nih.gov*
Health News Digest: *healthnewsdigest.com*
Mayo Clinic: *mayoclinic.org*

Depression-Related Websites: Tools

MySelfHelp: *myselfhelp.com*
Postpartum Health: *postpartum.net*
Teen Depression: *helpguide.org*
Psych Central: *psychcentral.com*

Relationship-Related Websites: Information and Tools

The Couples Institute: *couplesinstitute.com*
The Gottman Institute: *gottman.com*
Divorce Busting: *divorcebusting.com*
Smart Marriages: *smartmarriages.com*
American Association for Marriage and Family Therapy: *aamft.org*
Emotionally Focused Therapy: *eft.ca*

Therapy-Related Websites: Information and Tools

American Psychological Association: *apa.org*
Authentic Happiness: *authentichappiness.com*
Anxiety: *anxieties.com*
Psychology Information Online: *psychologyinfo.com/depression/help.html*

Acknowledgments

From a distance, writing a book looks like a solitary endeavor, a process shared only between a writer and his or her computer. But, looks are deceiving. In fact, writing this book and getting it into your hands is only made possible through the combined efforts of many people. I'd like to express my gratitude to them.

First, as always, is my wife, Diane. For more than three decades, we have shared our ideas, our dreams, our goals, our love, our lives. No one has taught me more than Diane about the responsibility we all have to spread the best of ourselves into each interaction.

My family, the Yapkos and Harrises, shows how strong and healthy family relationships are vital to a sense of well-being. I am incredibly lucky to share close and loving bonds with them.

My best friends, Wendy and Richard Horowitz, continue to be profound sources of both comfort and inspiration. I'm deeply grateful for their love and lifetime friendship. I couldn't love or be proud of their daughter, Megan, any more than if she was my own. They are the best of all antidepressants.

My network of colleagues and friends includes many wonderful people who have encouraged me to sharpen and better articulate my ideas. I am especially grateful to Erv Polster, Peter Sheehan, and Jay Haley.

A number of experts were wonderfully generous with their time and expertise in discussing their research and ideas with me. Many thanks to David Burns, M.D. (Stanford University), Constance Hammen, Ph.D. (University of California, Los Angeles), Aimee Hunter, Ph.D. (University of California, Los Angeles), and Susan Nolen-Hoeksema, Ph.D. (Yale University).

Acknowledged with great appreciation are three esteemed colleagues who gave generously of their time and expertise to review and help improve my work: Sharon Crosby, Miriam Iosupovici, and Albina Tamalonis.

Special thanks go to my literary agent, Stephanie Tade, who is exceptional in what she does. Her enthusiasm for this book and her efforts to make sure it made it into print are gifts I greatly appreciate.

Finally, my sincere thanks to my editor at The Free Press, Leslie Meredith. Her belief in the importance of this book was unwavering and her exquisite attention to detail vastly improved upon my efforts.

Index

Economic status, depression and, 6
Educational system, 100
Effectiveness, price of, 175
Effexor, 7
Electroconvulsive therapy, 15
Emory School of Medicine, 186
Emotional reasoning, 35
Emotional support, 173
Emotionally focused therapy (EFT),
    163
Empathy, 18, 172
  of therapist, 2–3
Entitlement, sense of, 18, 63, 96, 100,
    101–102, 109
Erectile dysfunction, 176
Exercise, 90
  benefits of, 16, 82–83
  as coping behavior, 72
Exercises. *See* "Learn by Doing" exercises;
    "Pause and Reflect" exercises
Expectations
  about parenting, 195
  case studies, 47–51
  defining, 46–47
  depressed people and, 45–46
  internal orientation and, 48–51
  unrealistic, 45, 46, 67, 115, 144, 151
  what do you notice in others, 51–55
Eye contact, 51, 56, 93

Facebook, 17, 180
Family reenactment, 161
Family therapy, 102–103
Fatigue, 10
Fear, 102
Feelings, as choice, 101–102
Few Good Men, A (movie), 121
Financial impact of depression, xvii,
    103
Financial schemes, 56
Flattery, 153–154
Flexibility
  in children's problem solving,
    188–189

as goal, 39–40
  in thinking, 119–120
Focus, quality and direction of, 71
Focusing on Feeling Good program, 42,
    84
Food and Drug Administration (FDA),
    7, 196, 197
Form over substance, 17–19
Frames of reference, 29–32, 34–37, 39,
    40, 43, 102
Friendships, 22, 27. *See also* Depression,
    effect on others
Frustration tolerance, 27, 41, 126, 144,
    159, 163, 172
Fun, as casualty in depression,
    110–111, 163–165
Functional magnetic resonance imaging
    (fMRI), 172

Gang members, 99
Gender
  depression and, 26, 78–79
  rumination and, 78–79
  socialization and, 78
*Generation Me: Why Today's Young
    Americans Are More Confident,
    Assertive, Entitled—and More
    Miserable than Ever Before*
    (Twenge), 18
Genetic predisposition, 178
Genetic variance, 178
Genetics, xvii, 1, 14, 178
"Getting it off your chest," 98
Ghostwriting, 8
Global thinking, 124, 167, 173, 186, 195
Gloucester, Massachusetts, 190
Gottman, John, 162
Grades, 18
Guilt, 152–153

Hammen, Constance, 191
Hand-me-down blues, 21, 177,
    178–198. *See also* Children and
    depression

About the Author

Michael D. Yapko, Ph.D., is a clinical psychologist and internationally recognized expert who lectures widely on depression, psychotherapy, and clinical hypnosis. He is the author of ten books, including *Breaking the Patterns of Depression, Hand-Me-Down Blues,* and *Suggestions of Abuse.* He lives with his wife, Diane, in Fallbrook, California.

Printed in the United States
By Bookmasters